CHANGING HANDS:
ART WITHOUT RESERVATION 2

Contemporary Native North American Art
from the West, Northwest & Pacific

CHANGING HANDS: ART WITHOUT RESERVATION 2

Contemporary Native North American Art
from the West, Northwest & Pacific

David Revere McFadden
Ellen Napiura Taubman

Museum of Arts & Design

Museum of Arts & Design
40 West Fifty-third Street
New York, New York 10019

Published on the occasion of the exhibition
Changing Hands: Art Without Reservation 2
Contemporary Native North American Art
from the West, Northwest & Pacific
organized by the Museum of Arts & Design, New York

Exhibition itinerary:

Museum of Arts & Design, New York, New York
September 22–January 22, 2006

Institute of American Indian Arts Museum, Santa Fe, New Mexico
March 4–April 30, 2006

Eiteljorg Museum of American Indians & Western Art, Indianapolis, Indiana
May 20–August 20, 2006

Naples Museum of Art, Naples, Florida
October 3, 2006–January 7, 2007

Philbrook Museum of Art, Tulsa, Oklahoma
January 28–April 22, 2007

Anchorage Museum of History & Art, Anchorage, Alaska
May 17–September 16, 2007

Weisman Art Museum, University of Minnesota, Minneapolis, Minnesota
October 26, 2007–January 6, 2008

Changing Hands: Art Without Reservation 2 has been made possible through a
grant from the National Endowment for the Arts as part of the American
Masterpieces Program and the Dobkin Family Foundation. Additional support
has been provided by the Achelis Foundation and Alice and David Rubenstein.
The national tour is supported in part by Lowry Hill. Accompanying public
programs are underwritten by the American Express Company.

Library of Congress Control Number: 2005932664

ISBN 1-890385-11-5

Designed by Linda Florio and Dima Todorova/Florio Design
Edited by Stephen Robert Frankel
Printed and bound by The Studley Press, Dalton, Massachusetts

Front cover: Steve Smith, *Pieces of the Puzzle*, 2004
Back cover: Brian Barber, *At What Cost?*, 2004
Frontispiece: Robert Davidson, *Identity* (detail), 2005

CONTENTS

LENDERS TO THE EXHIBITION

Alcheringa Gallery
Victoria, British Columbia

Anchorage Museum of
History and Art
Anchorage, Alaska

Lynn and Marc Appelbaum

Robert G. Argall

Andy Benjamin

Donald E. and Robert C. Bergstrom

Margit Biedermann

Chris Bredt and Jamie Cameron

Nadia Bruce

Russell and Suzy Campbell

Canada Council Art Bank
Ottawa, Canada

Adam and Kyle Canepa

Mary Cavanaugh

Court and Meg Clara

Coastal Peoples Fine Arts Gallery
Yaletown, Vancouver, British
Columbia

Barry Coffin

Nancy and Phillip Cohen

Jim and Todd Cowart

Department of Indian and
Northern Affairs Canada
Gatineau, Quebec

Eric and Barbara Dobkin

Douglas Reynolds Gallery
Vancouver, British Columbia

Eiteljorg Museum of American
Indians and Western Art
Indianapolis, Indiana

Pam and Scott Evans

John and Tawna Farmer

David Filer

Thomas G. Fowler

Froelick Gallery
Portland, Oregon

Daniel Greenberg and
Susan Steinhauser

Hallie Ford Museum of Art
Willamette University, Salem,
Oregon

Richard M. Hanson

Heard Museum
Phoenix, Arizona

Home & Away Gallery
Kennebunkport, Maine

Inuit Gallery of Vancouver
Vancouver, British Columbia

Kiva Indian Arts and Gifts
Fort Collins, Colorado

Lattimer Gallery
Vancouver, British Columbia

Andria and Chuck Lawson

The Legacy Ltd.
Seattle, Washington

Pierre and Anne Marie L'Hertier

Lovena Ohl Gallery
Scottsdale, Arizona

Dr. Elizabeth McLean

David Mollett

Janice Moody

Jean Mulder

National Museum of
the American Indian
Smithsonian Institution
Washington, D.C.

Donald and Noël Neely

Dr. and Mrs. Mark R. Olsen

Michelle Parker

Carla Potter

John and Joyce Price

Price Dewey Galleries, Ltd.
Santa Fe, New Mexico

Barbara and Paul Primeau

Alice Rogoff Rubenstein

St. Pierre Galleries
Anchorage, Alaska

Dolores Schapiro

Arlene and Harold Schnitzer

Stephen and Jazmin Signer

Helene Singer and Seymour Merrin

Dr. M. Jane Smith
Gitxsan Nation

Sonosky, Chambers, Sachse,
Endreson & Perry, LLP
Washington, D.C.

Shuzo Uemoto

University of Alaska Museum
of the North
Fairbanks, Alaska

Gloria Ury

Van Zelst Family

Mr. and Mrs. Michael Wahlig

Guinotte Wise

Medora Woods

Bruce and Kristine Yerigan

Dr. James and Diana Zirul

Anonymous Private Collectors

EXHIBITION ADVISORY COMMITTEE

Nadema Agard
Director, Red Earth Studio
Consulting/Productions, New York,
New York

Dan and Martha Albrecht
Paradise Valley, Arizona

Jill Alden
Millwood, New York

Steven Alvarez
Cultural Education Director, Alaska
Native Heritage Center, Anchorage,
Alaska

Janeen Antoine
Piedmont, California

Linda Arthur
Professor and Chair, Department of
Apparel Merchandising Design and
Textiles, Washington State University,
Pullman, Washington

Kathleen Ash-Milby
Assistant Curator, National Museum
of the American Indian, New York,
New York

Gary Avey
Publisher, *Native Peoples Magazine*,
Phoenix, Arizona

Joe Baker
Lloyd Kiva New Curator of Fine Art,
Heard Museum, Phoenix, Arizona

Jonathan Batkin
Director, Wheelwright Museum of
the American Indian, Santa Fe, New
Mexico

Janet Catherine Berlo
Professor of Art History and Visual
and Cultural Studies, University of
Rochester, Rochester, New York

Bruce Bernstein
Assistant Director for Cultural
Resources, National Museum of
the American Indian, Smithsonian
Institution, Washington, DC

Ian Berry
Curator, The Tang Teaching Museum
and Art Gallery, Skidmore College,
Saratoga Springs, New York

Joanna O. Bigfeather
Curator, Pauma Valley, California

Martha Black
Curator of Ethnology, Royal British
Columbia Museum, Victoria, British
Columbia

Sharla Blanche
Exhibits Registrar, Anchorage Museum
of History and Art, Anchorage, Alaska

Nancy J. Blomberg
Curator, Native American Art, Denver
Art Museum, Denver, Colorado

Marsha C. Bol, Ph.D.
Director, New Mexico Museum of
Fine Arts, Santa Fe, New Mexico

Dr. Barbara Brotherton
Curator, Native American Art, Seattle
Art Museum, Seattle, Washington

Steven C. Brown
Sequim, Washington

Christina E. Burke
Research Collaborator, Department
of Anthropology, National Museum
of Natural History, Smithsonian
Institution, Washington, DC

Jean Carlo
Fairbanks, Alaska

Dexter Cirillo
Snowmass, Colorado

Ralph T. Coe
Santa Fe, New Mexico

Jane Colman
Santa Fe, New Mexico

Colleen Cutschall
Professor, Visual and Aboriginal Art
Studies, Brandon University, Brandon,
Manitoba

Leslie Dawn
Department Chairperson, University
of Lethbridge, Lethbridge, Alberta

John A. Day
Dean, College of Fine Arts, University
of South Dakota, Vermillion,
South Dakota

David J. de la Torre
Manager, Art in Public Places Program,
State Foundation on Culture and the
Arts, Honolulu, Hawai'i

Eric and Barbara Dobkin
New York, New York

Rebecca J. Dobkins
Faculty Curator of Native American
Art, Hallie Ford Museum of Art,
Willamette University, Salem, Oregon

Margaret Dubin
Scholar, Native American Studies,
University of California

Lois S. Dubin
Curator and author, New York,
New York

Karen Duffek
Curator of Art, Museum of
Anthropolgy at the University of British
Columbia, Vancouver, British Columbia

Kate C. Duncan
Professor, School of Art, Arizona State
University, Tempe, Arizona

Natalie Fitz-Gerald
Santa Fe, New Mexico

Merrily Glosband
Curator, Peabody Essex Museum,
Salem, Massachusetts

John R. Grimes
Director, Museum of the Institute
of American Indian Arts, Santa Fe,
New Mexico

Mary G. Hamilton
Publisher, *American Indian Art
Magazine*, Scottsdale, Arizona

Emma I. Hansen
Curator of the Plains Indian Museum,
Buffalo Bill Historical Center, Cody,
Wyoming

Barbara Harjo
Oklahoma City, Oklahoma

Bruce Hartman
Director, Johnson County Community
College Gallery of Art, Overland Park,
Kansas

Michael Hice
Santa Fe, New Mexico

Greg A. Hill
Assistant Curator of Contemporary Art,
National Gallery of Canada,
Ottawa, Ontario

Lynn Hill
Vancouver, British Columbia

Rick Hill
Ohsweken, Ontario

Marita Hinds
Institute of American Indian Arts
Museum, Sante Fe, New Mexico

Alan Hoover
Manager of Anthropology, The Royal
British Columbia Museum, Victoria,
British Columbia

Joe D. Horse Capture
Associate Curator, Africa, Oceania, and
the Americas, The Minneapolis Institute
of Art, Minneapolis, Minnesota

Rock Hushka
Associate Curator, Tacoma Art Museum,
Tacoma, Washington

Ira Jacknis
Research Anthropologist, Phoebe
A. Hearst Museum of Anthropology,
University of California, Berkeley,
California

Twig Johnson
Curator, Native American Art, Montclair
Art Museum, Montclair, New Jersey

Aldona Jonaitis
Director, University of Alaska Museum
of the North, Fairbanks, Alaska

Christine Knop Kallenberger
Director of Collections and Public
Programs, Philbrook Museum of Art,
Tulsa, Oklahoma

Carolyn Kastner, Ph.D.
San Francisco, California

Andrea LaForet
Director of the Canadian Ethnology
Service, Canadian Museum of
Civilization, Ottawa, Ontario

G. Paulette LaGasse
Program Curator, Museum of the
Red River, Idabel, Oklahoma

Lucy Lippard
Galisteo, New Mexico

Barbara Loeb
Associate Professor of Art History,
Oregon State University, Corvallis,
Oregon

Margaret MacKichan
Director of Great Plains Art Institute,
Sinte Gleska University, Mission,
South Dakota

Robin Mader
Cultural Trade Commissioner,
International Trade Canada,
Ottawa, Ontario

Molly F. McCracken
Community Services Outreach
Assistant, National Museum of the
American Indian, Smithsonian
Institution, Suitland, Maryland

Gerald McMaster
Deputy Assistant Director, The
National Museum of American
Indian, Smithsonian Institution,
Washington, D.C.

Jennifer Complo McNutt
Curator, Contemporary Art, Eiteljorg
Museum of American Indians and
Western Art, Indianapolis, Indiana

Bill Mercer
Curator, Portland Art Museum, Portland,
Oregon

Floyd Nez
Instructor, Sinte Gleska University,
Great Plains Art Insitute, Mission,
South Dakota

John W. Nunley
The Morton D. May Curator of the Arts
of Africa, Oceania, and the Americas,
The St. Louis Art Museum, St. Louis,
Missouri

Barbara W. Overstreet
Associate Director, Alaska Native Arts
Foundation, McLean, Virginia

Diana Pardue
Curator of Collections, Heard Museum,
Phoenix, Arizona

Zena Pearlstone
Associate Professor, Art History,
California State University, Fullerton,
California

David W. Penney
Vice President of Exhibitions and
Collections Strategies and Curator
of Native American Art, Detroit Institute
of Arts, Detroit, Michigan

Ruth B. Phillips
Canada Research Chair and Professor of
Art History in Modern Culture, School
for Studies in Art and Culture, Carleton
University, Ottawa, Ontario

Meg Quintal
Institute of American Indian Studies,
University of South Dakota, Vermillion,
South Dakota

Laurel Reuter
Director, North Dakota Museum of Art,
Grand Forks, North Dakota

David Roche
Santa Fe, New Mexico

Alice Rogoff Rubinstein
Chair, Alaska Native Arts Foundation,
Bethesda, Maryland

Allan J. Ryan, Ph.D.
New Sun Chair in Aboriginal Art
& Culture, Carleton University,
Ottawa, Ontario

Brother Simon. S.J.
Director, The Heritage Center, Red Cloud
Indian School, Pine Ridge, South Dakota

Pat Soden
Director, University of Washington
Press, Seattle, Washington

Marlys and Harry Stern
Bloomington, Indiana
Gaylord Torrence
Fred & Virginia Merrill Curator
of American Indian Art, the
Nelson-Atkins Museum of Art,
Kansas City, Missouri

Charleen Touchette
Artist and author, President, TouchArt
Books, Santa Fe, New Mexico

Charlotte Townsend-Gault
Associate Professor, Department of Art
History, Visual Art and Theory,
University of British Columbia,
Vancouver, British Columbia

Roslyn Tunis
Curator, Oakland, California

Walter Van Horn
Curator of Collections, The Anchorage
Museum of History and Art, Anchorage,
Alaska

Elizabeth Weatherford
Head, Film and Video Center, George
Gustav Heye Center of the National
Museum of the American Indian,
Smithsonian Institution, New York,
New York

Rebecca West
Curatorial Assistant, Plains Indian
Museum, Buffalo Bill Historical Center,
Cody, Wyoming

Kathleen Whitaker
Director, Indian Arts Research Center,
School of American Research, Santa Fe,
New Mexico

Dr. Peter Whiteley
Curator of North American Ethnology,
American Museum of Natural History,
New York, New York

Robin K. Wright
Curator, Thomas Burke Memorial
Museum, University of Washington,
Seattle, Washington

Gwen Yeaman
President, Native Appraisal, LLC,
Indianapolis, Indiana

GALLERY ASSOCIATES

Helen Carlson
The Legacy Ltd., Seattle, Washington

Geoff Cline
Cline Gallery, Santa Fe, New Mexico
& Scottsdale, Arizona

Lane Coulter
Lane Coulter Antiques, Santa Fe,
New Mexico

Nancy Davenport
Stonington Gallery, Seattle, Washington

Julie Decker
Decker/Morris Gallery, Anchorage,
Alaska

LaTiesha Fazakas & Douglas Reynolds
Douglas Reynolds Gallery, Vancouver,
British Columbia

Christina Ferki
Art no Art, Philadelphia, Pennsylvania

Svetlana Fouks
Coastal Peoples Fine Arts Gallery,
Vancouver, British Columbia

Charles Froelick
Froelick Gallery, Portland, Oregon

Leroy Garcia
Blue Rain Gallery,
Santa Fe & Taos, New Mexico

Mark Glover
St. Pierre Galleries, Anchorage, Alaska

Denise Grogger
Lovena Ohl Gallery, Scottsdale, Arizona

Peter Lattimer
Lattimer Gallery, Vancouver,
British Columbia

Robb Lucas
Case Trading Post, The Wheelwright
Museum of the American Indian,
Santa Fe, New Mexico

Kent McManus
Grey Dog Trading Company, Tucson,
Arizona

David Mollett
Well Street Gallery, Fairbanks, Alaska

Elaine Monds
Alcheringa Gallery, Victoria,
British Columbia

Robert Nichols
Robert Nichols Gallery, Sante Fe,
New Mexico

Derek Norton & Gary Wyatt
Spirit Wrestler Gallery, Vancouver,
British Columbia

Victoria Price
Price-Dewey Gallery, Santa Fe,
New Mexico

Cecily Quintana
Quintana Gallery, Portland, Oregon

Christina Ritchie
The Contemporary Art Gallery,
Vancouver, British Columbia

David Schultz
Home & Away Gallery, Kennebunkport,
Maine

Robert Scott
Eagle Spirit Gallery, Vancouver,
British Columbia

Melanie Zavediuk
Inuit Gallery of Vancouver, Vancouver,
British Columbia

ACKNOWLEDGMENTS

It is exciting and daunting to launch a series of exhibitions as complex as *Changing Hands: Art Without Reservation*. What was originally conceived as a single exhibition grew into a series that examines contemporary Native North American art from diverse geographical regions. This decision was mandated by our having found, much to our delight, that the field today was burgeoning with new and under-recognized talent, and that the sheer number of artists that merit attention in a survey of contemporary Native art greatly exceeded the spatial capacity of a single exhibition. We are proud and honored to present the second installment of this series, and deeply grateful for the time and expertise that many individuals and organizations have so generously given in the realization of the exhibition, the accompanying publication, and related educational programs.

To gain access to the artists, scholars, collectors, curators, and gallery owners was an overwhelming task in and of itself, something we could only have accomplished with a great deal of help. Without the artists' exceptional talents and their gracious collaboration in all stages of this project, nothing could have happened. For so generously sharing their lives and their art with us, and hence with those who see the exhibition or read this publication, we offer our profound thanks.

The assistance and cooperation of colleagues at other institutions and organizations has been crucial for the project's success. We are delighted to know that more and more contemporary art museums in the United States and abroad are now collecting contemporary Native North American art; this is something that could not have occurred without the perceptive intelligence and commitment of museum curators, directors, donors, and board members in this country.

The exhibition's distinguished Advisory Committee and the Museum's Gallery Associates have played important parts in researching and locating artists and collectors. Without their patient help, the exhibition would be incomplete. Many of our advisors are also lenders to the exhibition, and some are also donors to the Museum's permanent collection. Special thanks are due to two members of the Museum's Board of Governors, Natalie Fitz-Gerald and Eric Dobkin, who have advocated for this exhibition series since its inception.

The exhibition and publication have been made possible with the accomplished help of our dedicated museum team. Assistant curator Jennifer Scanlan's intelligence and talents can be seen in every detail of the catalogue and exhibition: she coordinated the efforts of all the team members, organized production goals and schedules, and effortlessly resolved countless problems and loose ends. We were fortunate to have Dara Metz as the project coordinator from the very beginning; she has dealt with the correspondence, loan agreements, and condition and installation queries, and has assembled biographical and art-historical information with her usual grace, intelligence, and patience. The third critical member of the exhibition team was curatorial assistant Jennifer Steifle, who served as the essential right hand to the two of us and to everyone else involved in the project—the many lenders and artists, the designers, and the museum staff. In addition, we are grateful to our project interns, Tessa Paneth-Pollak and Laura Stern, whose conscientious assistance was invaluable. All aspects of *Changing Hands: Art Without Reservation 2* show the deftness and nimble minds of our dream team.

Ken Mowatt
Egret Sculpture (detail), 2002

Other museum staff members who deserve special mention include our skilled and accomplished registrar, Linda Clous, and her assistant, Brian MacElhose, who choreographed the complex arrangements needed to assemble the exhibition. The Museum's curator of exhibitions, Dorothy Twining Globus, has brought her meticulous eye and her love of objects to bear on the presentation of this exhibition in our galleries and on tour. Traveling exhibition coordinator Stephen Mann has generated a stellar tour for the exhibition, which will assure that these magnificent works of art will be enjoyed by hundreds of thousands of people across North America. We extend our sincerest appreciation to the entire staff of the Museum for their extraordinary expertise and dedication.

Exhibition designer Todd Zwigard collaborated with Dorothy Globus to create a spectacular installation that presents each work of art to its best advantage. The handsome exhibition catalogue was the creation of Linda Florio, an exceptionally talented and innovative graphic designer who worked in close collaboration with her assistant Dima Todorova. The sensitivity and skill of our publication photographers deserves special acknowledgment; we wish to thank Maggie Nimken in particular, as well as David Behl, for their invaluable contribution to the catalogue. And, as every author knows, the final quality of a publication rests in the hands of its editor; in this instance, we are blessed to have the skillful services of the thoughtful and resilient Stephen Robert Frankel.

The authors who contributed to the exhibition catalogue have shared their knowledge and love of the field with us from the earliest days of the project. We cannot begin to thank them enough for enriching the understanding and appreciation of the art and the artists that are the raison d'être for the exhibition and publication. And finally, we want those artists to know how deeply grateful we remain to them for working with us on this labor of love.

Ellen Napiura Taubman
David Revere McFadden
Curators

FOREWORD

It is a great pleasure to present *Changing Hands: Art Without Reservation 2: Contemporary Native North American Art from the West, Northwest & Pacific*, the second of three exhibitions that explore the rich diversity of innovative contemporary art made by an exceptional group of highly talented Native North American artists. *Changing Hands: Art Without Reservation 1* highlighted the work of Native artists from the American Southwest; and *Changing Hands: Art Without Reservation 3* will conclude the series with an examination of indigenous art from the East, Southeast, Northeast, and Canada. Together, these exhibitions are dramatic and memorable evidence of the vitality and energy of Native art today, and demonstrate that we are living through a pivotal moment in its continuing evolution.

The mission of the Museum of Arts & Design is to reveal the profound engagement between materials and process that drives creativity in wood, glass, ceramics, metalwork, fiber, and mixed media, and to represent the artistic diversity of world cultures. The Museum celebrates the work of artists who transform mute materials into memorable and meaningful forms and who brilliantly combine their rich individual cultural traditions with a passionate commitment to making art. Nothing could better describe the artists featured in *Changing Hands: Art Without Reservation 2*. The art presented by these artists is compelling, engaging, and often challenging. It inhabits that magical territory in which beauty and meaning coalesce. Past and present are seamlessly merged in these objects, which embody the traditions of Native craftsmanship brought into the present. The Museum of Arts & Design is proud to take a leading role in bringing the work of these artists into a wider cultural arena.

The exhibition and accompanying publication document the exciting trajectory of Native art today. Both have been achieved through the generous assistance and cooperation of many individuals and institutions. Board members Natalie Fitz-Gerald and Eric Dobkin continue to champion this exhibition series. We are grateful to the exhibition's Advisory Committee and the Gallery Associates, who have been such an important source of information and recommendations. Their collective eye is reflected in the quality of the works shown and in the impressive number of young, emerging, and underrecognized artists who are shown alongside acknowledged masters. We also express our gratitude to all those—collectors, galleries, museums, and artists—who have so generously lent works for the exhibition, and have so graciously shared them with our visitors. Special thanks goes to Gallery W52, who agreed to participate in this exhibition, opening up their neighboring space so that we could include works by many of the artists working on a larger scale.

This exhibition would not have been possible without the assistance and cooperation of several organizations and individuals. A grant from the National Endowment for the Arts' American Masterpieces Program affirmed the importance of this project and will help underwrite public programs at each of our six additional venues. I would also like to offer thanks to the Dobkin Family Foundation, a longtime supporter of the *Changing Hands* series; the Achelis Foundation; Alice and David Rubenstein; Lowry Hill, a supporter of the exhibition's national tour; and the American Express Company, for underwriting accompanying public programs.

Rebecca Lyon
Tlinigit/Haida Woman (from Women of the North Series), (detail), 2004

I want to express our deepest appreciation to all the artists in *Changing Hands: Art Without Reservation 2*. The Museum of Arts & Design is committed to seeking out the most talented and creative individuals working today, and our criteria of quality of concept and excellence of execution have been admirably fulfilled in the works of these artists. Likewise, I wish to thank the catalogue authors and essayists whose words illuminate these inspired works.

My congratulations to guest curator Ellen Taubman and to David Revere McFadden, the Museum's chief curator and vice president for programs and collections, for their superb achievement in organizing the exhibition and the accompanying catalogue. Ellen Taubman has given the Museum of Arts & Design the benefit of her rich knowledge of both historical and contemporary Native art. Without her inspiration and passion, the exhibition and publication would both be diminished. The Museum is very fortunate to have the curatorial leadership of David McFadden. His wide-ranging passion and knowledge of the decorative arts, as well as his extensive network of contemporary Native artists, many of whom he met while he was director of the Millicent Rogers Museum in Taos, New Mexico, make him exceptionally qualified to curate this exhibition. I would also like to acknowledge the efforts of the team brought together by David and Ellen to accomplish this ambitious project, who represent an exceptional cross-section of talent and determination. In addition, the rest of the Museum's dedicated, hard-working, and enthusiastic staff deserve our heartfelt thanks for all the work that they have poured into the exhibition and catalogue.

As the Museum of Arts & Design begins to write a new chapter in its distinguished history and makes the transition into larger quarters and an even richer menu of public programs, it is gratifying to know that exhibitions such as *Changing Hands: Art Without Reservation 2* will continue to express our vision of the arts—one that is inclusive, accessible, and engaging.

Holly Hotchner
Director

Changing Hands: New Directions

David Revere McFadden and Ellen Napiura Taubman

Whenever we attempt to interpret a work of art, we are at once confronted with problems that are as perplexing as they are contradictory. A work of art is an attempt to express something that is unique; it is an affirmation of something that is whole, complete, and absolute. But it is likewise an integral part of a system of highly complex relationships. A work of art results from an altogether independent activity; it is the translation of a free and exalted dream. But flowing together within it the energies of many civilizations may be plainly discerned.
—Henri Focillon[1]

In this country, everyone has a definition of what an Indian person is already. Ask anyone on the street and they'll give you their version. I think this attitude emerges from all of the anthropological, ethnographic, etc., work that has been inflicted upon Native people over the years.
—Bently Spang[2]

Just as my ancestors continually adapted and incorporated technology and new materials, I adapt and incorporate technology and materials. I embrace tradition and yet I am not bound by tradition.
—Keʻalaonaonapuahīnano Campton[3]

WHAT DOES A WORK OF ART MEAN? Works of art function on many levels; their meaning and value change in response to the evolution of the cultures that create and preserve them. Are there significant differences between works that were made to meet practical needs and those that address more intangible emotional and spiritual issues? Do works of art, by their very nature as expressions of individuals and cultures, confound this division into the humbly useful and the eloquently poetic? Each work of art featured in *Changing Hands: Art Without Reservation 2: Contemporary Native North American Art of the West, Northwest & Pacific* functions as an expression of an individual worldview, and one that conveys overarching cultural and social contexts in which the work was conceived, created, commodified, and collected. Ideas and images, content and purposes are interwoven in every object.

Many of these are three-dimensional works in traditional materials—mediums identified with handcraft traditions, such as fiber, clay, metal, glass, and wood—which have been transformed by the creative vision of the indigenous artists who made them. Although the content may often be confrontational, political, provocative, or satirical, the interpenetration of two worlds—one maintaining powerful traditions and the other striving for contemporary innovations—is seamless and graceful. These works speak directly to the historical and cultural matrix that is so vital to the aesthetics and meanings of Native art, but they are spoken in art's timeless, international voice, transcending purely regional and ethnographic concerns.

Some of the artists have chosen to work in unexpected—or more aptly termed, nontraditional—mediums. These include installation, video art, performance art, fashion, and design, thereby asserting a new and greatly expanded definition of Native art. *Changing Hands:*

Art Without Reservation 2 offers a broad alternative view of recent and ongoing developments in Native art by emphasizing formal aesthetics as well as content. While tribal affiliations and cultural histories may remain vital to these artists, the works address issues far beyond the purely ethnographic and anthropological interpretations and boundaries imposed by the dominant culture.[4] Indeed, the exhibition raises important and provocative questions about cultural identity in a changing world, about the interface of tradition and innovation that informs contemporary Native art, and about the juxtaposition of reservation lifeways and contemporary urban life.

All of the artists examine and respond to their respective histories both critically and creatively, and, especially, confront the stereotypes and misconceptions that surround Native art. The fundamental intentions of Native artists have shifted from those of earlier generations; today, artists explore the interplay and impact of past and present from a more personalized perspective than previously, but also on a more universal level. Bruce Bernstein has pointed out that work by Native artists "reflects a commitment to self-determination, individual visions, and new storytelling devices. Cars, planes, and cellular phones define these artists' lives today as much as pots, baskets, and beadwork."[5]

Performance artist James Luna has stated: "I would live nowhere else, as my life is filled with variety. I truly live in two worlds. This 'two world' concept once posed too much ambiguity for me, as I felt torn as to who I was. In maturity I have come to find it the source of my power, as I can easily move between these two places and not feel that I have to be one or the other, that I am an Indian in this modern society."[6] Environmental and political issues, too, are embedded in the work of many artists, who examine and comment upon the essential, but fragile, relationships between the natural world and human intervention.

In the early stages of our research for the *Changing Hands: Art Without Reservation* exhibition series, we quickly realized that the sheer number of contemporary Native artists from the United States and Canada was daunting. To convey a greater understanding of this abundance and to acknowledge the talents of so many, we decided that the most logical approach would be to explore contemporary developments regionally. Three distinct geographic areas were proposed: the American Southwest (*Changing Hands: Art Without Reservation 1*); the Plains, Prairie, and Plateau regions west of the Mississippi River to the continental West Coast—including California, Oregon, and Washington—and further westward to Hawai'i and northward to include Canada's Pacific Northwest Coast and Alaska (*Changing Hands: Art Without Reservation 2*); and the regions east of the Mississippi, including the southeastern United States and northeastern Canada (*Changing Hands: Art Without Reservation 3*).

The areas covered in the present exhibition seem appropriate and further justified by the historical circumstance that many tribal nations spanned North America without the political borders that exist today. Canada and the United States, now two sovereign nations, were first inhabited by Native peoples who shared significant material and artistic cultures as well as many similarities in their beliefs regarding the material and spiritual worlds of land and nature.[7]

In contrast to the American Southwest cultures (the Rio Grande Pueblos, Hopi, Zuni, and Navajo), who lived in the same geographic region for generations, the artists in the present exhibition tend to be less heterogeneous. Tribal groups from the Plains, Prairie, and Plateau regions were most often forced without notice to abandon their Native homelands and were removed to far less habitable environments. There, they frequently faced challenging living conditions, and had to submit to attempts to erase their indomitable cultural pride and heritage, euphemistically described as "assimilation."[8] Exemplary of these changes is the situation of the numerous present-day tribes in Oklahoma that originally inhabited the American Southeast. Despite the need to reinvent themselves on so many levels, these resilient cultures managed to preserve their traditions by means of oral histories, music, and the visual arts. This steadfastness in the face of disenfranchisement enabled them to revive a frayed tapestry of powerful Native traditions by weaving them once again into a strong cultural and artistic fabric.

The repertoire of traditional Native materials used in making objects has changed dramatically over time: Skins and furs used for clothing were replaced by manufactured textiles; metal needles, thread, and thimbles replaced bone and sinew; decorative porcupine quills were outshone by a profusion of sparkling glass trade beads; and even buffalo robes gave way to Pendleton and Hudson's Bay blankets as ceremonial regalia. While many Native artists are rediscovering traditional materials in their work, an equal number have embraced new materials and techniques that ground the works in the present. Today it is not surprising to find plastics, digital equipment, automobile tires, and kitsch souvenir trinkets taking their place beside gold, silver, wood, and cedar bark.

> Speaking only for myself, I have to wonder just how much of the "traditional" in today's art actually applies to the lives of the Indian people who create art objects. I have questions about why there is such an attachment to a specific period of Indian history in art, but very little regard for contemporary perspectives. Tradition is a part of that deep cultural grounding that makes my art and the art of others unique and important. But it remains only a part.
> —Todd Defoe

The powerful intersection of past and present within the cultures from the Plains region has had dramatic cultural and artistic implications, as revealed in the mediums chosen by the artists and the messages their works communicate. Some of these artists are striking out on new and surprising paths of exploration of their inherited cultures—including Arthur Amiotte, creating sculpture from fiber; Charlene Teters, who often transforms objects from popular culture into works of powerful intention; Todd Defoe, with his virtuoso carving of traditional catlinite (pipestone); and Rick Bartow, who uses an astonishing variety of found materials in his animal sculptures. Others have chosen to work with the more typical or "traditional" Native materials, but have taken them to new levels, as Maynard White Owl Lavadour and Molly Murphy have in their innovative use of beadwork.

As noted earlier, the tribal groups that were relocated to Oklahoma have created a distinctive artistic culture, evident today in the emergence of such talented individuals as fashion designer and fiber artist Kimberly "Wendy" Ponca, goldsmith Kenneth Johnson, and ceramic artist Bill Glass, Jr. In California, many early traditions were slowly but surely disappearing, while at the same time the outspoken works of notable painters grew stronger and more significant. The work of California mixed-media artist Jean LaMarr is emblematic of the composite nature of materials being used by artists today; she has created wall-hung boxes that contain a wide range of found objects, commercial ephemera and graphics, and photography, much in the spirit of Joseph Cornell.

To a great extent, the indigenous Hawaiian cultures have similarly struggled to maintain their distinctness and cultural integrity despite ongoing and long-term efforts by certain groups to obscure or eradicate their tribal ancestry and cultural practices. Today there is a vocal and passionate group of Native Hawaiian artists actively reissuing, reviving, commemorating, and celebrating customs and traditions thought by many to have been forgotten. A vital new chapter in the history of Hawaiian art is emerging. The work of many of the leading exponents of this renewed cultural energy and pride is represented in the diversity and quality of the works by contemporary Hawaiian artists chosen for the exhibition, as seen in the sculptures of Kaili Chun, Sean Kekamakupaʻa Lee Loy Browne, and Ivy Hāliʻimaile Andrade, in the feather works of

Paulette Nohealani Kahalepuna and the Domingo family, and in the mixed-media works of Moana K. M. Eisele. This movement of renewal is also multi-generational: photographer and feather artist Natalie Mahina Jensen-Oomittuk is following in the path established by innovative artists such as her father, Rocky Kaʻiouliouliokahihikoloʻehu Jensen.

In contrast, many Native groups residing along the coast of the Pacific Northwest have experienced more or less unbroken cultural continuity and territorial stability for generations. With a temperate climate throughout the year, ample foodstuffs from the sea and land, and a bounty of raw materials available around them, Pacific Northwest societies have flourished. Their rich and diverse cultural heritage has served as a powerful catalyst for creativity; highly complex and sophisticated traditions and conventions (such as richly carved wood sculpture) continue to inform and inspire contemporary sculpture in the region today. Modern master carver, metalsmith, and jeweler Bill Reid (1920–1998) was integral in paving the way for an entirely new generation of artists by breaking down barriers of materials, scale, technique, and content. In his hands, traditional imagery and iconography were incorporated into vital contemporary designs that eradicated artificial boundaries between tradition and innovation. Today's master artists—including sculptor Robert Davidson, who works in wood and metal and is also a painter and printmaker; Dempsey Bob, known for the monumentality and refined carving style of even his small-scale sculptures; and Susan Point, Joe Feddersen, Preston Singletary, and other artists who are working in the new medium of glass—continue this legacy of experimentation and evolution.

The 1960s was an era of change for Canadian First Peoples, a time when their full citizenship was confirmed and their cultural autonomy recognized. In the United States, 1962 marked the founding of the Institute of American Indian Arts in Santa Fe, New Mexico under the visionary guidance of Lloyd Kiva New (1916–2002), among others. This institution rapidly became the launching pad for a new generation of professionally educated painters and sculptors who studied with him and with Allan Houser (1915–1994) and Fritz Scholder (1937–2005). The Emily Carr Institute, which was founded in Vancouver, British Columbia in 1925, served a similar role in Canada. Both Hawaiʻi and Alaska achieved full statehood only in 1959, bringing the Native cultures of these regions into a new light. However, critical acceptance of a more modernized view of Native art did not follow immediately: although private and institutional collecting of traditional Native art flourished throughout the twentieth century, it was not until the 1970s and beyond that contemporary Native art began to be widely considered, celebrated, and collected, more by private collectors at first, and subsequently on an institutional level.[9]

The works of art in *Changing Hands: Art Without Reservation* 2 have been grouped under four general themes to highlight the prominent ideas or motifs characteristic of each theme: "The Human Condition," "Material Evidence," "Beyond Function," and "Nature as Subject." These categories are intended to serve primarily as

thematic doorways of interpretation and are not mutually exclusive. In truth, the themes tend to overlap, interact, and cross-fertilize one another; and, while they are especially pertinent to Native art of both past and present, it should be remembered that they also highlight universal issues and concerns. The works featured in the exhibition and catalogue were all created by Native North American artists and reflect their personal and cultural worlds, but they transcend the barriers of geography and culture that have often interfered with an accurate perception of the artistic intent and cultural context of Native art. Fundamentally, *Changing Hands: Art Without Reservation* 2 seeks to show how these works of art fit into the art world at large.

The Human Condition

"The Human Condition" and "Nature as Subject" are themes that serve as figurative "bookends" for the exhibition, spanning works of art with a highly individual and subjective point of view at one end and works that explore the more objective aspects of the natural world at the other.

"The Human Condition" comprises the largest and probably most provocative body of work in the exhibition. Here, challenging questions are raised about issues that have the most profound relevance to the content of the works of art: personal and cultural identity in the twenty-first century; historical, political, and social commentary; environmental concerns; and systems of belief and mythology that place an individual within her or his cultural context.

British Columbia multi-media artist Peter Morin confronts complex issues of identity and cultural affiliation in his *Dirt Jacket*, 2004 (page 73). The off-the-rack suit jacket has been covered with mud that was collected by Morin when he returned to his birthplace, his ancestral cultural reserve. In its original condition, this ready-made jacket is one that could be worn without notice in virtually any culture or any setting, a metaphorical reference to the uniformity and anonymity of urban life today. At the same time, the dirt embedded into the fiber is specific to a personal experience fully appreciated only by the artist. The jacket is a costume appropriate to two different scenarios—as a generic garment suitable for quotidian life, and as a talisman that confirms a unique identity. In the artist's own words, "I wear this jacket to be safe."

Alaska-born sculptor and writer Susie Silook uses walrus ivory, whalebone, and other traditional materials to create compelling figures (primarily female) from ancestral myths and stories to address broad-based issues such as the threatened natural environment, or those of a more intimate character such as her personal journey toward self-awareness. In *Looking Inside Myself*, 2002 (page 37), a stylized portrait head is suggestive of a timeless archaic image and equally archetypal ornamental patterns. The head is "split" open to reveal the inside, but the calm, self-possessed face suggests that questions of identity and purpose have been confronted and resolved. On the issue of dual identity—a constant in contemporary Native life—Silook has asserted, "I am able to partic-ipate in and become acquainted with many cultures, many views. Contrary to popular conception, I am not caught between two worlds. I am walking in many simultaneously."[10]

Questions of personal and cultural identity are raised by a sig-nificant number of works included in "The Human Condition." Artists approach the theme from a highly subjective, self-revelatory point of view, which is atypical in Native art. Alaskan artist Jack Abraham's autobiographical work *Personal Armor Revisited*, 2004 (page 28), exemplifies the role of art as a means of reuniting fragmented identity, in this case his dual identity as a Native artist and that of a contemporary individual in a more global setting. This powerful work (diminutive in scale but monumental in impact) uses the crumbling framework of architecture as the fragile support system for a (self-?) portrait mask. The architecture suggests the ruins of a building, the function of which has long been forgotten. While the building no longer serves a practical purpose, it is still able to evoke strong memories and associations that serve as a backdrop for the human face, but the precise narrative contained in these memories is not specified. The remnants of the past continue to buttress the present. Abraham comments, "Coming from the edge of the world, to some people I have made the effort to learn as much about the world and its people as I can. Just wish more people would do the same, so I don't have to keep explaining that I don't live in an igloo and we don't rub noses."

Self-awareness on a more abstract level is conveyed in *Identity*, 2005 (page 30), by internationally acclaimed British Columbia artist Robert Davidson. This cast-bronze head, based on a pair of similar wood sculptures by Davidson, merges the indigenous with a timeless quality. His ability to achieve such a seamless synthesis parallels his exceptional abilities to move easily among mediums and techniques in the pursuit of his art. Davidson's take on identity is self-assured and confident.

Hawaiian artist Rocky Kaʻiouliokahihikoloʻehu Jensen's highly stylized figural sculpture *Hinahanaiakamalama*, 2004 (page 51), is based on traditional Hawaiian ancestor figures that served impor-tant ceremonial and spiritual needs. For Jensen, an important element of his identity is found through his identification with Hawaiʻi's cultural past and his recognition that his art serves as the mediator between that past and his artistic present. Through sculpture, the spirits of his ancestors live comfortably in the modern world—heritage is given new life.

Two other artists, Bently Spang from Montana and James Luna from California, approach the question of cultural identity in somewhat more abstract terms. Spang's *The Four Stages of Dried Meat*, 1998 (page 71), is composed of a mixture of reservation dirt and silicone, rolled out and flattened to simulate pieces of dried buffalo meat. The work is rich with metaphorical associations: Dried buffa-lo meat was a dietary mainstay for the Cheyenne people and serves as a reminder of Spang's heritage, but the "meat" in this instance is a modern synthetic material combined with the "real" dirt. The four numbered strips of meat seem to suggest the four stages of life.

Suspended on commercial trouser hangers, they may imply that the hunting of buffalo, once essential for life among his people, is no longer necessary; today we can "buy" our food (and our identity) "off the rack."

For more than three decades, James Luna has devoted his creative energy to installation and activist performance art. Luna uses familiar objects identified with Indian culture—"Native" objects such as rattles, pipes, shirts, moccasins—in combination with found and ready-made "outsider" objects ranging from umbrellas and guitars to digital equipment and consumer-product packaging such as Jell-O boxes. Appropriating objects from both his Native world and that of popular American culture, Luna achieves a delicate balance between the solemn and the humorous, between the sublime and the ridiculous. The subjects that Luna addresses—life and death, transformation, racism, and imperialism—are of the utmost seriousness, but often presented with wit and humor. His installa-tion *The Spirits of Virtue and Evil Await My Ascension*, 1999 (page 25), is at once meditative and celebratory, with its visually arresting, boldly patterned umbrellas.

Reflecting on the human condition from a socio-political point of view are artists who transform the ordinary and the trite into provocative visual statements. David Bradley's *Land O Bucks, Land O Fakes, Land O Lakes*, 2003 (page 59), is an outsize Warholesque butter package that comments on the market-driven commodification of Indian culture, in which a "fake" version of their material and cultural history, translated into stereotypical advertising imagery, assures that those who exploit it will rake in the "bucks." Indiana artist Martha Gradolf uses Japanese-made ceramic figurines of "Indians" in her work *Made in Japan*, 2002 (page 70), to address "Native American issues such as history, stereotypes, and spirituali-ty," and to "nurture this ancient legacy as it re-creates itself again in a new and contemporary form." Gradolf's woven strips evoke memories of the woven fringe-pendants on early bandolier bags; each strip now serves as the support or background for Japanese-made kitsch figurines depicting stereotyped images of Indians.

Gambling games and other games of chance have been employed by several of the artists to serve as metaphors for the negotiations that are required whenever multiple cultures overlap and compete. California artist Gerald Clarke's sardonic installation work *Ethnopoly*, 2000–present (page 60), is an adaptation of the board game Monopoly, familiar worldwide; versions of the game are available in languages ranging from Croatian and Chinese to Hebrew and Swedish. Clarke's *Ethnopoly* transforms the game of power and real estate into one that deals with race relations in America today. The game pieces are white, red, yellow, and black to represent stereotypical views of racial groups. When a player chooses a signature color, she or he is intended to assume the identity of the indicated race. The goal of Clarke's game is to save $1,200 for the down payment on a home; along the way, players earn or lose money, and experience prejudice, favoritism, and problems involving health and family, among other issues. Virginia artist Donald Tenoso's *One Bull's Chess Set*, 1997 (page 49), is based on the Battle of the Little Bighorn and features doll-like chess pieces in the form of Indians and soldiers, horses and mules, and an Indian king and queen juxtaposed with a figure of Custer and a saloon-hall dancer. Tenoso poses the question, "Does the Battle of the Little Bighorn have relevance today? I think so. Despite the fact that people tried to exterminate us, we are still here. I guess we are meant to be here. We were here to greet the other people who came to America. We weren't inhospitable until the other people were bad to us." Oklahoma-born John Hitchcock's *Ritual Device (Give Away)*, 1997–2005 (page 69), explores issues of land, politics, technology, and intercultural identities by means of video projection, sound, screen-printed ephemera, and digital printmaking, with a ring-toss game at its center.

Minnesota artist Todd Defoe is acclaimed for his virtuosity in carving catlinite, a soft argillaceous rock historically used to make pipe bowls for ceremonial tobacco pipes. Prior to becoming a full-time artist, Defoe worked in the casino and hotel-management industry, which gave him an insider's view of the business. Defoe's *The New Four Directions*, 2001 (page 57), makes reference to the historic significance of the ceremonial pipe within Plains cultures, where the "peace" pipe served as an object of exchange, negotiation, and collaboration. This work is an acid commentary on the impact of gambling casinos throughout Indian country: the pipe bowl takes the form of a slot machine, while poker chips decorate the stem.

Mixed-media artist Judy Chartrand challenges stereotypical views associated with gender roles in Indian and non-Indian cultures. Each of her gender-bending *Buffalo Soldiers*, 2003 (one shown on page 151), consists of a framed chamois thong bordered in red satin, embellished with traditional-style dyed porcupine quillwork and the addition of several tufts of buffalo hair. Chartrand explains, "I have lined the thongs with a rich red satin to accentuate the sexual characteristics often found in women's lingerie and to project the idea that men also desire to communicate their appeal via a peacocklike display of attractiveness. The works are entitled *Buffalo Soldiers* due to the tufts of buffalo hair sticking out at the crotch area."

In *Lovely Hula Hands*, 2005 (page 34), Hawaiian installation artist Puni Kukahiko finds expression for social and cultural concerns through the unusual medium of cast chocolate. Originally part of a large-scale installation, the work as shown here consists of multiple figures of hula dancers cast in milk chocolate, made from a mold taken from a commercial Hawaiian souvenir figure of an amply endowed, bare-breasted performer. The figures serve as a commentary on the ways in which traditional Hawaiian culture has been commodified and sold as tourist souvenirs. Kukahiko has remarked that, as "a native Hawaiian woman, indigenous to the islands of Hawai'i, I am not inspired but provoked to create work that addresses the pride and shame of a rich cultural heritage and a socially and economically disenfranchised people in our own homeland."

Another Hawaiian artist, Kaili Chun, engages the viewer by presenting iconic objects related to Hawai'i, isolated in vitrines made of *koa* wood, a Hawaiian species of acacia (see page 72). One of the rarest and most precious trees found on the Hawaiian islands, *koa* carries with it rich cultural associations. In one of her works, the objects in the vitrines are a *kāhili* (ceremonial feather staff) and a white cross (symbolic of the Christian religion introduced into Hawai'i). Through these devices, Chun deals with issues of revelation and concealment, the viewer and the viewed, and the sacred and the secular.[11]

Environmental concerns are also addressed by many of the artists in *Changing Hands 2*, ranging from the abuse and destruction of the natural world to the dangers of rampant, uncontrolled development. *Clearly Salmon*, 2004 (page 62), by Idaho artist Thelissa M. Redhawk, is a transparent fish of acrylic epoxy containing the man-made detritus that is contaminating the rivers in which the salmon swim—telephone parts, a railroad spike, a hammer head, Christmas lights, tin-box lids, and a plastic six-pack holder. The traditional Wasco twined basket (known as a Sally Bag) is the format adopted by Oregon artist Pat Courtney Gold. Gold works in traditional fibers—dogbane, cattail, tule, and sedge grasses, which she harvests and prepares using traditional methods—as well as more innovative and unorthodox "fibers," including barbed wire, bicycle chains, plastic bags, and audio tape. Gold's *Honoring Women, The Victors of Breast Cancer*, 2003 (page 31), is a poignant narrative of loss. A more political tone is struck in her *Indigenous People, Obstacles in the Way of Progress*, 2004 (page 76).

Mixed-media and installation artist Corwin "Corky" Clairmont's *Split Shield*, 2001 (page 63), is part of an ongoing series in which he addresses the destruction of Native homelands and the natural environment by highway development. The "shield," hung with paper feathers painted with trucks, consists of large fragments of cast paper made to simulate shredded automobile tires. It encircles a collage of photo-transferred images on cotton cloth, featuring landscapes, tire tracks, and the imprint of a human hand, with the cloth split into two jagged pieces by a "lightning bolt" of white space.

Material Evidence

> Traditionally, Indians embraced new materials with which to create and new ideas to express.
> —Marcus Amerman

The works in *Changing Hands 2* are exemplary of the Native artists' profound engagement with traditional and innovative materials and processes. The Museum of Arts & Design has recognized that the boundaries and hierarchies that kept craft and design separate from art are no longer valid; the artists whose works are included in this exhibition provide ample and convincing proof of this timely model. With skill and finesse, they give a fresh new voice to mute materials, from the historic and traditional (such as pipestone, antler, seal gut, and fur) to the modern (acrylics and neon). The traditional ones are sometimes associated with regional practices (beadwork from the Plains, wood carving from the Northwest); however, more often than not, they are freely used by artists across the board for the aesthetic integrity of the material itself and the profound engagement with the material that is fundamental to all art, design, and craft.

> In order for traditions to remain traditional, they must always change and adapt to present ways. Otherwise they become part of dead cultures.
> —Ronald Senungetuk

In *Guarded Secrets*, 2005 (pages 108–09), Alaskan artist Sonya Kelliher-Combs combines traditional walrus gut and porcupine quills to make spiky cellular forms that simultaneously attract and threaten the viewer. Wilma Osborne, a fellow Alaskan, employs a wide range of indigenous materials—primarily animal skins and fur—to create contemporary accessories that are her unique fashion statements, including hats and carrying bags, such as *Messenger Bag*, 2003 (page 97). A more traditional skin-sewer, Rosalie Paniyak, has employed similar materials for *My Love, This Liberty*, 2005 (page 105), her personal interpretation of a national icon, the Statue of Liberty, basing her impressions on television coverage of the terrorist attacks in New York on September 11, 2001.

Montana artist Molly Murphy's *Parfleche Abstraction, Cool Tones Warm Tones*, 2005 (page 126), features a pair of bandolier bags constructed in a classic form that can be aligned with the modern "shoulder bag." She has used brightly colored cloth appliqué and incorporated motifs most closely associated with those on historical Plains beadwork, now translated into purely abstract, geometric designs. Murphy believes that "many aspects of traditional Native art and design dovetail with contemporary art theory and color theory." Her work presents "what I learned from tribal bead workers on equal footing with design masters such as Matisse and Mondrian."

Moana K. M. Eisele, a mixed-media collage artist from Hawai'i, has combined traditional Hawaiian *kapa* (bark cloth) with a *kua pōhaka* (stone anvil) and a branchlike wooden element in her *Mohala Mau (Forever blooming forth)*, 2001 (page 108), a mysterious but engaging sculptural composition that underscores the timeless link of the past to the present. Fellow Hawaiian artist Keʻalaonaonapuahīnano Campton is represented in the show by a series of four small black-and-white panels in acrylic resin and aluminum on canvas, also 2001 (page 112), each of which contains between one and five astronomical glyphs. Each panel represents a line from a prayer, recontextualized by the choice of materials and the simple, reductive style: what was spoken silently or in a more intimate setting is presented here as a universal abstraction that encourages a more subjective interpretation.

The relationships between artists, their materials, and their unique cultural heritages is exemplified more literally in the

skillfully woven *Anoni Hats*, 2004 (page 122), fitted with colorful and traditionally constructed leis made of brightly colored bird's feathers, by Kilohana Domingo and his mother Lehua Domingo, thereby providing a visual transition from one generation to the next.

Also explored in "Material Evidence" are the values assigned to both common and precious materials. The appeal of simple or ordinary materials to convey a personal message has been beautifully exploited by California artist Brian Tripp in his *Necklace*, 2000 (page 119). At first glance, the necklace appears to be made of exotic stones and silver; closer inspection reveals an assemblage of smooth river pebbles held together with commercial duct tape and separated by plastic beads. On the opposite end of the spectrum is the work of artist and master jeweler Kenneth Johnson, renowned for his work in gold, platinum, and precious and semiprecious stones. His elegant *Three-Tiered Turtle Gorget Necklace*, 2004 (page 94), evokes an ancient form of pectoral ornament, now translated into an opulent wearable sculpture.

Oklahoma artist Juanita Pahdopony used found objects—standard aluminum car hubcaps and tractor-clutch springs—to create *Plains Shield II*, 2002 (page 114), a work that is infused with numerous meanings, both literal and abstract. In choosing these materials, Pahdopony, like Tripp, also reflects on the changing nature of materials in an ever-evolving world in which the term "natural" must be constantly redefined. These artists underscore the potential of new or rediscovered materials while reminding us that Indian art has always changed and evolved while retaining historical authority.[12]

Materials readily identified with the Native craft traditions—wood, feathers, skin, and fiber—are prominently represented in this section, but so too are more unusual materials, such as the water laser–cut and anodized aluminum used with consummate skill by Robert Davidson in *Meeting at the Centre*, 2004 (page 117), or the recycled plastics found by Dan Worcester and reconfigured in his unique and colorful knife handles (page 119). Bridging past and present is the exemplary work of Maynard White Owl Lavadour, whose *Purse*, 2003 (page 219), combines faceted gold-plated metal beads with traditional glass beads to suggest the sparkle of water in which his beaded fish swim.

> We as people and artists are constantly in need of change—of finding new ways to interpret old knowledge and express traditional values in a new format.
> —David Ruben Piqtoukun

Glass, whether blown, cast, or cold worked, is a relatively new material for a significant number of Native artists today,[13] who are using it to create a diverse array of objects.[14] Since being adopted by artists such as Larry Ahvakana and Preston Singletary, to name but two, it is a medium that has been propelled into the mainstream of Native art, not only among Native artists in the Northwest but in other areas too, today including Southwest artists

Tony Jojola and Tammy Garcia, whose skilled work in ceramics was featured in the Museum's *Changing Hands* 1 exhibition in 2002.[15]

While some of these artists work primarily, or even exclusively, in glass, others incorporate it into multi-media works. Preston Singletary replaces traditional carved wood with delicately sand-engraved glass in works such as his *Bentwood Chest*, 2004 (page 110), and Hawaiian artist Bernice A. Keolamauloa oʻnalani Akamine uses glass in combination with other materials for her organic underwater forms, such as *ā pele*, 2001 (page 111).

Turned and carved wood, now exceptionally popular worldwide, appear more and more frequently within the context of Native arts. While they are fundamentally traditional, Native artists give them new life using techniques such as lamination and lathe turning (Alan Bell, *Bowl*, 2004, page 125), inlay (Nathan Hart, *Turned and Inlaid Bowl*, 2005, page 209), carving (Ivy Hāliʻimaile Andrade, *Nā Niho ʻoki*, 2005, page 114), and as a canvas for painting, as in the work of Steve Smith, Carl Stromquist, and Bradley Hunt.

Pattern is also a quintessential feature of traditional Native work, but the tradition flourishes with new vigor today. Whether using glass beads, woven or twined fiber, or inlaid stone, abstract pattern making is an important tributary in the international artistic mainstream. The stone and silver inlay patterns created by Montana-born artist Robert Gress in his belt buckles and other ornaments evoke the geometry of early painted parfleche designs. Oregon artist Joey Lavadour uses twined fiber to create bold staccato rhythms of color and shape in his baskets. Dan Worcester's laminated plastic knife handles, mentioned above, also derive their visual impact from boldly contrasting colors.

Beyond Function

In our culture there was no word for art. In the past, everything we did in our everyday life had aspects of art involved in it. Our houses were works of art, we traveled in canoes that were monumental art pieces, we ate our food from works of art, and our celebrations of story, song, and dance revolved around the art. But I do not believe we should stay in the past with the art. We must take who we are today and our experiences and move the art to new levels. While I use the traditional forms and structures of my ancestors, I also have the vision of new ideas and new materials to make the art speak to me today.
—Bradley Hunt

The paraphernalia of daily life often function on two or more levels simultaneously. Such quotidian objects—clothing, tools and implements, recreational devices—are necessary adjuncts for contemporary life; however, they may also be imbued in their making and use with cultural signifiers that give them a position and importance far beyond that of the merely practical. These signifiers may include the choice of materials, whether local or imported, rare or commonplace; the specialized and often virtuoso skills needed to transform the materials into recognizable forms; and

the diversity of visual and symbolic colors, patterns, and textures with which they are embellished.

Everyday objects such as these are also potent reminders of specific cultural histories, personal aesthetics, and visual vocabularies of motif and form. Many of the artists whose works have been selected for *Changing Hands* 2 explore the unlimited potential of practical objects to elicit memories, confirm the expected, inspire, and amuse. They can range from ordinary items of clothing and dress, tools, implements, and even communications equipment, to objects that evoke a powerful sense of ritual by serving as tangible manifestations of cultural and spiritual values.

Some expressions of form "beyond function" may be literal. Demonstrating the triumph of visual effect over functional requirements, Hawaiian artist Dean Kaahanui's *Surfboard*, 2004 (page 160), is ornamented at the top with extraordinary carved motifs, a life-size talisman commemorating and celebrating his deep cultural links to the Pacific Ocean. Alaskan-born artist Jerry Jacob Laktonen's beautiful and fragile *Dream Paddles*, 2004 (page 160), were created as objects that are to be viewed more as abstract sculpture, a contrast to the paddles that were integral to daily life and survival for previous generations of Native Americans. The spindle whorl used by the indigenous peoples of the Northwest Coast to twine fibers for weaving is the starting point for *Return*, 2003 (page 168), a sculpture in glass, wood, and steel by Vancouver artist Susan Point. She has translated the form of a simple hand spindle into an oversize version of the implement, constructed of fragile glass and unabashedly modern stainless steel.

Many artists featured in *Changing Hands* 2 have drawn on familiar historical forms as reference points for new work, as is evident in the basketry forms favored by Oregon artist Joe Feddersen, which echo decorative elements seen on traditional twined basketry. Feddersen's glass baskets—for example, *Parking Lot*, 2004 (page 169)—are at once visual and tactile: the textured surfaces he achieves with the technique of wheel cutting is reminiscent, but not derivative, of the surfaces of vessels designed by twentieth-century Italian master Carlo Scarpa using the *battuto* ("hammered") technique.

At the other end of the spectrum are materials that have remained constant for generations, but which today are used in innovative ways by contemporary Native artists. While the materials may indeed be identified with that which is more traditional, their uses by current artists are often unexpected. For example, Vancouver master carver Gary Olver used catlinite to create his diminutive, elegant, and purely decorative and emblematic *Halibut Hook*, 2003 (page 152), while Minnesotan artist Todd Defoe has used the same material to make astonishing, witty objects that explore the notions of function and dysfunction. Defoe merges his skill at carving with his love of music in a series of musical instruments—violins, woodwinds, and keyboard instruments—made of this stone. His *Improvisation #5*, 2005 (page 167), is a fantastic but ostensibly playable musical instrument that recalls the dreamlike melting shapes in several paintings by Surrealist artist Salvador Dali.

In this ongoing exploration of conventional and unconventional uses of materials, *Tele Box*, 1999 (page 166), by Northwest Coast artist YáYa (Charles Peter Heit), is unusual. The push-button telephone is housed in a hand-carved box made largely from prized and costly materials—birds-eye and curly maple, ebony, and mahogany—most of them not indigenous to the Northwest Coast. Details such as the abalone-shell inlay recall the nacreous shell used for decorating headdresses and other regalia displayed at potlatches and other ceremonies. YáYa's account of making the piece reveals his wry sense of humor: "In 1999 I got my hands on some really nice-lookin [sic] wood. Bird's-eye maple and curly maple. I thought I should offer to do the new owner's initials on the sides, if they like. Until someone bought the phone, I decided to put Billy Gates' initials on one side for display. I don't know who bought it, but they didn't ask me to put their own initials on. I enjoyed making the piece, but it wuz [sic] a lot of trouble and too much time."

Another group of artists whose work is included in "Beyond Function" have focused on the metaphorical meanings and cultural memories embedded in traditional garments and ceremonial regalia, sometimes reinterpreting garments and accessories in witty and surprising ways. The series of *Miniature Hat Pendants*, 2002 (page 170), twine-woven from spruce root by Northwest Coast artist Primrose Adams and painted by her son Alfred Adams, feature exaggerated and stylized animal motifs inspired by traditional wide-brimmed hats worn for ceremonies and special occasions. The Adamses' "hats," though, are diminutive pendants made to be worn at the neck. Extending the concept of wearable art to a highly theatrical level, Alaskan artist Peter Lind's *Aleut Chief's Hat*, 2004 (page 156), is modeled after the visorlike headdresses traditionally worn by Aleutian hunters to protect their eyes from the strong sunlight; these were often decorated with elaborate talismans to ensure success in the hunt.

Fiber artist Lisa Telford's *A Night on the Village*, 2004 (page 157), is woven from red cedar bark, a traditional material used in Northwest Coast basketry. However, that is where the similarity ends. Whereas traditional native dress is generally modest, and the wearer appropriately concealed, this garment provocatively spotlights the female body rather than offering warmth or protection from the elements—more suitable for partying at a dance club than for a fishing expedition. Alaskan artist Rebecca Lyon, for her *Women of the North* series, 2004 (pages 154–55), has made full-scale versions of traditional garments worn by Tlingit/Haida, Yup'ik, Athabascan, and Aleut women, in hand-hammered copper. Explaining that they are dedicated to her late mother, Lyon observed, "As I have looked back to make a connection with past generations of women in my family, I lament that no personal artifacts or mementos from either of my great-grandmothers or the woman before them have been passed down in my family. Even though I wear Gap jeans and live a non-traditional lifestyle, one day some part of me will join [these four women] inside this symbolic copper vessel too, because I have found that I wear traditional clothing on the inside."

Historian and beadwork artist Tom Haukaas has created a pair of elaborate garments—*Special Boy's Shirt*, 2004, and *Special Girl's Dress*, 2005 (page 147)—commemorating the death of a significant individual in his life. Within the framework of a traditional Creation story, Haukaas has embellished both the shirt and dress with highly personal images of flora and fauna that are simultaneously spiritual, abstract, and decorative.

Noted South Dakota artist and scholar Arthur Amiotte takes non-functionality to a new level in his *Woman's Dress: An Impressionistic Sketch in Fiber*, 2005 (page 150), a wall piece based on a traditional, early-style Plains dress. Amiotte has reinterpreted the garment as pure line, texture, and color (blue and white), using natural and synthetic fibers, glass trade beads, brass hawk bells, seashells, tanned elk hide, tin cones, and an elk tooth. The strong presence evoked by this piece suggests that the ancestral women of the Plains are also emblems of a living culture that remains vital.

Two artists—Canadian Keri-Lynn Dick and Alaskan Paula Rasmus Dede—have each chosen to make unwearable wearables in the form of high-heeled shoes. Keri-Lynn Dick's *Pair of Shoes*, 2003 (page 156), employs shredded cedar bark fiber (traditionally used for basketry and woven panels) for an unconventional purpose, and embellishes each shoe with a small, carved wooden mask. Rasmus Dede's *Not Your Mama's Mary Janes*, 2003 (page 174), with their monumental platform soles and heels and a baroque flurry of decoration, offers a wry commentary on contemporary street gear. Referring to the frequently "over-the-top" flourishes that give her works a special character, Rasmus Dede says, "I love using a riotous mix of colors in creating objects. I also use heavy ornamentation and fringe to push an object beyond the ordinary."

Ritual objects in *Changing Hands 2* are commemorated for their compelling visual presence as well as their symbolic content. Often these objects become the basis for an exploration of form, color, and pattern in their own right. Hawaiian artist Paulette Nohealani Kahalepuna's *Hand Kāhili*, 2005 (page 105), are modern versions of the elaborate feathered standards that signified the presence of royalty. Historically, such kāhili were made from a variety of extremely rare, colorful, or distinctively patterned feathers, were given individual names, and their use was strictly limited to ceremonial purposes.

Drums, too, serve both symbolic and artistic purposes, and have been used more frequently by contemporary artists as canvases for painted imagery. Among these is the traditional-style box drum that Lawrence "Larry" Ahvakana deconstructed into a four-paneled wall relief for his *Qatluaqaq Tim-Inua, Spirit of the Box Drum*, 2004 (page 171), combining red and yellow cedar, red oak, and horsehair with glass, acrylic, and fluorescent tubing.

Ceremonial dance masks—carved in wood and made for specific rituals or narratives—have long been identified with Native cultures, most specifically with those from the Northwest Coast and Alaska, and are ubiquitous in the work of contemporary artists who employ the form as a reminder of historical precedent, but also to serve more subjective and contemporary aesthetic goals. *Negaquaq (North Wind Spirits)*, 2003 (page 146), by Phillip Charette (also known by his Native name, Aarnaquq), consists of a pair of imposing and theatrical masks intended as wall sculpture rather than for active use. Among the materials that Charette has used are raku-fired clay pendants that serve as wind chimes, adding another sensory experience.

Taken as a whole, these objects eloquently, and often poignantly, transcend traditional hierarchies of function. The materials chosen by each artist, the techniques employed, and the suggestive presence of historical prototypes make them compelling statements of contemporary vision.

Nature as Subject

Just as our spirit is being revived, so can the spirit of nature. Are we *xaa.aadaa* (humanity) ready to take on the challenge of rethinking how we view our world?
—Robert Davidson

The works presented in this section refer to the primary elements of air, earth, and water, but from diverse, subjective points of view. Native art celebrates the full range of the natural world, from prairie flora to coastal fauna, evoking universal themes that can be traced through the history of all cultures. However, the personal and spiritual relationship with the land among Native peoples, even with the social disruption and isolation that came with the forced move of tribes from their ancestral lands, cannot be underestimated as a special source of inspiration for Native artists. Colleen Cutschall emphasizes the importance of nature in the Plains cultures, and the belief in "the earth as a site or space in which . . . reconnection occurs. Reconnection implies a need to connect, to know, to become a part of, to have direct involvement, and to affect. It is the impulse to bring thought or consciousness into action or form or both."[16] Using an impressive variety of traditional and non-traditional materials, these artists achieve a delicate and graceful balance between subjective and objective nature, demonstrating the skill that unites hand, eye, and mind in the production of a work of art.

The progression of the seasons has informed many of the ancient traditions and rituals of all Native cultures, including those in the Northwest. Specific activities, such as fishing, are often assigned to a specific month and carried out under the guidance of the moon associated with that month in Native mythologies. Canadian Northwest artist Tim Paul's series of masks from 1999–2000 (page 186) represents this lunar cycle and some of the events and activities governed by the changing moons over the course of the year. Paul has revived the forms of early ceremonial masks, but has translated them here into a contemporary narrative.[17] His *December Moon* is painted with stylized snowflakes and symbolizes the month "when the moon sits on the surface of the water for four days"; *April Moon* is carved and painted with images of migratory geese flying in a flock; *May Moon: The Month the Fur Seal Is Hunted* is painted with his

abstract versions of appropriate marine forlines. The spiritual presence of nature is underscored in a work by New Mexico jeweler and sculptor Keri Ataumbi, *Tah'lee's Parents*, 2004 (page 202), a necklace made of silver and gold, and cast from a living oak branch—a tree whose leaves are identified with her cultural ancestors and incorporates a reference to Sun Boy, the offspring of the sun and the earth.

Images of fish and water are found in several works, including one by New Mexico artist Ed Archie NoiseCat, whose *Spirit of the Salmon I*, 2002 (page 227), is an homage to the mainstay food of the Pacific Northwest. NoiseCat frequently uses images drawn from nature as signs of his people's continuing relationship with nature. Oregon artist Lillian Pitt, generally known for her work in clay, today uses a wide variety of materials in her sculptures, including painted copper and aluminum, as in *Fish Rattle*, 2003 (page 219). The core of meaning in Pitt's work is found in the world of nature: "In the spring, I walked up to the hills to lie down on the ground and watch the plants grow. The smallest, most minute flowers were beautiful. No one else seemed to see them. Time seemed to stop in the open country."[18] *Fish Rattle*, based on an ancient rattle form, celebrates the existence of the Pacific salmon, which has played such an important role in Native history.

Forest Dweller: The Bear, 1998 (page 215), by Missouri artist and designer Margaret Roach Wheeler, is both a fashion statement and a costume. It consists of a coat and headdress that simulates, in color, texture, and detailing, the essence of a bear—a fundamental component of Native imagery and mythology. Wheeler created this work to be used in performance; accompanied by sound and light, the garment is animated both literally and figuratively by the wearer.

Other fauna appear in numerous works in this exhibition. Two of Kevin Pourier's unusual spoons carved of buffalo horn feature animal motifs: the power of the buffalo stampede and the vast stretches of the Plains are suggested in his *White Buffalo Spoon*, 2003 (page 210), while his *Butterfly Spoon*, 2002 (page 207), captures the dramatic flight of monarch butterflies. Pourier is one of the few Native carvers now working in this medium; his delicately carved and engraved motifs are inlaid with a variety of finely ground stones—such as malachite, turquoise, and coral—for their rich, natural colors. The archetypal buffalo also appears on the lid of Colorado artist Pahponee's dramatic vase *New Age*, 2003 (page 211), intended as a symbol of what she calls "an age of transformation."

Oregon artist Rick Bartow's animals, such as his *Dog Pack Series*, 2003 (page 213), are composed of found wood, recycled nails, and paint. These sculptures are highly schematic yet exuberant, infused with the energy of life conveyed through pose and gesture, and with the intention to "honor the diverse cultural images that helped spawn these sculptures." They recall totemic objects of the Northwest and highly charged nail fetishes from Zaïre,[19] but they are also imbued with Bartow's idiosyncratic sense of humor, which along with "curiosity rest[s] just beneath the surface of metal, hair, and nails."

The panoply of creativity evident in the works of art presented in *Changing Hands 2* provokes an important question: Is there a "renaissance" of creativity found in the Native North American community of artists that was not there earlier, or is it more that the works that these innovative artists are creating are at long last being reevaluated as more than cultural artifacts? In reality, it is both. The evolution of the arts that began with a group of artists who initiated a new chapter in the history of Indian art—Bill Reid, George Morrison, Fritz Scholder, Alan Houser, Charles Loloma, and James Schoppert, to name but a few—continues with extraordinary vitality and diversity today. Native artists now have opportunities to launch their careers in new territories and pursue new ideas to an extent perhaps only imagined by an earlier generation. We are becoming aware of the large number of talented individuals of Native heritage who are currently creating art of global significance. The most crucial aspect of this "renaissance" is expressed by one of the artists included here, Preston Singletary: "It is important to realize that Native cultures are alive and it is we who are declaring who we are and what new traditions are developing." Native art, we believe, has been de-regionalized and is no longer defined by tribal stereotypes or by a romantic revision of history. We are deeply grateful to all of these creators, and honored to have contributed to a new understanding of Native art through this series of exhibitions.

NOTES

1. Henri Focillon, *The Life of Forms in Art* [*Vie des formes*, 1934], translated by Charles B. Hogan and George Kubler (New York: Wittenborn, Schultz, 1948; New York: Zone Books, 1992), p. 31.

2. Bently Spang, quoted in Ian Berry, *Staging the Indian: The Politics of Representation*, with essays by Jill D. Sweet, Katherine Hauser, and Barry M. Pritzker (Saratoga Springs, N.Y.: Tang Teaching Museum and Art Gallery, Skidmore College, 2002), p. 129.

3. Unless otherwise specified, all commentaries from artists are excerpts from recent written or verbal communications to the authors of this essay.

4. Probably the first efforts to position Indian art within the framework of modern art was the exhibition *Indian Art of the United States* at the Museum of Modern Art, New York, January 22–April 27, 1941 (organized by the Indian Arts and Crafts Board of the U.S. Department of the Interior, under the direction of the museum's general manager, Rene d'Harnoncourt, in collaboration with Frederic H. Douglas, curator of Indian art at the Denver Museum). However, it should be noted that the works were presented in the same way that African art was then generally regarded, as another body of "primitive" art that was resonant with the modern art movement.

5. Bruce Bernstein, "Community as Context," in Gerald McMaster, ed., *Reservation X* (Seattle: University of Washington Press, and Hull, Quebec: Canadian Museum of Civilization, 1998), p. 13.

6. Berry, *Staging the Indian*, p. 72 (see n. 2, above).

7. *Changing Hands: Art Without Reservation 3* (scheduled for 2009) will examine developments east of the Mississippi River, the southeastern and northeastern United States, and eastern Canada.

8. "The key to even the most basic understanding of native communities is to move beyond stereotypes to the realization that native people today are making change happen for themselves. Virtually all North American native societies have suffered military conquest, mass murder, disenfranchisement, relentless cultural attacks, exploitation, and neglect. This treatment left grim legacies resulting in despair, hopelessness, poverty, and dependence. Even so, in many cases, great strides are being made. Far from having vanished into the sunset, native people across North America are defending their rights, revitalizing their cultures, an attempting to live with dignity as native people in the twenty-first century." Barry M. Pritzker, "A Current Political Perspective," in Berry, *Staging the Indian*, p. 39 (see n. 2, above).

9. The Museum of Contemporary Crafts (later called the American Craft Museum, and now renamed the Museum of Arts & Design) acquired its first piece of native American ceramics, a black-feather decorated plate made in 1968 by Maria Martinez and Popovi Da (1977.2.57), in the 1970s. It is significant that this object was among the works circulated in a landmark crafts exhibition, *OBJECTS: USA*, funded by the Johnson Wax Company in 1977, which served as a bellwether for the new and rapidly expanding world of craft as art.

10. From a statement written for the Eiteljorg Museum artist's competition in 2002, and quoted in Janet Catherine Berlo, "Susie Silook: 'Simultaneous Worlds' and the Yupik Imagination," in *After the Storm: The Eiteljorg Fellowship for Native American Fine Art 2001* (Indianapolis, Ind.: Eiteljorg Museum, 2001), p. 80.

11. James Jensen, *The Contemporary Museum Biennial Exhibition of Hawai'i Artists*, 2003 (Honolulu, Hawai'i: The Contemporary Museum, 2003), p. 6.

12. "[A]s in all the elements that go to make up any particular material culture tradition, the change in technique or tools and the substitution or addition of foreign materials do not necessarily alter the total traditional aspect of an object," J. C. H. King, "Tradition in Native American Art," in Edwin L. Wade, ed., *The Arts of the North American Indian: Native Traditions in Evolution* (New York: Hudson Hills Press, 1986), p. 68.

13. There is, of course, a long and distinguished tradition of Native art using commercial glass beads beginning at the time of contact and trade with Anglos.

14. See Carolyn Kastner, ed., *Fusing Traditions: Transformations in Glass by Native American Artists*, with essays by Roslyn Tunis, Preston Singletary, Kate Morris, and Lloyd E. Herman (San Francisco: Museum of Craft & Folk Art, 2002).

15. *Tammy Garcia: Visions in Glass: A Collaboration with Preston Singletary* (Santa Fe and Taos, N.M.: Blue Rain Gallery, 2005).

16. W. Jackson Rushing III, ed., *Native American Art in the Twentieth Century: Makers, Meanings, Histories* (London and New York: Routledge, 1999), p. 191.

17. Peter Macnair, "Power of the Shining Heavens," in Peter Macnair, Robert Joseph, and Bruce Grenville, *Down from the Shimmering Sky: Masks of the Northwest Coast* (Seattle: University of Washington Press, 1998), p. 47.

18. Quoted in Elizabeth Woody, "Growing Up on the Reservation," *Bend Living* (Spring 2004), p. 43.

19. Nails, as used by Bartow, not only suggest African fetishes but may also refer to the harpoons of the whale hunt. Noted by Rebecca J. Dobkins in her monograph *Rick Bartow: My Eye* (Seattle and London: Hallie Ford Museum of Art, in association with University of Washington Press, 2002), p. 40.

THE HUMAN CONDITION

All art addresses issues of the human condition, whether as investigations of subjective states of awareness and psychological revelation or as those with ironic, humorous, or satirical intent. This theme—the richly diverse and multifaceted nature of our individual and collective lives—is necessarily the largest and arguably the most provocative in the exhibition. Here, challenging questions are raised about issues that have the most profound relevance to the content of the works of art: personal and cultural identity in the twenty-first century; historical, political, and social commentary; environmental concerns; and systems of belief and mythology that place an individual within her or his cultural context.

Note about measurements in the captions:
Height precedes width precedes depth, unless
specified otherwise.

C. MAXX STEVENS

b. in *Wewoka, Oklahoma; lives in Santa Fe, New Mexico*

"I was lucky I grew up around artists all my life. Tradition is heritage, custom, culture, belief, attitude. It is all that and more; it is what is inside you and how you get it out. Tradition is very important to me, but at the same time I really like change. Oral tradition was very important in my family when I was growing up, and as a very quiet person who would rather die than speak in public, I knew I had to do something to let my voice and stories out. I found installations to be the perfect vehicle and format for me to work in. I like people to go into one of my pieces and discover a story or be affected by the materials or process."

Memory Prom Dress, 2005

Printed digital images on paper, chicken-wire and metal-rod armature on wheels, wire, horsehair braid, found objects (wooden birdcage, ceramic, pewter Indian, plastic rats, electric lights) H. 60 in., Diam. 53 in. (152.4 x 134.6 cm)

Collection of the artist

JAMES LUNA

b. 1950, Orange, California; lives on La Jolla Indian Reservation, La Jolla, California

"In creating this work, I was very conscious of an Indian theme that would speak out to all humanity concerning something that we all share, the ritual of death—a ritual that is both solemn and joyous. *The Spirits of Virtue and Evil* represents a multicultural artwork. The installation is patterned after a 'traditional' but contemporary Luiseño funeral. The all-night wake starting at dusk begins with a Catholic rosary, followed by traditional Indian singers who sing a series of complex songs till sunrise. The graveside service continues with a Catholic blessing, then more Indian singing, and closes with old Christian hymns sung in English and Spanish."

The Spirits of Virtue and Evil Await My Ascension, 1999

Installation: One "Indian Lounge Suit," one "High-Tech War Shirt," wire armatures for costumes, umbrellas, found blanket, table stand for blanket, CD player with CDs, lighting with color gels
Dimensions variable

Collection of the artist

MARIANNE NICOLSON

b. 1969, Vancouver Island, British Columbia;
lives in Victoria, British Columbia

"In my works for public art spaces, I engage in the exploration of traditional concepts and incorporate contemporary mediums into the visual presentation of these concepts. While I consider that the formal aspects of Northwest Coast cultural production is well represented in museums and commercial galleries and will carry on well into the twenty-first century, the conceptual foundations of this work are endangered owing to radical acculturation and language loss. Creating artworks that address these issues and express traditional concepts in new ways in public art spaces is my way of perpetuating and preserving Kwakwak'wakw culture as well as sharing those concepts with a wider audience."

Portrait of Am'yax̱íd, 2001

Photographic transparencies, Plexiglas, acrylic, wood
62 x 51 1/2 in. (157.5 x 130.8 cm)

Canada Council Art Bank

TERI GREEVES

b. 1970, Wind River Reservation, Wyoming;
lives in Santa Fe, New Mexico

"A long time ago, a Kiowa woman brought bead-work to her Kiowa people. She was compelled to express herself and her experience as a Kiowa woman of her day. My grandmother was a bead-worker. She too was compelled to bead/express herself and her experience as a Kiowa living during her time. I am a beadworker. I am compelled to do it. I have no choice in the matter. I must express myself and my experience as a twenty-first-century Kiowa, and I do it, like all of those unknown artists before me, through beadwork."

Gkoy-Goo: The Story of My People,
2000

Brain-tanned deerskin, glass beads, brass and nickel studs, brass tacks, birchwood trunk
17 x 32 x 16 in. (43.2 x 81.3 x 40.6 cm)

Collection of Eric and Barbara Dobkin

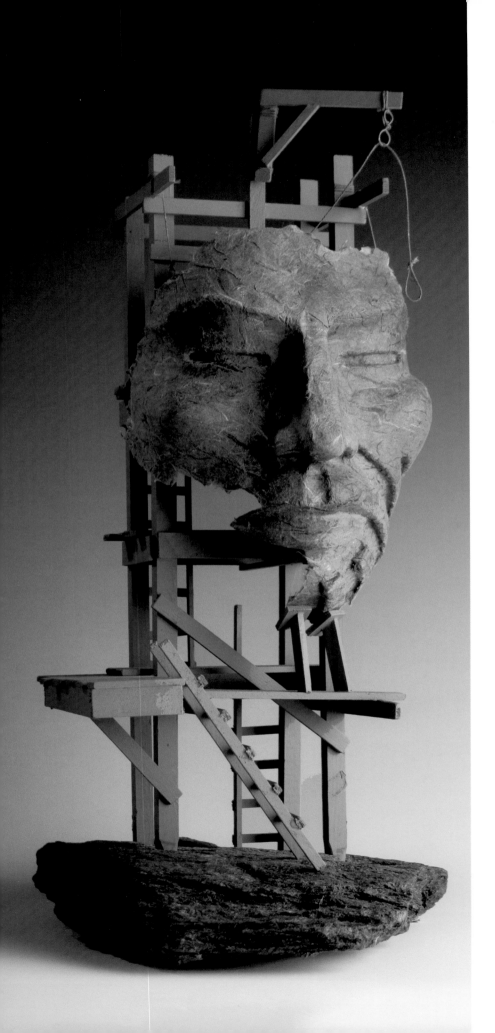

JACK ABRAHAM

b. 1956, Umkumiut, Nelson Island, Alaska;
lives in Anchorage, Alaska

"As a contemporary artist, I feel privileged
to draw from a rich heritage. I try to convey
something in most of my work other than
the aesthetics."

Personal Armor Revisited, 2004

Paper, bass wood, cedar,
acrylic spray paint,
found rock
16 x 7 x 9 in. (40.6 x 17.8 x
22.9 cm)

Courtesy of St. Pierre Galleries

NICHOLAS GALANIN

b. 1979, Sitka, Alaska; lives in Sitka

"Tradition is a gift; diversity is a form of wealth. Tlingit historic arts provide a solid foundation to build upon. Coming from a culture with a strong visual language, I risk cutting myself free from this when I work away from these forms. Through my current works, I am exploring issues of indigenous identity—a living culture portrayed through scholarly books, often written with a foreign perspective."

What Have We Become? Vol. II,
2004

Paper
11 x 7 x 8 in. (27.9 x 17.8 x 20.3 cm)

Collection of the artist

JAMES MADISON

b. 1973, Tulalip, Washington; lives in Marysville, Washington

"After studying European Art and growing up watching my father paint in abstract form, I became very interested in that particular style of art. Artist legends such as Van Gogh, Dali, and Picasso became a great inspiration to me. Using a combination of Northwest Coast carving and design methods along with contemporary abstract design, I was able to bring my culture to a new level. One side of the face represents my Tlingit Indian heritage. This is done using Tlingit formline design, stylized elements. The opposite side of the face represents my Snoqualmie/Snohomish heritage, which is Salish. Here, I use stylized Salish elements to form my design."

Self-Portrait, 2003

Bronze
$9^1/_2$ x 7 x $3^7/_8$ in.
(24.1 x 17.8 x 10 cm)

Collection of the artist

ROBERT DAVIDSON

b. 1946, Hydaburg, Alaska; lives in Surrey, British Columbia

"We Haida were once surrounded by art. Art was one with the culture. Art was our only written language. It documented our progress as a people, it documented the histories of the families. Throughout our history, it has been the art that has kept our spirit alive."

OPPOSITE
Identity, 2005

Bronze
25 x 14 1/2 x 3 3/4 in.
(62.5 x 36.8 x 9.5 cm)

Collection of the artist

PAMELA BAKER

b. 1959, Vancouver, British Columbia;
lives in North Vancouver, British Columbia

"Tradition is very important. My elders and my parents' ancestry have most affected my artistic vision and work—just their will and strength alone. I was drawn to my elders and listened; now I share with my children, nieces, nephews [our] culture, tradition, potlatch. I am aware of what I cannot show; that is why my work is contemporary with traditional influences."

Chilkat Cape, 2005

Wool, dutchess satin,
glass beads
22 x 37 in. (56 x 94 cm)

Collection of the artist

PAT COURTNEY GOLD

b. on Warm Springs Reservation, Oregon;
lives in Scappoose, Oregon

Honoring Women, the Victors
of Breast Cancer, 2003

Cotton, wool, cloth fiber remnant,
ribbon, glass beads, charms
H. 9 in., Diam. 6 in. (22.9 x 15.2 cm)

Collection of the artist

DUANE SLICK

b. 1961, Waterloo, Iowa; lives in North Providence, Rhode Island

"In our information-saturated world, perception becomes truth. *The Meaning of Art* examines the use of context to make a decision and offers a direct challenge to popular perceptions by mainstream America about Native dress and hairstyle as identity signifiers. It provides as a backdrop the weight of histories of tribal nations in images and oral traditions as the criteria for interpreting current events and issues of identity formation.

"As a demonstration of context, the text follows and connects traditional Meskwaki rules with ruminations on events and ideas of identity and assimilation: What does it mean to be 'traditional?'"

The Meaning of Art, 2003
(3 of 6 panels shown here)

Acetate imprinted with photocopied images, acrylic, Plexiglas, human hair, industrial nuts and bolts, hinges
6 panels, *each* 17 x 11 in. (27.9 x 43.2 cm)

Collection of the artist

JUANITA PAHDOPONY

b. in Portland, Oregon; lives in Lawton, Oklahoma

"Although there is no word for 'art' in the Comanche language, it was something that everyone did in so many ways. Tradition is not important to my work if it means how something was done in the generation(s) before our time. American Indian art has been too heavily influenced and defined by the art of the 1950s, characterized by decorative, commercial, and repetitive art and patterns. In actuality, art is adaptable and changeable, just as it has been for all other cultures in the world—we used the materials that were accessible in our environment or we traded to get them. The tradition was change."

Native Woman's Dreams:
Autobiographic Tipi, ca. 1994

Canvas, photographs, paper, acrylic paints, oil pastels, fabric paint, ink
60 x 84 in. (152.4 x 213.4 cm)

Collection of the artist

PUNI KUKAHIKO

b. 1975, Kailua, Oahu, Hawai'i; lives in Honolulu, Hawai'i

"I am a native Hawaiian woman, and it is this position that most affects my artistic vision. I am not inspired but provoked to create work that addresses the pride and shame of a rich cultural heritage and a socially and economically disenfranchised people in our homeland. The separation in Hawai'i between traditional art and contemporary art is a manifestation of the social identity conflict that we as Hawaiians face in every aspect of our lives. Tradition is a continuum of which we are all part; it grows and changes as we do, and our values dictate how tradition is perceived. For Hawaiians especially, we must protect our identity from the external pressures that mean to disregard our ancestors, but also from the internal pressures that can label our ancestors 'authentic, museum-quality, and dead,' because it is our customary belief that our ancestors live on with us in our work and all we do. Beauty is an issue I deal with in my work often. My inheritance as a Polynesian woman is the image of beauty that is 'exotic, erotic, and for the conquering.' Much of my work addresses the 'hula girl' image, and I question my own formations of beauty, womanhood, and sexuality."

Lovely Hula Hands, 2005

Chocolate (plus cakestand, not shown in photo)
each 9 x 3 x 3 in. (22.9 x 7.6 x 7.6 cm)

Collection of the artist

REG DAVIDSON

b. 1954, Massett, Queen Charlotte Islands (Haida Gwaii), British Columbia;
lives in Old Massett, Queen Charlotte Islands

"If you look at Haida art, there are guidelines that you need to follow. I was taught that I must learn the rules before I can bend them. The questions of what is 'traditional' always baffles me. Who is to say whether something is traditional or not? The question I ask is 'When does contemporary become traditional?'"

LEFT
Mercedes, 2003

Red cedar, horsehair,
abalone, seed beads
12 x 14 x 7½ in. (30.5 x
35.6 x 19.1 cm)

Collection of Andria and
Chuck Lawson; courtesy of
Inuit Gallery of Vancouver

RIGHT
Royce, 2003

Red cedar, horsehair,
operculum shells
12 x 12 x 6½ in. (30.5 x
30.5 x 16.5 cm)

Collection of Andria and
Chuck Lawson; courtesy of
Inuit Gallery of Vancouver

SUSIE SILOOK

*b. 1960, Gambell, St. Lawrence Island, Alaska;
lives in Anchorage, Alaska*

"All my life, everywhere, someone was busy making something, so I took it for granted eventually
that I could make something. No one discouraged
me or discriminated against me in any way, when
it came to art work. Instead there was always
encouragement, and materials were freely given.
I'm moved to create angular, bony, sensuous
forms, suited for my materials of bone and ivory.
I prefer that they convey some emotion, some
power, be alive. Rage can be a beautiful thing
to behold, as can sadness.

"Traditionally, one of the purposes in creativity
was to appease spirits. That was beautiful,
although many of yesterday's objects seem
strange or frightening today, if one is not familiar
with them. Are we not still seeking to appease
spirits, albeit of a different sort?"

OPPOSITE
Looking Inside Myself, 2002

Whalebone
13 x 13 x 6 in. (33 x 33 x 15.2 cm)

Collection of Thomas G. Fowler

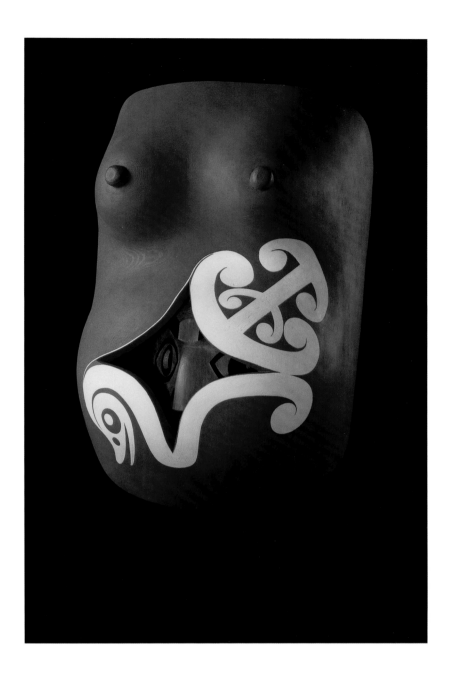

JOE DAVID

*b. 1946, Meares Island, British Columbia;
lives in Vancouver, British Columbia*

"I have no agenda in regard to having a career as
an artist, I'm not interested in seeing my picture
or reading my thoughts in glossy magazines or
receiving arts awards. The life and joy expressed
in my works is the life and joy I experience in my
life, my family, my friends, and my people."

Mother and Child, 2003

Red cedar, cedar bark rope,
human hair, dry earth
pigments, paint
24 x 13¹/₂ x 12 in. (61 x
34.3 x 30.5 cm)

Collection of John and
Joyce Price

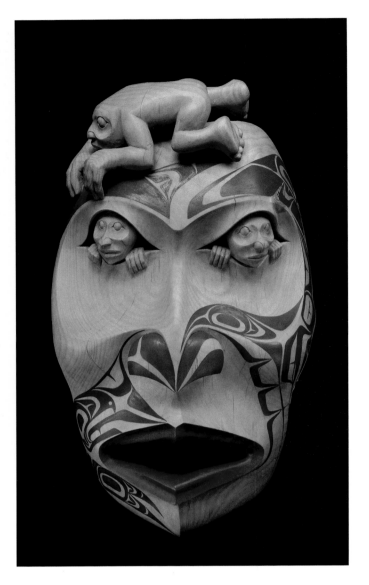

BARRY COFFIN

b. 1947, Lawrence, Kansas; lives in Santa Fe, New Mexico

"As an Indian artist, I think it is time to look to the future. It is time for Indian artists to create new images. To me, it is exciting and inspiring to create something that no one has seen before. It is time for all artists to create art to honor Mother Earth and all of the people living on her. I have been very blessed to be an artist. I hope my artwork has the ability to bring some joy and happiness into everyone's lives."

Ancient Heart Warrior, 2004

Bronze
11 x 8 x 7 in. (27.9 x 20.3 x 17.8 cm)

Collection of the artist

WAYNE YOUNG

b. 1958, Prince Rupert, British Columbia; lives in Victoria, British Columbia

"All of my pieces are directly influenced by the tribal, clan, and family crests and their stories. Tradition is very important in my work, and my interest in sculpture has brought contemporary elements into my carving."

Three Brothers Mask, 1998

Alder, acrylic paint
16 x 9 x 5 in. (40.6 x 22.9 x 12.7 cm)

Private collection; courtesy of Alcheringa Gallery

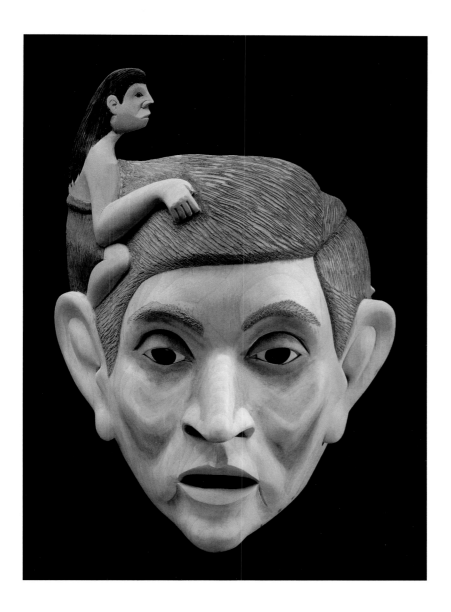

KARITA COFFEY

b. 1947, Lawton, Oklahoma; lives in Santa Fe, New Mexico

"The *Moment of Impact* pin of cast silver is a metaphorical work dealing with two worlds colliding. My brother, Bill Gover, was killed when the car he was riding crashed into a tree in Pawnee, Oklahoma, on March 21, 1981. Three men were killed in that accident, and the forty-year-old tree died, too. From this experience comes the *Moment of Impact* pin: a face (representing my brother) with twigs coming out of the head (the tree). These works are from an ongoing series on memory and place."

STAN GREENE

b. 1953, White Rock, British Columbia;
lives in Chilliwack, British Columbia

The European, 2001

Alder, acrylic paint
13 x 11 1/2 x 5 in. (33 x 29.2 x
12.7 cm)

Courtesy of Lattimer Gallery

Moment of Impact, 2003

Sterling silver
2 x 1 in. (5.1 x 2.5 cm)

Collection of the artist

Wa Wokiye (Helping Hands), 2004

Clay, acrylic paint, painted turkey feather, commercially made plastic hands, white leather, abalone, wax thread
26 x 5 x 3¹/₂ in. (66 x 12.7 x 8.9 cm)

Collection of the artist

Ta Oyate Waokiye (Helps Her People), 2004

Clay, acrylic paint, turquoise 4-direction crosses, glass beads, thread
26 x 5¹/₂ x 3¹/₄ in. (66 x 14 x 8.3 cm)

Collection of the artist

Ta Oyate Wica Gluha (Keeps Her Nation), 2004

Clay, acrylic paint, clear fishing string, glue, glass beads, plastic beads, thread
26 x 5¹/₂ x 3³/₄ in. (66 x 14 x 9.5 cm)

Collection of the artist

MURIEL ANTOINE

b. 1932, Herrick, South Dakota; lives in Mission, South Dakota

"Reflecting on my place in this universe, I add my dedication to preserving the harmony of this country's insight by embodying my art (masks) and poetry as a bridge between the logical thinking and paradox. The masks bring their own power of suggestion that need no words or explanation. Artistic utilization as an indirect teacher is a powerful source of unconscious communication. It touches that part of one's self that responds to the ancient use of symbols from the distant past."

Tahcha Luta (Scarlet Deer), 2004

Clay, acrylic paint, wool, shell buttons, glass beads, abalone buttons, thread
26 x 6 3/4 x 3 3/4 in. (66 x 17.1 x 9.5 cm)

Collection of the artist

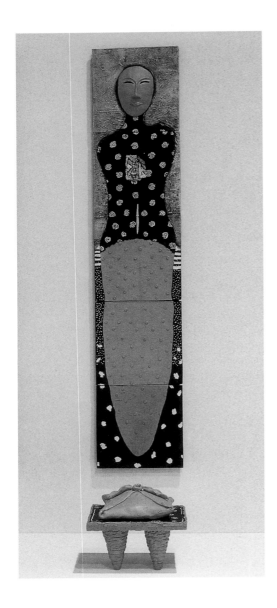

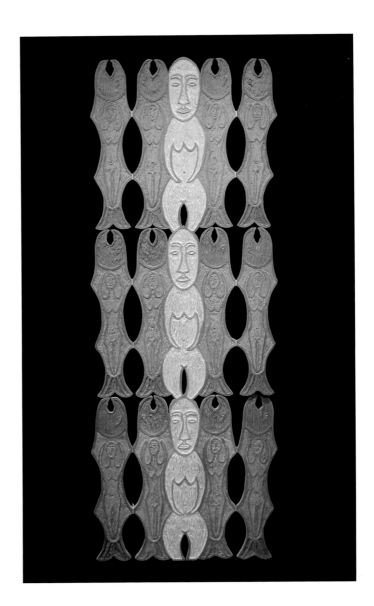

ANITA FIELDS

b. 1951, Hominy, Oklahoma; lives in Stillwater, Oklahoma

"I am inspired by all kinds of experiences—where I come from, my family, ancestors, and the essence of who we are as Osage people. The culture is passed from one generation to the next in order to perpetuate our way of being human. My work is informed and inspired by the emotion invoked through tradition."

Regarding the Elements of Being #2, 2000

Earthenware, terra sigilata, gold leaf
wall piece: 75 x 15 in. (190.5 x 38.1 cm); floor piece: 12 x 15 x 15 in. (30.5 x 38.1 x 38.1 cm)

Collection of the artist

JOHN HOOVER

b. 1919, Cordova, Alaska; lives in Grapeview, Washington

"The Okvik Madonnas were found in Eskimo villages. They were thousands of years old. I felt a sense of wonder and attraction to someone who could carve such beautiful images in ivory."

Okvik Totem, 2000

Cedar, oil paint, commercial brass hinges
69 x 24 x 1¼ in. (175.3 x 61 x 3.2 cm)

Collection of the artist; courtesy of Well Street Art Company

KATHLEEN CARLO KENDALL

b. 1952, Tanana, Alaska; lives in Fairbanks, Alaska

No maaqh hut'aanenh
(Storytellers from the Coast),
2003

Yellow cedar, brass, copper,
gold leaf, pigment
each 28 3/4 x 29 1/8 x 7 1/8 in.
(73 x 74 x 18.1 cm)

Anchorage Museum of History
and Art; Rasmuson Foundation
Art Initiative

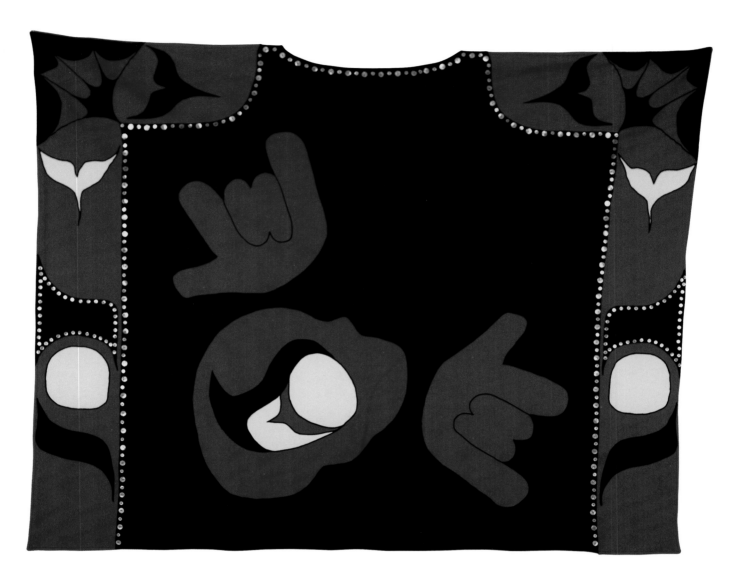

SONNY ASSU

b. 1975, Vancouver, British Columbia; lives in Vancouver

"As an artist, I've set out to balance two distinct voices, trying to come to some understanding of who I am and how I want to display my persona. Creating identity by challenging the notion of tradition explores the paradigm of the Indian person in the twenty-first century. My tradition/identity is made up not only of my 'Indian-ness' but also of TV, comic books, pop culture, and the effect of mass media/advertising: by using the images I use now, I begin to empower the aboriginal culture by appropriating from the appropriator. Creating identity by challenging the notion of tradition will not only provoke thought and discussion of who a real Indian is, but will bring awareness to a new movement in First Nations art and political thought."

When Raven Becomes Spider Embrace (Blanket Series #2), 2003

Akoya shell buttons, melton wool, synthetic gabardine, cotton jogging fleece
78 x 98 in. (198 x 249 cm)

Collection of the artist

LINDA AGUILAR

b. in Santa Barbara, California; lives in Fort Collins, Colorado

"Sometimes I hide bells inside or underneath a basket while the outside is very calm and conservative in form. I choose to weave with horsehair and thread. I like to play with materials, ideas, and titles and poke fun, sometimes having several titles for one basket."

Red Men: Diamonds in the Rough,
2003

Horsehair, waxed thread, beads, shells, metal washer
H. 3¹/₄ in., Diam. 5¹/₄ in.
(8.3 x 13.3 cm)

Courtesy of Kiva Indian Arts and Gifts

PERRY EATON

b. 1945, Kodiak Island, Alaska; lives in Anchorage, Alaska

"For me, tradition is what elders handed you to begin life with. There is an obligation to know it and understand when deviation occurs. Abstractions of tradition are not bad, unless they are done without a strong grounding in tradition. My masks are traditional and cultural in form, allowing me to examine contemporary issues and questions in a timeless format."

Assimilation or Affiliation, 2004

White spruce, automotive lacquer, oil paint, twine
30⁷/₈ x 13³/₁₆ x 4¹/₂ in. (78.4 x 33.5 x 11.4 cm)

Collection of the artist

CONNIE WATTS

*b. 1968, Campbell River, British Columbia;
lives in Port Alberni, British Columbia*

"The perspective of the artist is only a beginning. The connection between the participant and the work gives the work life, and a deeper understanding is achieved.

"Northwest Coast First Nations artwork started by tying a whole set of realistic, emotional, and abstract content into the final pieces. Because this language was developed early on, people have come to assign this complex system of understanding into a superficial means of looking only for the animals, myth, and the past cultural tradition it is linked to.

"My work to date has encapsulated this state of similarities and differences of the two merging cultures. I would like to understand the path in which the Northwest Coast artwork was heading pre-contact and continue this development as freely as I can, immersing myself into the past to look with unjaded eyes. In that state, my works then gain their life."

LEFT TO RIGHT

Indulgence, 2005

Black walnut, cedar, mirror glass, found synthetic fabrics
60 x 14 x 14 in. (152.4 x 35.6 x 35.6 cm)

Collection of the artist

Flirtation, 2005

Black walnut, cedar, mirror glass, found synthetic fabrics
60 x 14 x 14 in. (152.4 x 35.6 x 35.6 cm)

Collection of the artist

Posing, 2004

Black walnut, cedar, mirror glass, found synthetic fabrics
60 x 14 x 14 in. (152.4 x 35.6 x 35.6 cm)

Private collection

VICTORIA ADAMS

b. 1950, Oakland, California;
lives in Santa Fe, New Mexico

"The jewelry I create comes from
my life view, in which ritual, culture,
ancient and contemporary experiences play significant roles. These
items are talismans of my own
participation and consciousness."

*Deer Dancer Wears His New
Striped Leggings*, 2004

18k gold, sterling silver,
walrus tooth, ammonite
fossil, citrine, garnet, jasper
5 3/4 x 2 1/2 x 3/4 in.
(14.6 x 6.3 x 1.9 cm)

Collection of Donald
and Noël Neely

JACKIE LARSON BREAD

b. 1960, Conrad, Montana; lives in Great Falls, Montana

"It sounds trite to say that I like to create something beautiful. But by creating something that
reflects the parts of my life, I am sharing the
tradition, the humor, the ideas I hold close,
and that is beautiful."

Connections, 2005

Smoked buckskin, glass
beads, earth paint,
nylon thread
4 x 4 x 4 in. (10.2 x
10.2 x 10.2 cm)

Collection of the artist

DONALD TENOSO

b. 1960, Riverside, California; lives in Arlington, Virginia

"Does the Battle of the Little Bighorn have relevance today? I think so. Despite the fact that people tried to exterminate us, we are still here.

"The chessboard is a square sheet of rawhide. It is warped and uneven to symbolize the fact that Indians are still playing on an uneven field. The struggle goes on. The Indians still fight cowboys. Every once in a while, we redraw the lines, we group up again, and we go at it.

"As a Lakota doll artist, I have used both traditional and non-traditional themes in my dolls, drawing from my experience with my own and other Native cultures. I see beauty in the enduring nature of our traditions in transition. We have gone from hunting buffalo to raising them, from a pre-horse society to a horsepower society, from craft to art, but still the roots of our traditions in transition thrive."

One Bull's Chess Set, ca. 1997

Human hair, rawhide,
brain-tanned deerskin, leather,
buffalo hair, buffalo hide,
ermine, tradecloth, porcupine
quills and claws, bone, pipestone, wood, feathers, shell,
beads, silver, gems
H. of chess pieces: 3$^1/_2$ to 6 in.
(8.9 to 15.2 cm);
chessboard (not shown):
27$^1/_4$ x 25$^1/_4$ in. (69.2 x 64.1 cm)

Collection of the artist

DOUG COFFIN

b. 1946, *Lawrence, Kansas; lives in Abiquiu, New Mexico*

"The video cuts that I have selected for *Cigar Store Indian* show typical Hollywood heroes that often become role models. The more ammo used or people killed, the better chance of making money. Maybe feeding people would get better results than killing them."

Cigar Store Indian, 1998

Wood, oil paint, television, video
73 x 14 x 14 in. (185.4 x 35.6 x 35.6 cm)

Collection of the artist

TANIS MARIA S'EILTIN

b. 1951, *Skagway, Alaska; lives in Bellingham, Washington*

"To query one's identity in this ever-changing world is an unrelenting challenge. As a member of the Tlingit Nation and a Native corporation, I have witnessed recent social and economic changes that contributed to new standards for tribal recognition. We are strong in attitude and possess the knowledge of our past. We continue to practice potlatch, speak our language, and recognize one another through our grandmother's and great-grandmother's clan. This piece reflects our ability as indigenous people to retain our cultural heritage despite corporate and U.S. Government standards of identification. The Tlingit war helmet pictured on the drum represents our ability to resist entities that threaten self-awareness and cultural identity."

War Head, 2003

Rawhide, wood, beaver fur
30 x 30 x 5 in. (76.2 x 76.2 x 12.7 cm)

Eiteljorg Museum of American Indians and Western Art

ROCKY KAʻIOULIOKAHIHIKOLOʻEHU JENSEN

b. 1944, Honolulu, Hawaiʻi; lives in Keaau, Hawaiʻi

"Art communicates the philosophy and unique nuances of a people. In the traditional times of our Hawaiian culture, the arts were an integral part of the fabric of our society, an integral part of our daily life, an essential element of the political, scientific, and spiritual order. All elements were interwoven and inseparable, an extraordinary metaphoric language.

"What is Hawaiian art? A definite language expressed through the working of the mind, and hands; an eye and heart for fine detail; and the clever and meticulous translation and perpetuation of metaphor twenty-four thousand years in perfecting—requirements cultivated by millennia of artist ancestors who came before me. Perpetuating their traditional philosophy is the hallmark of my work—I speak for those who cannot speak!"

Hinahanaiakamalama, 2004

Mango, *koa* (Hawaiian acacia wood), mother-of-pearl, fiber, feathers
54 x 8 x 8 in. (137.2 x 20.3 x 20.3 cm)

Collection of the artist

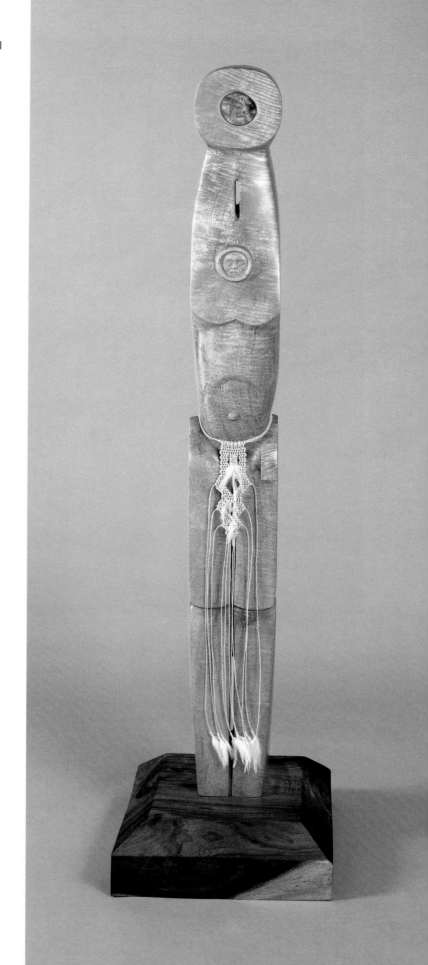

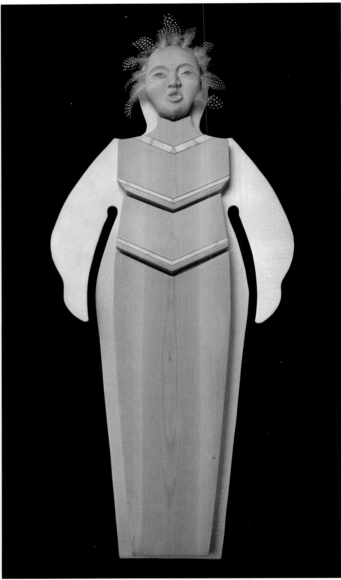

SUSIE BEVINS-ERICSEN

b. 1941, Beechey Point, Alaska; lives in Anchorage, Alaska

"Inspiration for this work comes from ancient ivory carvings of the Bering Straits Eskimo cultures. The okvik torso human forms were engraved and etched with geometric patterns and curved lines.

"I believe that each person has memories etched in the soul that are imparted through the ancestral lineage in the form of creative, spiritual, and intuitive impressions. Like the etched patterns on the torso figures, we carry these memories in the soul."

LEFT
Primal Origins: Male, 2003

Aluminum, brass, poplar, bass wood
40 x 15 x 1¹/₂ in. (101.6 x 38.1 x 3.8 cm)

Collection of Alice Rogoff Rubenstein

RIGHT
Ancient Memories: Female, 2003

Aluminum, poplar, bass wood, ivory, feathers
34 x 15 x 1¹/₂ in. (86.4 x 38.1 x 3.8 cm)

University of Alaska Museum of the North

SEAN KEKAMAKUPA'A LEE LOY BROWNE

b. 1953, Hilo, Hawai'i; lives in Honolulu, Hawai'i

"*Puna/Oji-san* (which means "grandparent") refers to the life cycle of the Hawaiian *'ohana* (family unit), something that is of primal importance not only to Native Hawaiians but to all cultures throughout the world. The execution of these works in granite, the most difficult of stones to work, reinforces the endurance and perpetuity of the *'ohana*.

"The vertical format of *Puna/Oji-san* characterizes the strength, firmness, and wisdom of the *'ohana* elder."

Puna/Oji-san: Ha'awi I ka ike,
2003

Belfast granite (from South
Africa), akasaka granite
(from Japan)
H. 42 in., Diam. (of base): 12¹/₄ in.
(106.7 x 31.1 cm)

Collection of the artist

JUDY CHARTRAND

b. 1959, Kamloops, British Columbia;
lives in Coquitlam, British Columbia

"Artistically speaking, I consider myself to be working within a contemporary First Nations art tradition, where much of my work confronts issues of colonization, assimilation, and identity politics. As a socially conscious person, I make art to express my realities. In resistance to these stereotypical identifications, I am reinventing some of these labels in accordance with my way of knowing and understanding the world."

Metis Soup Cans, 2004

Low-fire clay, underglaze colors, glaze, luster, wood
31¹/₂ x 18¹/₂ x 4 in. (with frame)
(80 x 47 x 10.2 cm)

Collection of the artist

STAN NATCHEZ

b. 1954, Los Angeles, California; lives in Mesa, Arizona

"I feel fortunate to have been raised in the city because of the perspective it gave me on life. Without an awareness of our heritage, we have no identity. By taking the best of both worlds, the modern and the traditional, we are more able to find balance in our lives. As a student, dancer, and advocate for the Native American community, I continue to find time for my art. Painting is a way of life for me. I paint the life I live, so every painting I do is a self-portrait. My art is about you and the way I respond."

Capturing the Flag on Campbell Soup, 2005

Oil paint, glass beads, found objects, paper
24 x 30 in. (61 x 76.2 cm)

Collection of the artist

MARCUS CADMAN

b. 1970, Shiprock, New Mexico; lives in Shiprock

"I assemble things—old photographs, cloth, buckskin, money, bingo sheets, pages from the Bible, and other found objects—onto my canvas or paper. This technique of collage is vital to my work, because it thrusts upon the viewer the differing images and realities of the modern world and the tribal world. The powerful images that I create are my willingness to let the spirit of each piece flow through me onto the canvas or paper. I let no social, political, or religious standards interfere with this process. I create from my own truth."

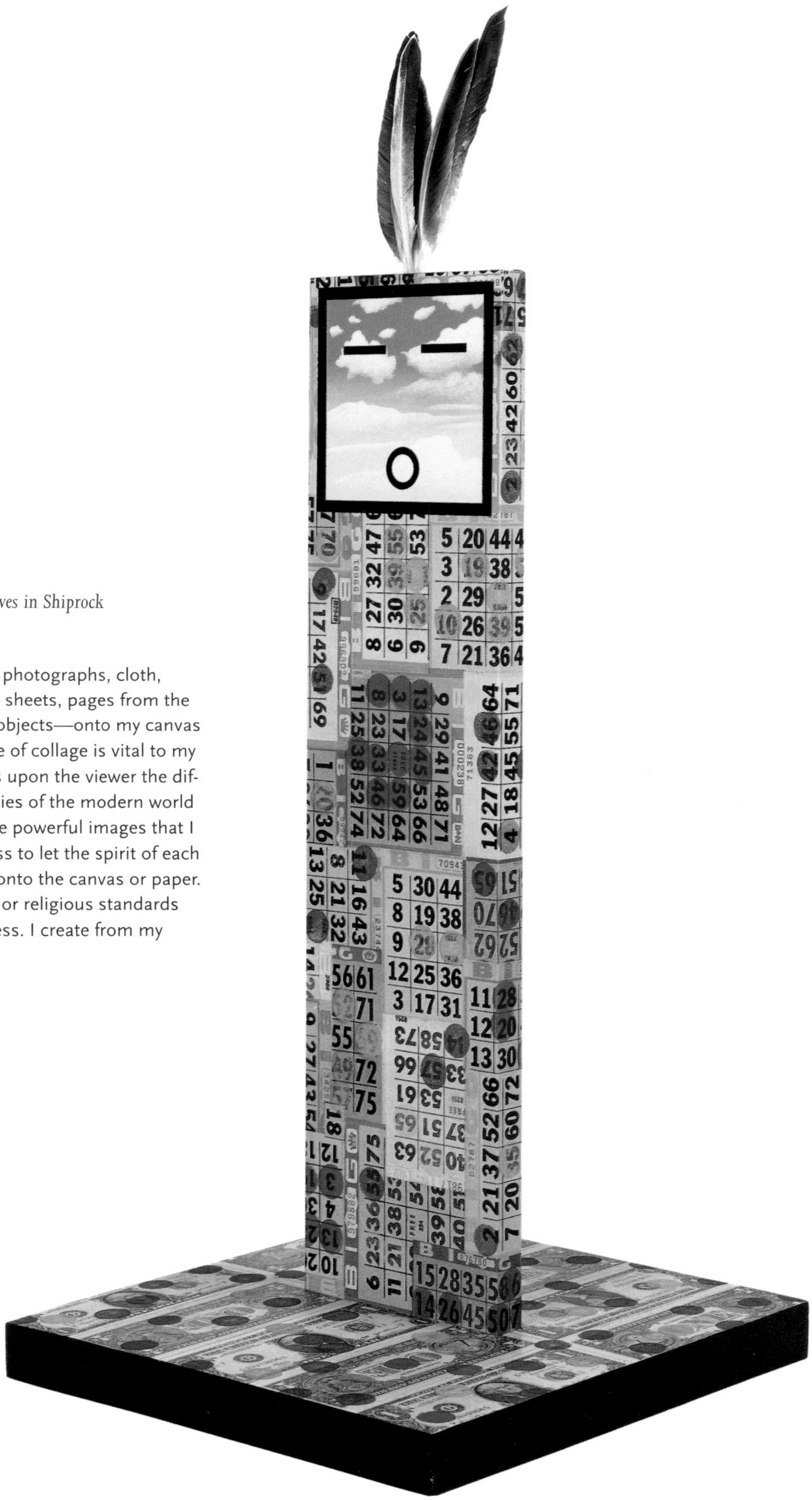

Kachina: Bingo Sheet—
"Please God Let Me Win,"
2005

Bingo sheets, currency, duck feathers, acrylic paint, wood
30 1/2 x 12 x 12 in. (77.5 x 30.5 x 30.5 cm)

Collection of the artist

MARCUS AMERMAN

b. 1959, Phoenix, Arizona; lives in Santa Fe, New Mexico

"So many events in my life and people that I know, and have known, have been choreographed to manifest my ability to communicate through the creation of power and beauty.

"Traditionally, Indians embraced new materials with which to create and new ideas to express. Our art comes from spirit and not so much from sense impressions, so our creativity isn't limited by material realities. Beauty, to me, is the balanced amalgamation of 'form' and 'content.'"

Postcard, 2002

Glass seed beads, antique glass beads, nylon thread, rubberized cotton
11 x 17 in. (27.9 x 43.2 cm)

Private collection

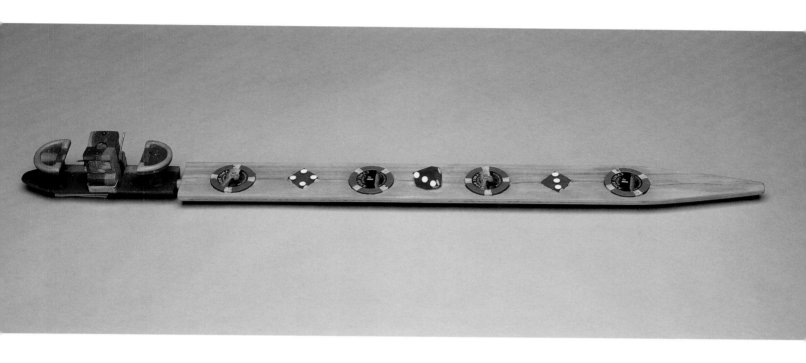

TODD DEFOE

b. 1970, Fond du Lac, Minnesota; lives in Cloquet, Minnesota

"Through my art, I explore my own identity, the identity of my tribe, and the identities of Native people everywhere. In my work, I respond to the repeated depictions of stereotypical Native images, which perpetuate the belief that we are trapped in a time long ago. I want the viewer to gain insight into the lives of modern Native people. The objects which I create can be viewed as both 'traditional' art and as 'contemporary' art—a renewal of a continuum of Native art as it may have evolved in an environment free of the attitudes of authenticity and 'Indian-ness' that have arrested the evolution of Native art in America for at least one hundred years. All around me are the conveniences, and hazards, of modern society. Standing alongside these things are the history and worldview of my tribe, the Ojibwe. Reconciling this combination of cultures is a subject of my art."

The New Four Directions, 2001

Catlinite, silver, wood, commercially manufactured dice, gaming chips
L. 25 3/4 in., W. 2 in., H. 2 1/4 in.
(65.4 x 5.1 x 5.7 cm)

Collection of Nancy and Phillip Cohen

JOSEPH SENUNGETUK

b. 1940, *Wales, Alaska; lives in Anchorage, Alaska*

"I feel that the art produced for the tourist is not that creative, or original, or worthy of too much mental exercise understanding it.

"My art is the product of much thinking before execution, and it needs to be of artistically sound material, color, finish, movement, composition. I then wonder about the future of it. Will it become stale, outdated, outmoded, dusty, ignored at some point in its own life? Native art (among other disciplines) is capable of being considered the world's best art, contemporary or otherwise. People just need to recognize it beyond their small ways of looking at things."

Multicultural Breast Plate, 2000

Fused glass (plate by Catherine Senungetuk), ivory, ebony, plastic, birch (turned wood forms by Buz Blum), antler, steel, acrylic color plate horizontal: 6 x 15 ¹/₂ x 12 ¹/₂ in. (15.2 x 39.4 x 31.8 cm)

Collection of the artist

DAVID NEEL

b. 1960, *Vancouver, British Columbia; lives in Vancouver*

"The early curators and collectors had these erroneous ideas in mind when they established the collections we see today. They desired artifacts that portrayed the past rather than the period during which they were collecting. As Northwest Coast artists, we have the right and responsibility to discuss and revise the understanding of our culture. The best art is achieved by leaving the channels of creativity open and allowing the finest work, that which comes from our insides, our soul or our heart, into the wood, canvas, or page. Then artists, Native or non-Native, may fulfill their potential."

International Mask of Commerce, 1999

Alder, cedar bark, copper, silver, gold, abalone, operculum shell, bank notes 27 x 11 x 9 in. (68.6 x 27.9 x 22.9 cm)

Courtesy of Lattimer Gallery

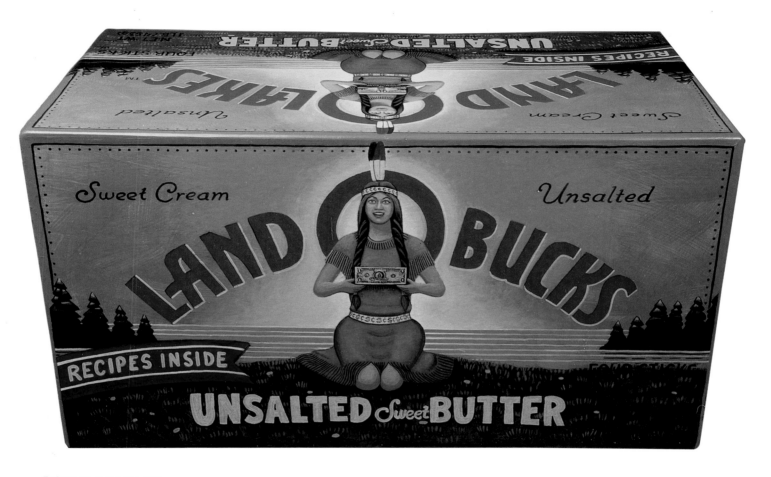

DAVID BRADLEY

b. 1954, Eureka, California; lives in Santa Fe, New Mexico

"Throughout my art career, I have been an American Indian rights activist. Art is about freedom, and with that freedom comes responsibility. Injustice must first be exposed before it can be overcome. Some of my work deals with socio-political issues, such as identity and racial stereotypes.

"Historically, America has had a love/hate relationship with Indian people. The stereotype of the 'Noble Savage' is often perpetuated by non-Indian companies for an Indian logo or mascot, which they use to sell their product or sports team. For 500 years, non-Indians have stolen our land and resources, and now that Indian identity has become a marketable commodity, they want to steal that, too. I say no, enough is enough."

Land O Bucks, Land O Fakes,
Land O Lakes, 2003

Paint, paper, wood
16 x 31 x 16 in. (49.5 x
91.4 x 49.5 cm)

Collection of the artist

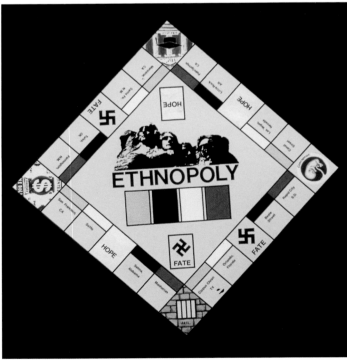

GERALD CLARKE

b. 1967, Hemet, California; lives in Anza, California

"This game is like life. You can become rich, die, or go bankrupt at any time. To win, you must save up $1,200 for a down payment on a house. Along the way, you will have to pay taxes, face racism, get a job, and try to achieve some quality of life for you and your family. I made this 'game' because of the damaging effects of political correctness on real and honest social discourse, particularly when examining racial relations in America today. You may not be able to say what you really think at work, but you can while playing ETHNOPOLY— after all, it's only a game!?!"

Ethnopoly, 2000–present

Wood, plastic, acrylic paint, polyester resin, paper, vinyl lettering, steel, oil spray enamel, found objects (metal folding chairs, folding card table, play money)
Installation dimensions variable;
board: 24 x 24 in. (61 x 61 cm)

Collection of the artist

CHARLENE VICKERS

b. 1970, Kenora, Ontario; lives in Vancouver, British Columbia

"My work concerns memory and expression of Aboriginal identity, where materials carry social and cultural significance. My moccasins focus on the commodity aspect of Aboriginal culture and selling an idealized First Nations body. Issues of racism and marginalization are exposed in the works, presenting a realistic rather than romanticized reality for Aboriginal peoples. I reinvent typical Native objects sold to tourists, such as the moccasin, and combine them with personal comments on urban living for aboriginal peoples. The moccasins tell stories of power relations, loss of culture, and finding personal strength."

Not for Trade, 2004

Camouflage denim, glass beads, paper, cotton cloth quilt, found photograph, glass frame, copper wire, found wooden chair
33 1/2 x 14 x 16 in. (85.1 x 35.5 x 40.6 cm)

Collection of the artist

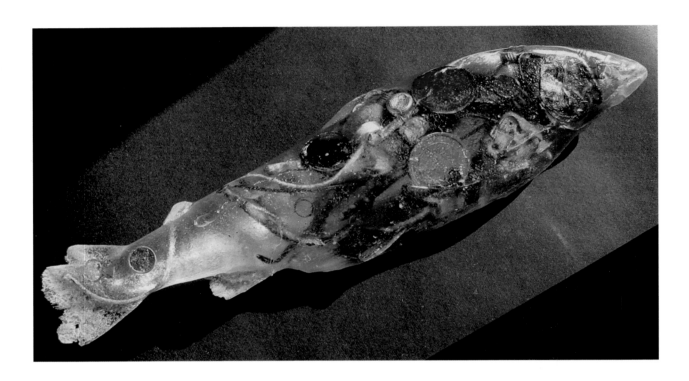

THELISSA M. REDHAWK

b. in Portland, Oregon; lives in Elk City, Idaho

"My art expresses the reverence I have for the sacred landscapes as they were when my ancestors walked the same paths. Much of my art comes from life experiences on the Umatilla and Columbia rivers. My subjects in any medium reflect the spirituality and preservation of what is fast disappearing.

"The contents of *Clearly Salmon* show visible remnants of modern conveniences leading to the disappearance of our salmon. Now we have polluted rivers, rearranged sacred landscapes, and less salmon. This piece reflects my heartfelt concern for the salmon habitats and the rivers that have sustained my tribe for generations."

Clearly Salmon, 2004

Acrylic epoxy, found objects (barbed wire, railroad stakes, beer bottle caps, Copenhagen tobacco lid, hammer, Christmas tree lights, plastic six-pack holder, telephone jack)
L. 25 1/2 in., W. 6 1/2 in., H. 3 1/8 in. (64.8 x 16.5 x 7.9 cm)

Collection of the artist

CORWIN "CORKY" CLAIRMONT

b. 1947, St. Ignatius, Montana; lives in Ronan, Montana

"My ultimate goal as an artist is to remind people of our shared humanity. I wish to give Indian culture back the humanity that has been taken from it by stereotypes created over the past five centuries. Neither the super-shaman nor the drunken Indian do anything to convey what we as a people feel. I want to express the passion, pain, and reverence I feel as a contemporary Native person."

Split Shield, 2001

Cotton fiber, paper, ink
84 x 49 in.
(213.4 x 124.5 cm)
Eiteljorg Museum of
American Indians and
Western Art

RANDALL BLAZE

b. 1949, Townsend, Montana;
lives on Pine Ridge Reservation, South Dakota

"I am creatively aware of the secret workings of nature and natural materials. Every medium manipulated by an artist has its own distinct and special nature. Creatively exploring variations in nature has been my motivation as an artist until 9/11. *Metamorphosis* is about introspection into human frailty."

Metamorphosis, 2001

Earthenware
H. 30 in., Diam. 13 in.
(76.2 x 33 cm)

Collection of the artist

STEVEN DEO

b. 1956, Claremore, Oklahoma; lives in Rio Rancho, New Mexico

"As a contemporary artist of Native American descent, identity has been a constant point of reference for me. Often, I've looked in the past through the eyes of the camera at images of my personal family or images that are provided in the context of Western history. In this examination and comparison of the Indian of the distant past to the present, the Native American is a reflection of his environment. As our environment has changed through the processes of modernity, so has our self-perception. When nature was our only environment, we told stories of our values. Today, nature has been covered with concrete, steel, and asphalt. We have been relocated, dislocated, grouped and regrouped, numbered and scattered. The one commonality we have left is an extended family called 'Indian.'"

America's Child, 2004

Plastic toy army men, tank, and American flag Installation: dimensions variable; figure: 14 x 8 x 9 in. (35.6 x 20.3 x 22.9 cm)

Collection of Nadia Bruce

KAPULANI LANDGRAF

b. 1966, Pu'ahu'ula, Kaneohe, Hawai'i; lives in Kaneohe

"We must always be engaged in creative forms of resistance to help prevent further erosion and the destruction of *nā wahi kapu* (sacred place), whose presence binds us to our ancestors, our oral and written traditions, our spiritual world, our land, its living entitities, and our indigenous history, as well as our future."

Make i ke kai hohonu (*Death in the Deep Sea*), 2001

Kā'ai (sennit casket) of silver-gelatin prints wrapped in *kapa* (mulberry bark cloth), fiber, fishhooks, lead weights, fishing line, red volcanic cinders
Installation: dimensions variable; height of figure: 72 in. (182.9 cm)

Collection of the artist

BRIAN BARBER

b. 1975, Flint, Michigan; lives in Seattle, Washington

"The most significant influences in my life have come from my family. They have helped me define who I am and are a connection to my heritage. I think it is a very exciting time to be a Native artist working in glass, because we have the unique opportunity of exploring the parameters of a new tradition. We are essentially defining a new tradition by bringing a new voice to an ancient medium."

At What Cost?, 2004

Glass, steel, dammar varnish
4 1/4 x 6 x 4 in. (10.8 x 15.2 x 10.2 cm); base: 12 x 12 in. (30.5 x 30.5 cm)

Collection of the artist

JEAN LaMARR

b. 1945, Susanville, California; lives in Susanville

Postcards in Box Windows
top row, left to right: *Indian Princesses,
Knott's Berry Farm, Washo Indian Woman
and Papoose*
bottom row, left to right: *Minnehaha,
Fine Feathered Friends, Dolly Dingle's
Friend,* 1997–98

Handmade paper, acrylic paints, color
photocopies of postcards, iron wire,
pine, Plexiglas, flicker feathers, clay,
wood beads
each 12 x 12 x 6 in. (30.5 x 30.5 x 15.2 cm)

Collection of the artist

JOHN HITCHCOCK

b. 1967, Lawton, Oklahoma; lives in Madison, Wisconsin

"After the death of my grandparents to cancer, I began a series of print-based installations and drawings that ask questions about the quality of the U.S.D.A. commodity foods distributed by the United States government for food assistance to indigenous lands, welfare programs, and to Third World countries. I appropriated the silhouetted logos from commodities (a cow from a can of beef and a chicken from a package of powdered eggs) to question notions of assimilation and control, leading to broader questions about the proliferation of images in popular culture and mass electronic media: What are the societal, psychological, and physiological consequences of globalization? What have we learned from progress? I re-contextualize images from culture, electronic media, and food to question social and political systems."

Ritual Device (Give Away),
1997–2005

Found wool blanket screenprinted in acrylic ink, Lone Star Beer glass bottles screenprinted in acrylic ink, plastic hoops, cotton paper screenprinted in acrylic ink

Installation: dimensions variable; blanket: 77 x 66 in. (195.6 x 167.6 cm)

Collection of the artist

BENTLY SPANG

b. 1960, *Crow Agency, Montana; lives in Billings, Montana*

"By juxtaposing natural sculptural materials with artificial, I am able to create a metaphorical and symbolic representation of myself. The tension that inherently exists between the natural and the artificial characterizes the difficulty of finding a balance between the two worlds that I exist in. Achieving that balance becomes the ultimate challenge. The specific materials I use also serve a metaphorical function in that they support the layers of meaning built into each piece. Each material, and the motif it assumes, has its own diverse symbolic life. This layering of meaning is a fascinating and integral part of Native American culture; everything has its place, one thing leads to another, things are not always what they seem."

—from *The Spirit of Native America (1989)*

OPPOSITE
The Four Stages of Dried Meat
(from *Meat* Series), 1998

Silicone, reservation dirt, commercial pants hangers, metal numbers
overall 48 x 26 1/2 x 1 in. (121.9 x 67.3 x 2.5 cm)

Collection of the artist

MARTHA GRADOLF

b. 1955, *Indianapolis, Indiana; lives in Nashville, Indiana*

"As I weave, I use many of the same traditional techniques to create a contemporary form. Weaving connects me to the ancient ones, those who have gone before and those who guide me now. My wall hangings often embody a subtle message. Ironically, the 'unseen' message can unravel and reveal itself 'visually' just as I am finishing the piece. Other energies intertwine with our own in the same way fibers wrap around each other to make a length of yarn. Native American issues such as history, stereotypes, and spirituality lend themselves to us. It is my duty and desire to nurture this ancient legacy as it re-creates itself in a new and contemporary form."

Made in Japan, 2002

Wool, antique salt and pepper shakers, feathers, antique brass bells, brass cones, silver beads
38 x 22 1/2 in. (96.5 x 57.2 cm)

Collection of the artist

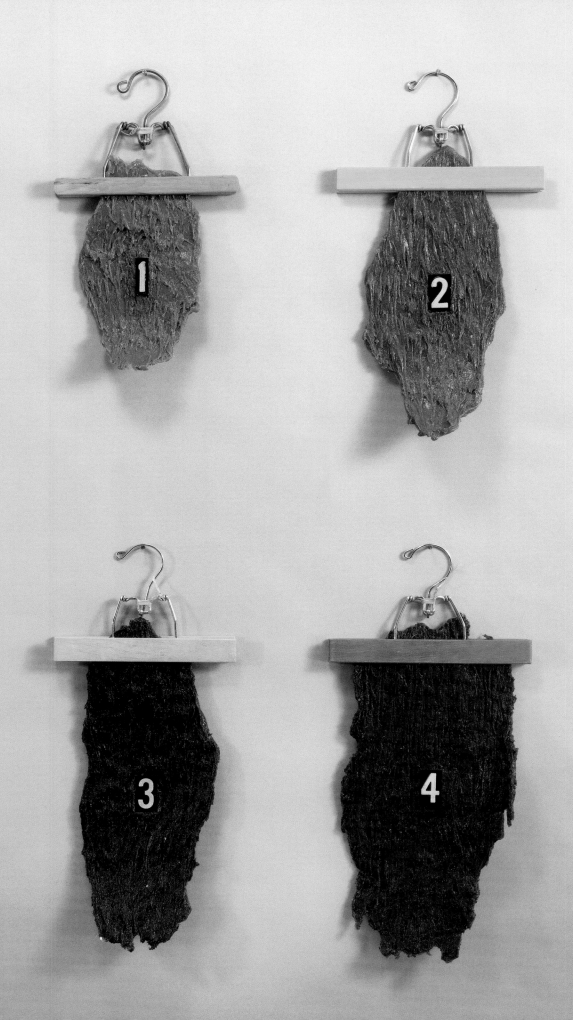

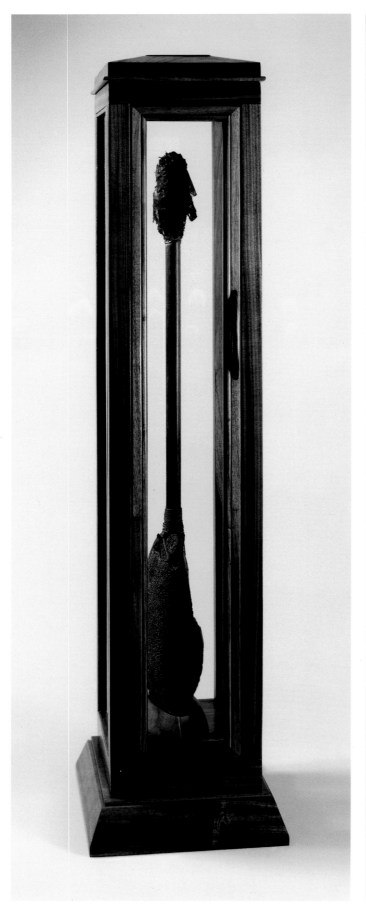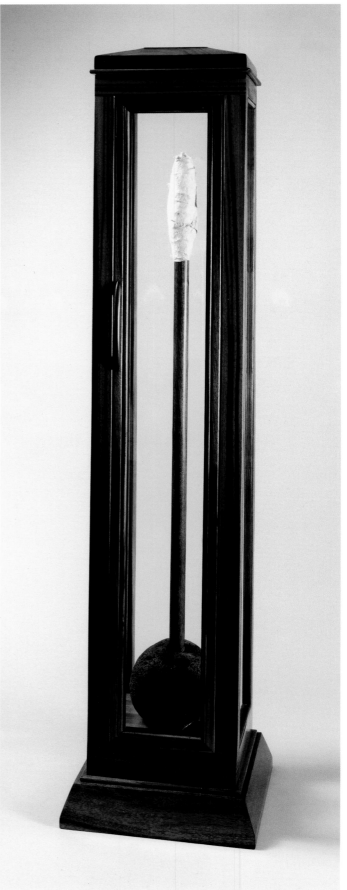

KAILI CHUN

b. 1962, Honolulu, Hawai'i; lives in Honolulu

"I have heard of you by the hearing of an ear. But now my eye sees you. Like Job, the Hawaiian people suffered difficult and bewildering times, losing a large portion of their population and, for many, becoming strangers in their own land. But as we have endured the insensitivity and genocidal practice of others, trying to fit into the boxes they build for us, we maintain our vision."

OPPOSITE
E hana mua a pa'a ke kahua mamua o ke a'o ana aku ia ha'I (Build yourself a firm foundation before teaching others), 2003 *

Glass, *koa* (Hawaiian acacia wood), *ōhi'a* (Hawaiian wood), *kapa* (mulberry bark cloth), *kukui* (Hawaiian nut oil), stones
Two vitrines, *each* 53¹/₂ x 13 x 13 in. (133.4 x 33 x 33 cm)

Collection of the artist

*Only in the catalogue; another work by this artist is in the exhibition.

PETER MORIN

b. 1977, Prince George, British Columbia; lives in Vancouver, British Columbia

"I will take a rock like she said,
  I will find the right rock and place it on my hurt.
  I will walk holding the rock on my place of hurt.
  I will ask the grandmother rock for help."

Dirt Jacket, 2004

Found wool jacket, dirt, found wooden hanger
30 x 24 x 5 in. (76.2 x 61 x 12.7 cm)

Collection of the artist

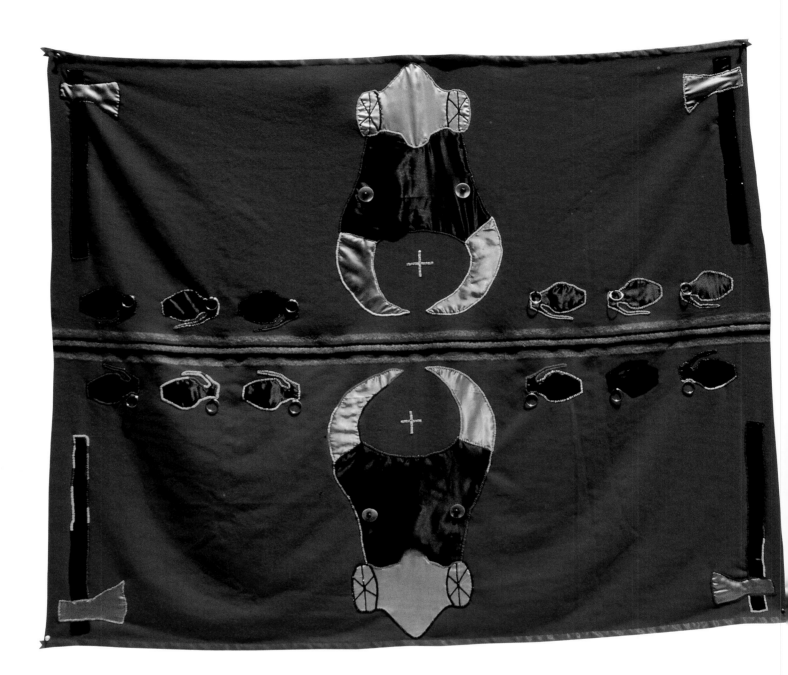

KIMBERLY "WENDY" PONCA

b. 1960, Odessa, Texas; lives in Fairfax, Oklahoma

"In my world, there is no separation between art and life. All of life is art, and nothing is without art."

Gulf War Man's Wearing Blanket,
2005

Glass beads, freshwater shells, satin, tradecloth, metal keyrings, mescal beans
60 x 72 in. (152.4 x 182.9 cm)

Collection of the artist

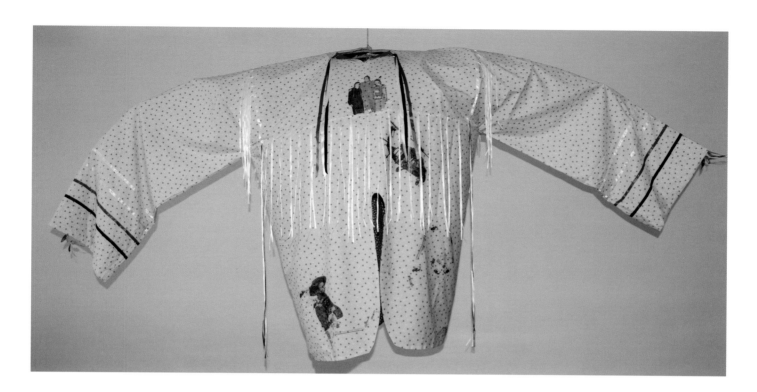

CHARLENE TETERS

b. 1952, *Spokane, Washington; lives in Santa Fe, New Mexico*

"My reference comes from history and world events, and is a Native woman's response to these events. The shirts refer to a time in history when the most holy of holy lands, the Black Hills, were invaded for gold and land. The invasion was followed by a desperate period of starvation, germ warfare, and military dominance of indigenous peoples. The Ghost Dance and other Dreamer religions were a Native response to these most desperate of times. This installation refers to these historic events, and brings them into the present context."

Shirt, 2001
(detail of installation)

Cotton, wood, silk ribbon
84 x 120 x 36 in. (213.4 x 304.8 x 91.4 cm)

Collection of the artist

PAT COURTNEY GOLD

b. on Warm Springs Reservation, Oregon;
lives in Scappoose, Oregon

"Native art cannot be separated from culture and tradition. Historically, trade was very important among the Columbia River people. The rivers connected all the nations who used canoes, much as we use cars to travel the highways.

"My Native American heritage and culture, Wasco Nation, has been handed down for many generations. This heritage and tradition define who I am. Cultures are dynamic, and my contemporary work reflects my view of the world that I live in: the good, the bad, and the ugly. Each of my baskets tells a story."

Indigenous People, Obstacles in the Way of Progress, 2004

Mixed fibers, cotton, hand-spun wool, acrylic yarn, metallic yarn, plastic bag
H. 12 ¹/₂ in., Diam. 7 ¹/₂ in.
(31.8 cm x 19 cm)

Collection of the artist

EMIL HER MANY HORSES

b. 1954, Pine Ridge, South Dakota; lives in Washington, D.C.

"Wanagi Yuhapi, or the Keeping of the Soul ceremony, is one of the seven ceremonies of the Lakota. A tipi was set up to keep the soul of a deceased family member. A lock of hair from the deceased would be kept in the tipi. After about a year, the family would invite people to gather at the site of the tipi. The soul of the deceased would be released at this time. Gifts and food would be shared in memory of the departed soul.

"I created this tipi as a tribute to the people killed on September 11, 2001. I did not know anyone personally who lost their lives, but this event has touched all of our lives."

9/11 Tipi, 2002

Tanned deerskin, glass beads, wood poles
H. 31 in., Diam. 18 in.
(78.7 x 45.7 cm)

Collection of Pamela R. and C. Scott Evans

KIM MAMARADLO

b. 1958, Crescent City, California; lives in Klamath, California

"I was born on the Yurok Reservation in Northern California where the Klamath River and the redwoods meet the Pacific. Since the beginning of time, the Yurok Indians have called this beautiful place home, and my subject matter and imagery are drawn from strong familial ties to this heritage. I am one of the last generations to have had the opportunity to experience the 'old' people. Today, I use their photographs, humor, personal recollections, traditional art, language, legal battles, and history as the focus for my work. Although the medium is contemporary, the strength of the warm color palette, layered imagery, and visual gesturing all work to create visual narratives infused with a vanishing way of life."

Stay Inside the Lines, 2000

Cotton, fabric paint, spray paint, mat board
31 $\frac{1}{2}$ x 37 $\frac{1}{2}$ x 2 in. (80 x 95.3 x 5.1 cm)

Collection of the artist

KEVIN MCKENZIE

b. 1961, Regina, Saskatchewan;
lives in Vancouver, British Columbia

"The task of taking on an entirely new medium becomes my springboard for commentary and the development of a new vocabulary in creating a dialogue between ancient themes and societal norms. The buffalo skull is a sacred object in my culture, the centerpiece of ceremony and ritual. It has also been the spiritual icon of the Plains Indians for eons, and this cultural significance has made the buffalo skull treasured for many ethnological collections. Depending on the social context, the functional can become sacred, and vice versa. Within the context of an industrial age, the corporate, military, cultural, and popular culture makers each offer unique expressions that contribute to the Native American image. The fusion of the industrial with First Nations aesthetics allows me to bridge the past with the present, and the industrial with the spiritual. For my new project, I have taken an inverted approach to this process, casting a buffalo skull in urethane and polyurethane resin, a common material in the manufacturing of countless prefabricated industrial products that we use every day. With this new sculptural project, the prefabrication of an object considered sacred allows me to bridge art and ritual with everyday life."

Ghost and God, 2003

Urethane and polyurethane resin, acrylic, neon lights 48 x 36 x 12 in. (121.9 x 91.4 x 30.5 cm)

Collection of the artist

On Inspiration

Susie Silook

WHEN ASKED TO WRITE ABOUT THE SUBJECT of my source of inspiration, I had to mull the twenty years of my career over in my mind, and go beyond my dusty studio to find something intangible, something frustratingly elusive to define.

Let's establish immediately that I do what I do to support myself and my family. My materials stem from this fact; the walrus continue to nourish the Native people of Alaska as they have for centuries, and the ivory has always been used to produce tools, housewares, religious items, and toys. Since European contact, the demand for ivory has shifted its use toward objects made for cash. It's an extension of the subsistence economy.

Initially, not having intimate knowledge of the sea mammals as men do, I made awkwardly carved figurines of people in parkas. How embarrassed will I be when I inevitably stumble across one of my early creations? That aside, I found that creating artwork was a rush, a solitary process that suited my independent nature. I was amazed that people liked the pieces that I made and were buying enough of them for me to live, however modestly. It was challenging work and kept my attention engaged.

Soon, I wanted my work to more accurately reflect the consciousness I'd become aware of around me as a child growing up Yup'ik. Somehow I needed to convey some of this complexity evident in language, in stories and legend, and in philosophy.

I was working on a carving of a woman in a *qiipaghaq*—a long, loose, cloth garment for women, which used to be made from flour sacks traded from whaling ships, and is now made from all kinds of colorful prints. My feet were dragging, and I was anxiously staring at my children while considering other options for our survival. They were growing up as children of a single parent (and starving artist) and I was glad they were too young to know it.

In a moment of youthful resolve, I removed the woman's *qiipaghaq* and gazed breathlessly at a slim, bald, naked woman, the ivory smooth and creamy white in my hands, and knew there would be no turning back. I imbued her with the skeletal design of my ancestor's dolls, and gave her curly hair of whale sinew. In this respect, I had a wealth of material to draw from, since ancestral ivory dolls from my island are abundant, elegant in form and design. No one really knew what to make of her, however, and I took a loss, so unconventional was she to the marketplace. Art was teaching me courage and political assertiveness.

The iconoclast had passed through the Arctic, instilling fear and shame. Not without a little trepidation about internal backlash, I began depicting pre-colonial spirits and concepts from all around the Arctic, including those outside my village and region of origin.

My mother is Inupiaq, my father Siberian Yup'ik—the two major circumpolar Arctic people. The Arctic is rich with culture, with the "supernatural," as real as the air we breathe, co-existing with "reality." We've been written off many times, and our current art is said (by some anthropologists and art critics) to be contaminated, no longer pure.

This is contrary to my life, where my parents' stories and way of living, hunting, singing, speaking, etc., were that of Yup'ik people adapting to new things but remaining very Yup'ik—in my father's case, remaining consciously spiritually Yup'ik, and unapologetically so. When I was a child, we'd moved away from the intensely communal, and back again. After a stint in the military, I went back to the village, only to find that I could no longer live there, so I moved to the city, where I took up art exclusively.

I believe that I will always feel a sense of responsibility toward my village—I want to say "tribe," but we don't use such language here. Sometimes I rebel against this, surrounded as I am by an individualistic culture, which finds its way into my work. Sometimes my struggle with alcoholism destroys all creativity. Sometimes I get in the way.

In writing this, I'm struck by the difference between what motivates and what inspires. The necessity of survival and the streak of rebelliousness are motivational forces, but they do not inspire. They serve to navigate me through the tremendous physical effort required of a sculptor of stubborn mediums. Inspiration is a whole different sort of impulse.

Enough people have asked me in sincerity where my ideas come from for me to regard them as gifts. Yet I've had to coax this gift along through the years, and it's had to blossom amid fear and doubt. Books, friends, other artists, galleries, the ancestors, my parents—they all serve as my instructors. When I finally sit with my material, be it ivory, bone, or stone, inspiration is some force that fills me with a natural high, enabling me to "see" something not yet there, and so I make my mark into hard material and begin to create, excited with new possibility. It's an exciting new beginning, keeping me coming back for more.

After all, I could find a "real job," and then could do what motivates and fulfills me—organize protests.

This is a long and inadequate answer for what should be a short response, and for that, I apologize. It has followed the route of much of my work; I've simply followed its course.

Savage Humor Is Still Alive

Doug Coffin

TO ME, ONE OF THE THINGS THAT MAKES AMERICA GREAT is our sense of humor. Sometimes it's outrageous and inappropriate, such as making jokes about a natural catastrophe. I have observed crude, but nonetheless funny, facets of light shed on some very dark subjects. Maybe it's like putting a Band-Aid on a wound—it helps it heal. I will say that 9/11 was the only event in my life where no humorous quips were made at the time it occurred.

Humor, it seems, allows the healing process to start. This is America, and the red man is part of its history—and the red man, from my knowledge, has a pretty good sense of humor. Among the works in this exhibition, my friend Marcus Amerman's *Postcard* (page 56) is an excellent example.

I was born in 1946 in Lawrence, Kansas, where I was raised. Lawrence is home to Haskell Institute, a boarding school for Indians. It recently celebrated its 120th anniversary (now as Haskell Indian Nations University). Our house was on the Haskell campus grounds, and my father was a very successful sports coach there. Growing up, this was my universe, surrounded by Indians. Many had never been off their reservation before and were very homesick.

As soon as I was able to get into trouble, I began roaming the campus with my younger brother, looking for little adventures. It didn't take us very long to discover the humor that thrived among the students; it was everywhere. I suspect that white people would not have imagined this picture of the stoic red man, constantly pulling pranks and *always* joking around. These moments were not readily seen or shared with the outside world. At the Haskell campus, such humor was nonstop and always done with sensitivity—not mean-spirited at all. As I grew older and experienced more of the outside world, this good-natured activity seemed to have fewer participants than in my world at Haskell.

Throughout my life, I have maintained contact with the Indian world, and am constantly reminded how joking around and telling funny stories creates an immediate bond and an open door in a new relationship. In any culture, wherever I've traveled in the world, you can see that humor is like a magnet: you are pulled in by it and it feels good. Good humor is usually a double-edged sword: it makes a point of enlightening as well as provoking a smile.

The Koshare clowns of the Southwest are an example of recognizing humor as a contribution to the well-being of the tribe. During the Feast days at the Pueblos, the role of the Koshares is twofold: first, of course, as entertainment; and second, using humor to correct and encourage those who need it, for the betterment of the tribe. The Feast Days are a time when it is proper for the Koshares to shed light on the shortcomings of individual tribal members whose behavior has been detrimental to the tribe as a whole, and, by so doing, the misbehaving member is "joked" back onto the right path.

Another observation in life is that money, lots of money, does not usually provide a good environment for spontaneous, genuine humor. What's more boring than talking about money? Maybe lack of money has provided a skewed, funny point from which to look at life. If this is true, then red people are rich with resources.

The Wellspring of Native Creativity:
The Origins of A.I.C.A

Janeen Antoine

Founded in 1983, American Indian Contemporary Arts (A.I.C.A.), a nonprofit Native arts organization based in San Francisco, California, has been a small part of the Native arts renaissance that we all have the good fortune to be witnessing today. Its essential mission was to provide contemporary Indian artists an opportunity to present their works. To that end, A.I.C.A., during the twenty-plus-years it has been in existence, has organized more than one hundred on-site exhibitions and five traveling exhibitions (to many museums in the U.S. and to Mexico, Central and South America, and France), presenting the works and voices of hundreds of Native artists working in a variety of mediums and disciplines. As director and co-founder, I was generously invited by the curators of Changing Hands 2 to write an essay about the creation of A.I.C.A. and its participation in the Native arts movement. This essay evolved into a more personal narrative, since, in this field, writing has historically been from an outsider's point of view. While academia and Native authorship are not mutually exclusive, I wanted to contribute from the perspective of the community of emerging Native voices only now being heard.

THAT NATIVE ART IS BEING CREATED AT ALL TODAY is a testament to the tenacity of Indian people. Before 9/11, before America, before Columbus, before every significant marker in this country's oft-miswritten history, indigenous peoples lived widely across this land. For millennia, we survived and thrived in every conceivable region and climate—Arctic, swamp, desert, plateau, woodland, prairie, and mountain—in co-existence with our environments and generally, with one another. In time's layered passage of seasons and generations, knowledge changed hands, flowing from one generation to the next, and highly symbiotic relationships with the land developed. It was known by reading the environments the best times to plant or harvest; what plants served what purposes; when animals, birds, and fish would migrate; how the changing seasons affected the plants and animals; and, from all this, how best to sustain ourselves. We understood that by caring for the environment, it would in turn care for us. Creator's hand was visible and manifest in all life, and for this reason we regarded all life as sacred and connected.

This reverence for life extended naturally to the resourcefulness of making objects from any and all materials at hand. As diverse as the lands themselves, objects emerged from trees and rocks, fire and water, from plants, animals, and marine life, from the earth itself. Created from the environment, they took shape as pottery, bark and plant basketry, feather work, shell beadwork, stone and wood carving, weaving, hide painting, quillwork, leatherwork, bone and horn carving, earth-pigment painting, and many other forms. There was no useless material—everything in the environment served a purpose.

It is said that there is no word for "art" in Native languages, and, by extension, neither is there a word for "artist." Creation was something done by everyone, men and women, young and old, as a natural outcome and progression of life. One could look around and see artistry everywhere. We created all items, ceremonial and utilitarian, to be simultaneously beautiful and functional. A lovingly beaded cradleboard was a thing of beauty created to hold our most cherished, our children—*wakanyeja* (the sacred beings), as they

are known in the Lakota language. A wondrous pipe and stem were elaborately carved and quilled for communion with Creator. The geographic and tribal origin of an object could be identified by its materials and styles. What has come to be known as "the arts" emerged from a context of purpose and relationship; each "art" object had a history, a place, a form, and a function.

Many tribes create beautiful objects for the purpose of sharing and giving. The original instructions of most of our cultures are that we share with others. Substantial giveaways to honor and memorialize were and are conducted, in which we present many gifts to other clans or to those most in need. Often, families and clans acquire status according to the extent of their giving; we carry on this tradition both to help us survive and to redistribute wealth. Giveaways were an established practice at the time of contact with the Europeans, who unfortunately had an inverse practice.

With contact came conflict, a purposeful attempt to exterminate Native peoples and, in the process, take everything we had. Colonization, occupation, oppression, genocide, disease, alcohol, forced removal from the land, suppression of language, and the breaking up of families were all strategic tactics used against the survival of Indian people by invading foreigners. (Based not on their appearance but on their behavior, the Lakota early on aptly named them *wasicuns*—literally "takes the fat.") The foreigners repeated these practices with every tribe they encountered, uprooting us from our traditional homelands or confining us to reservations, reducing us to destitution and squalid living conditions, beggars in our own lands. Despite this enduring poverty, Indian people are still known for and value generosity. We share whatever we have as a matter of custom.

The devastating effect of Manifest Destiny greatly diminished Native artifacts along with Native populations and lands. Legislation such as Canada's Indian Act (1876, modified in 1884), which authorized the seizure of items intended as potlatch gifts, robbed our communities. Near total extermination of the buffalo deprived us of subsistence and the creation of related cultural materials. With the imposition of Christianity, our religious practices were banned and, along with our ceremonial objects, were forced underground. Young Indian people were confined to boarding schools, where they were required to learn domestic skills and trades rather than the traditional skills of our ancestors. Our material culture was purposefully eroded at every turn.

Today, Indian people are recovering from the ravages of centuries of systemic racism. In the wake of the civil-rights movement and Indian activism all across Turtle Island, we are experiencing a resurgent pride in Native identity, politics, and art. In the midst of a Native arts renaissance, with growing recognition of indigenous art forms, our own voices are needed to contribute to the dialogue about our arts and our place. From our own perspectives, we must explain how our traditional and contemporary arts are part of our histories and lifeways, and demonstrate why they are important, both for the outside world and for our own communities. We must discuss how and why they are excluded from the broader art world and remain unrecognized, whether this is important to Native peoples, and if so, what must be done to redress the process of exclusion.

I grew up in Winner, a small, white farming town that was then part of, but now bordering, the Rosebud Reservation in South Dakota. Reservation border towns engender the most racist attitudes toward Indians, and this one was no exception. Indian resident and medicine man John Fire, in his book *Lame Deer: Seeker of Visions*, threatened suit for failure to provide basic services such as plumbing and paved streets in "Indian Town" and talked about how bad the discrimination was there. Anyone who ventured beyond the comfort of family and Indian community would find themselves confronting a hostile world outside. For a child, shame was a subtle, daily burden. As I grew older, I began to recognize the racist origins of the endemic poverty and witness the consequent alcoholism so common in my community. Constant messages of inferiority became self-fulfilling prophecies as we struggled to exist in a mean, white world.

In middle school, I left Winner to attend an Indian boarding school in Mission, the main town on the Rosebud Reservation. At the time, Indian boarding schools were being dismantled or merged with public schools. Most children were bussed to school, and those from outlying areas or other towns and reservations were usually boarders. To fill the dormitories, white ranchers were allowed to place their children in this historically all-Indian school. Racism was apparent, as all white students were segregated in the dormitory and placed within closest walking distance to the other school buildings in the compound. Even in the Indian community, darker children received the worst treatment, only this time from fellow students and from a few misguided dormitory matrons, both Indian and non-Indian.

From there, aided by my grandfather's efforts, I was one of a number of young Indian people selected to attend college preparatory high schools on scholarship in the late 1960s, and was sent off to Verde Valley, a private non-Indian boarding school in Arizona. The school's enlightened anthropological orientation stressed cultural awareness and appreciation, and resulted in a culturally and ethnically diverse student body exposed to other cultures through field trips and brief annual stays with families in southwestern Indian reservations and in Mexico. It was startling to be educated about and experience the possibility of being different yet equal, and this exposure began a lifelong process of transformation in my self-perception and my understanding of racism. It also caused a cultural separation and loss from my own community, but the ideal environment—one that would enable such growth and transformation within one's Native culture—did not exist for me or many other Native youth at the time, so this was the next best path.

My personal experience reminded me of the times when I felt best and most appreciated—when I was participating in or exposed to creative expression. At home, I admired my grandmother's Lakota-inspired geometric hooked rugs fashioned into cushions for the church altar, my mother's elaborate first-place Halloween costumes hand-sewn for the children, and the beautiful star quilts that emerged from my aunties' and grandmas' quilting bees. From my mother's

work as a Girl Scout leader, I learned simple weaving and crafts and found satisfaction and a sense of accomplishment in my own art creations. In boarding school, I took up embroidery, beadwork, ceramics, and weaving, producing items that were valued by others and made me feel creative and connected to something larger than myself.

It was on those high-school field trips that I first encountered Native arts to collect, delighted to find gifts for my family that I could buy with the meager amount of money I had somehow saved: bowls and vases, wood boxes, hand-woven shawls, and blouses from Mexico; silver jewelry, miniature sand paintings, and weavings from the Navajo Reservation. Even just as a consumer of Native arts, my knowing that Indian people made them gave them a special significance, and made me feel proud to be Indian. There was a distinct satisfaction in the beauty of these items that store-bought, mass-produced gifts couldn't equal. Though not yet articulated, these positive feelings were essentially what motivated me to devote time to the creation and continuation of A.I.C.A.

In 1981, Ken Banks, a Southern California Native (Digueño) who had just gotten his B.A. in architecture from U.C. Berkeley, asked me to help him create an organization to work with Native artists. He was the visionary and I was the glue, I suppose, in helping to ensure its formation. With our mentors and founding trustees—Carmella Johnson (Pomo), Hartman Lomawaima (Hopi), Richard Trudell (Santee), and George Longfish (Seneca/Tuscarora)—we developed a broad mission: to demonstrate the cultural contributions of the Indian communities and to provide economic opportunities for Native artists. As an emerging organization with limited resources, we did what little we could to support the creation of Native art, and were more instrumental in addressing its visibility and recognition within the broader community. The beneficiaries were all of us: the diverse Native artists, the Native community, and the general public.

There was early discussion of how to organize A.I.C.A. We did not want to be a museum, because we did not have a collection; nor did we want to acquire a collection, because of the historic relationship of museums to Indian people. The only museums that really included Indians at that point were mostly museums of natural history intent on documenting the visions of a "vanishing race"—us. They perpetuated the white attitude of viewing Native arts as curiosities; and the belief that indigenous cultures were on the verge of extinction guaranteed Native artifacts a place in their curio cabinets. Furthermore, collections amassed for museums depleted these artifacts in Indian communities, who were left with little of their cultural patrimony to share with the coming generations. Many Indian people, including my own relatives, remember with sadness the family treasures they were forced to pawn or sell well below their real value in order to to buy much needed food and basic staples.

Even in the 1980s, most museums did not interact with the Native communities and contemporary Indian artists. There was a notable disconnect in the museum world between the creators of the artifacts they held and the descendants of these creators. It seems that there is something "romantic" about old Indians of yore, but seeing Indians of today is an unpleasant reminder to museum curators about how we have been removed from lands and historically abused. Archived objects don't talk back, but people do. After a lot of hard work, there is much more dialogue—and even in some instances, collaboration—between museums, tribes, and Indian artists. This process of communication and healing is ongoing and growing.

In working with Indian artists, it became clear that they needed and wanted facilities in which to exhibit their work. The Institute of American Indian Arts in Santa Fe was foremost in training artists, but on a national level, there were few sister organizations that provided promotional venues for these and other artists. American Indian Community House Gallery in New York, Daybreak Star in Seattle, and the Institute of American Indian Arts Museum in Santa Fe were the most notable, urban-based, Indian-controlled nonprofit organizations that provided venues for Native artists. There were few other venues other than the Southwest Association for Indian Arts annual Indian Market in Santa Fe or the contemporary art shows held at institutions such as the Gilcrease, the Philbrook, and the Heard museums. A lack of facilities within the Indian communities and the systemic exclusion of Native artists from "mainstream" art venues left little opportunity for presenting Native arts.

We designed the A.I.C.A. programs to include artists from across the country. We began by presenting on-site exhibitions, and then branched out to organize several traveling exhibitions that reached thousands of people across the country and beyond, including *Indian Humor* and *The Spirit of Native America*.[1] Although the presentation of visual arts has been our predominant activity, we have also been involved with artists who work in other art forms or genres, including dance, performance, spoken word, and youth arts. Our initial ambitious ten-year plan to present all these different art forms and acquire our own facility was never realized, because it took so much more energy than we anticipated, even "just" to present the exhibition program. Nevertheless, we are proud to have been able to work with hundreds of artists from all parts of the country in presenting their work, both on our own and in collaboration with many nonprofit arts centers, museums, tribes, and commercial entities. After several years of overambitious programming, we settled on an annual schedule of five exhibitions—organized by theme, art form, tribe, or region—plus one solo exhibition and one group exhibition.[2]

Among our most successful exhibitions were the group shows of works by artists from a single tribal nation at a time. Here, the collective voices illustrated both the artists' common values and the specific concerns of their communities. *Commemorating Wounded Knee* was made all the more poignant because it opened the day the U.S. armed forces began bombing Iraq. Muriel Antoine's poem *Flag of White*, about the Wounded Knee massacre, was written on the wall beside her masks, and showed how little U.S. imperialism had changed from a hundred years earlier. In the Seminole exhibition *Shaping Forces and Weaving Balance*, we contrasted that tribe's historical early clothing and weaving styles with some contemporary creations, and presented several of the distinctive styles fashioned during the

post-contact period, reflecting the Seminole people's innovations and their pride in their unique identity.

Two of our group exhibitions—*Akua, Ali'i A Me Kahuna* (*Gods, Chiefs, and Holy Men*), organized by Hawaiian artists Rocky and Lucia Jensen, and *The Contemporary and Traditional Expressions of the Amskapi Pikuni* (Southern Blackfeet), organized by Blackfeet artist Darrel Norman— were especially strong because so many of the artists were present at the opening events. Despite our limited ability to provide the artists' travel expenses, they raised their own funds to enable them to come and share with us the inspiration for their work. Their hugely successful openings, presented with song and ceremony, reflected the Native importance of creating within the context of community, showing how these artists are extensions of their Nations and how the cultural values are passed from one generation to the next. At every gathering I have attended where Hawaiian Natives have been invited, they come bearing gifts, often using the simplest materials made of the plants and flowers of Hawai'i, and presented with *aloha* and *mana*. It is important that we remember and speak about the struggles of the Hawaiian Natives whenever we speak of our own struggles for justice.

San Francisco is an ideal location for A.I.C.A. because it has a large and diverse Native community, consisting of people from across the country who moved here through the early B.I.A. relocation program of the 1950s, and subsequent waves of new arrivals who came for school and employment. In addition, San Francisco recognizes and consistently funds nonprofit arts organizations as way of promoting tourism. International visitors and the city's cultural plurality demonstrated the need to represent the diversity of the many tribes in the state of California and beyond. In the year 2000, with the explosive impact of the "dot-coms" on rental property, we lost our gallery. (My expletive of the moment is "dot-commit!") Without a permanent home, we began to do more work within the local community: supporting local artists and groups through fiscal sponsorship, proposal development, and promotion. In collaboration with other Native nonprofit groups in San Francisco, we are continuing to search for a new location.

From time to time, issues arose from inside and outside the Native arts community, such as exhibiting items of a culturally sensitive nature. These include photographs of ceremonial dances or objects, and the use of pipestone by certain artists for decorative or ornamental use. Ensuring that sensitive photos would not be exhibited and that we would not display objects made of pipestone became a strong indication to Native artists of our responsiveness to tribal concerns and of our respect for tribal values. Being the showcase for so many different cultural groups was a continual learning process, and we relied upon the expertise of the Native artists to help us proceed on the right path.

An oft-expressed criticism from outside our community was the charge of "ghettoizing" the gallery by focusing only on American Indian artists. When that happened, we explained that the gallery was an important cultural facility and gathering place to express and share the myriad Native cultures of the San Francisco Bay Area, while providing a way for our artists to gain access to non-Native venues. With so few places to call our own, particularly in urban environments, it was very important to have venues that focused on Native cultures and arts.

Another issue that our artists often had to address was the frequent classification of their work as "traditional crafts" rather than "fine arts." As Native artists living today, they may work in traditional mediums or in new mediums or both, and the varied ideas that they express reflect their contemporary experiences. We cannot exclude artists from the contemporary arts movement and place them into a historical vacuum because they use "traditional" mediums. Nor can we eschew those artists using contemporary mediums and reject their work as not being "Native enough." This discussion is ongoing within the general arts community and within the Native arts community as well, and is one that is beginning to recognize the cultural bias of valuing European art forms above those of indigenous cultures.

While it has been a struggle to ensure A.I.C.A.'s continuance, the activities of Indian groups in many parts of the country confirm that the cultural rebirth is accelerating. More tribal museums are being created to relate their own people's histories and affirm their cultures, to renew development of regional art forms such as basketry and carving, and to display and encourage their own members' artistry. The California Indian Museum and Cultural Center (which opened in San Francisco in 1996 and moved to Santa Rosa in 2001) focuses on California Native history and traditions. The National Museum of the American Indian showcases its fabulous collection of artifacts and simultaneously presents exhibitions by contemporary artists in its New York and Washington, D.C. locations, giving wide exposure to indigenous peoples from all over the Americas. Important exhibitions such as *Changing Hands 2* are being developed by the greater arts communities to recognize the artistic genius and diversity of Indian peoples. Native artists are gaining wider and more serious recognition for their work and are being included in exhibitions that represent all artists, including such prestigious venues as the Venice *Biennale*. Institutions such as the First Peoples Fund and the Eiteljorg Museum of American Indians and Western Art (in Rapid City and Indianapolis, respectively) are making financial support a reality, enabling artists to develop their own visions, rather than having to respond to a purely commercial market. We need to focus on providing more opportunities for creative expression in all our schools and bring this essential element into our communities. Native artists need more recognition and financial support, and we need to document their work by issuing catalogues, videos, and other materials.

The future direction of Native arts will be determined by the creative artists and what they do. From a marketing standpoint, the field is open to many new audiences. New outlets such as Internet auction sites, small co-ops, regional art shows, tribal and casino venues, artist collectives, and the established galleries and museums have emerged. Since the development of the Internet, a tool of globalization, Native artists have been increasingly able to remain in their own communities and create and sell work that is derived from within their own culture and less directed by the commercial markets of Santa Fe and Scottsdale. As venues become more geographically diverse and tribally specific and as art forms and facilities continue to be revitalized, developed, and promoted, other regions of the country will become more prominent in this effort. International collaborations are also occurring more frequently as indigenous artists from all parts of the world begin to share with one another their traditions, art forms, and collective knowledge.

I cannot close this piece without mention of the artists and the work they do. One of the greatest gifts of my life has been the opportunity to know so many talented and engaged Indian people from all directions of this country. In the past, everyone may have been allowed and encouraged to express their creative drive, but today this is not so. These artists are in touch with the drive to create, a flowering of their innate and natural desire to celebrate and express the Creator's mystery. On a practical level, they have their drudgery, they struggle with life and all its obstacles and complexity. But on another level they are inspired, and their work is the touchstone of creativity. To look at the images in this catalogue is testament to that. One of my favorite simple axioms is "Small things grow." Like a seed, they take hold, begin to root, and take form, whether they are good or bad. These artists nurture the good, the seeds that contain the mystery and wonder of life, and bring them to fruition to the benefit of all of us. In them is contained the universe, and our connection with it all.

Our religions and philosophies reflect our cultural knowledge. We are part of a greater cosmos, not more important than the smallest creatures. We are not plotting dominion over nature, nor are we preordained to be masters of the universe. We live in a symbiotic relationship with nature and recognize our complex and mutual needs and the responsibility we have been given as human beings to care for the plants and animals, for the waters and the land, for one another. We recognize and own our responsibility as much as our right. We are of the earth, and understand that the earth is truly our mother, for she gives us life and sustains us. This abiding belief is manifest in the inspiration and creations of many Native artists. New and extant works acknowledge our place and our function in our families, in our communities, in our nations. Artists assume important community roles in perpetuating our traditions and encouraging innovation. The potential to use all art forms in healing our nations is great, and encourages artists' involvement as Native communities grapple with abuse and violence arising from oppression, especially among our large populations of youth. By understanding and using this power to promote wellness and respect, our artists can—and do—send a message to all creative people to take up the call to help heal our nations and our world. For this, we are all blessed.

NOTES

To Ellen and David, the curators of *Changing Hands 2*, for your experience and dedication in giving this exhibition life; to the artists for your inspirational vision; to our ancestors for your perseverance; and first and last, to Creator for our lives and the abundant blessings we receive, I thank you. Pilamiya.

1. *Indian Humor*, featuring the works and words of the artists themselves, was accepted by the National Museum of the American Indian as their first outside exhibition, and is still presented on their Web site. *The Spirit of Native America* traveled to Mexico, Central and South America, and France for three years. Each exhibition included works by nearly forty artists, and provided them with opportunities to participate in opening receptions, presentations, and discussions about their own work and Native arts in general. The international exhibition was especially important for the opportunity it provided artists to travel and learn, and to see how differently the indigenous peoples of the U.S. were perceived by people from other countries.

2. Whether planning programming or dealing with problems, artists and A.I.C.A. staff worked together to devise solutions and to present programs and exhibitions. The hardworking programming staff over the years has included Ken Banks, Kathryn Stewart, Theresa Harlan, Denise Quitiquit, Robert Moore, Ray Moisa, Marsha Kosteva, Sara Bates, and Debora Iyall. Many board trustees and volunteers also gave much time and enthusiastic support, and special appreciation goes out to current trustees Zandra Bietz and Steve Kiser for their years of dedication. My own involvement would not have been possible without financial and emotional support from my partner, Richard Trudell, and the family support of his brother Less and my mother Muriel to care for our son Maurice. It is the combined efforts of all involved—the funders, the volunteers, the trustees, the staff, the artists, and family—that enable A.I.C.A. to continue and put forth our message that Native cultures still exist and deserve recognition and support in their own right and as a contribution to the human dialogue.

MATERIAL EVIDENCE

A profound engagement with materials is central to the creative process in the visual arts. It is the artists' inherent skill that links hand, eye, and mind while making art that transforms mute materials into visual poetry. These artists celebrate the physical world of materials, whether in the traditional craft mediums, such as textiles, ceramics, wood, metal, and glass, or in contemporary materials ranging from plastics and vinyl to digital imagery.

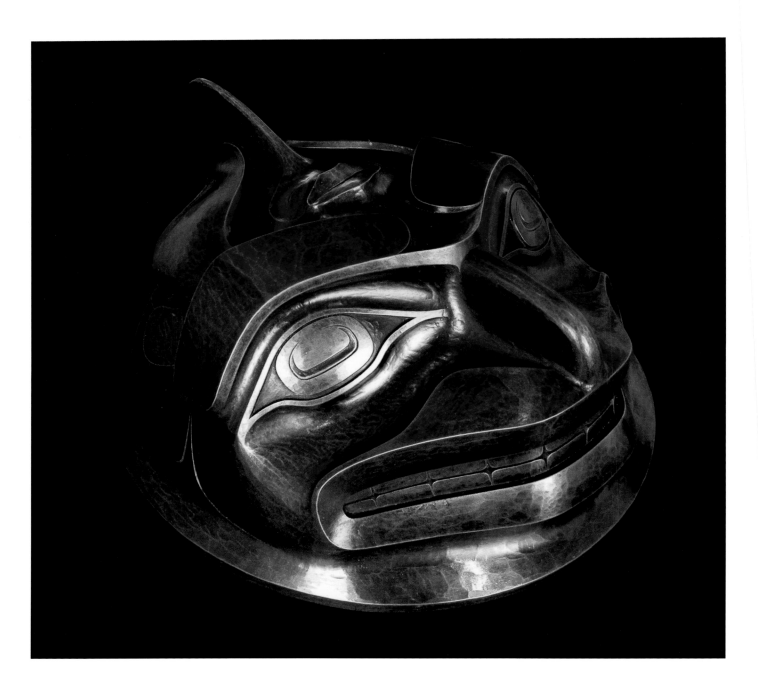

BENJAMIN DAVIDSON

b. 1976, *Vancouver, British Columbia; lives in Queen Charlotte Islands (Haida Gwaii), British Columbia*

Killer Whale, 2004

Resin
H. 7 1/2 in., Diam. 14 1/4 in. (19 x 36.2 cm)

Courtesy of Douglas Reynolds Gallery

LARRY ROSSO

b. 1944, Burns Lake, British Columbia;
lives in Vancouver, British Columbia

Grizzly Bear, 2002

Paper
28 x 29 x 7 in. (71.1 x 73.7 x 17.8 cm)

Courtesy of Douglas Reynolds Gallery

DARREN MCKENZIE

b. 1960, Regina, Saskatchewan; lives in Regina

"A main focus of Native art is Nature, our mother who binds all of life together and makes it flow, entwine, and mystify us. I define tradition as methodology and spirituality acquired over generations of ritual and necessity, for the greater understanding of our earth, sky, and selves. Tradition is important in my work because without it, what would I have?"

Natural Spirit, 2005

Red cedar, acrylic paint
24 x 8 x 5 1/2 in. (61 x
20.3 x 14 cm)

Collection of Pierre and
Anne Marie L'Hertier

CHRISTIAN WHITE

b. 1962, Queen Charlotte Islands (Haida Gwaii), British Columbia; lives in Massett, Queen Charlotte Islands

"I have been carving all my life. The pieces I create have stories that have been passed down through the generations. The art of storytelling was always a very important aspect of Haida culture. We as a people now are also creating history by carrying on our culture. We are practicing our traditional rites, remaining a vital part of the world culture."

The Power of the Shining Heavens,
2000

Argillite, catlinite, abalone
1 1/2 x 1 1/4 x 3/4 in. (1.5 x 1.3 x 0.6 cm)

Collection of Richard M. Hanson

RON TELEK

b. 1962, Vancouver, British Columbia;
lives in Prince Rupert, British Columbia

"A major theme of shamanic art is transformation. My culture believes that a transformation
from human to an animal, to the spiritual, is
always a possibility. Occasionally, my art captures
a terrifying vision. The vision represents the
struggle of the soul to create the good that will
conquer evil. All people, regardless of culture,
have faced this struggle. Through my art, I bring
the spiritual and cultural worlds of the Nisga'a
to others across the world."

*The Frog Who Always Wanted To
Be a Shark*, ca. 2002

Alder, string, bone, abalone
12 x 4 x 3 in. (30.5 x 10.2 x 7.6 cm)

Private collection

KENNETH JOHNSON

b. 1967, Lubbock, Texas; lives in Santa Fe, New Mexico

"My goal as an artist is innovation in the use of metal. I enjoy creating objects that are both beautiful and practical. There are so many facets to consider in a piece of jewelry. In many of my pieces, I see a story waiting to be told, or a meaning to be conveyed to the wearer. I draw from my background as I forge my future."

Three-Tiered Turtle Gorget Necklace, 2004

18k gold, platinum, peridot stones, diamonds gorget: 7 x 5 in. (38.1 x 12.7 cm); length of chain: 17 1/4 in. (44.5 cm)

Collection of the artist

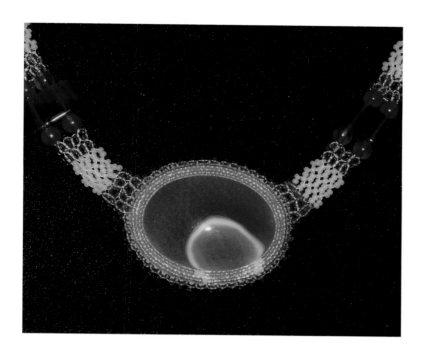

KATRINA MITTEN

b. 1962, Huntington, Indiana; lives in Huntington

"At the age of twelve, I wanted to learn an art
that is traditional to my people. I was drawn
to beadwork. Few people were practicing this
art in my area after the removal of Native
Americans from Indiana to 'Indian Territory'
in 1846. I found teachers in the master bead
workers of the past. The art that had survived
the removal helped me to understand the
technique, design, and colors used in creating
beautiful works of art."

Carnelian Necklace, 2004

Carnelian, glass beads,
beading thread, deerskin
L. 18 in. (45.7 cm);
medallion: 2 x 1½ in.
(5.1 x 3.8 cm)

Collection of the artist

JAMES FAKS

b. in Montana; lives in Santa Fe, New Mexico

Evening Purse, 2004

Sterling silver, amber
4¼ x 6¼ in.
(10.8 x 15.9 cm)

Courtesy of Price Dewey
Galleries, Ltd.

PAM KAWEHILANI BARTON

b. in Honolulu, Hawai'i; lives in Volcano, Hawai'i

"One of the countless pleasures of working with fibers is that I am able to span from the sublime to the ridiculous, and all with a clear conscience. Making *kapa* from mulberry bark parallels this pleasure. It is as meditative as it is intensive, and as satisfying as it is laborious, to experience the entire process of growing and harvesting the raw material, then fermenting and beating it (true to ancient Hawaiian tradition), then to produce fabric ranging from the likes of heavy cotton or linen to a delicate soft gossamer textile, which can be sewn, dyed, plaited, quilted, painted or printed on."

Pa'ipa'inahā no Hina (Cape for Hina), 2002

Kapa (mulberry bark cloth), wild ficus, iron oxide, wood rod
34 x 48 x 1 in. (86.4 x 122 x 2.5 cm)

Collection of the artist

WILMA OSBORNE

b. 1970, White Mountain, Alaska; lives in Tuluksak, Alaska

"Skin sewing is a traditional skill and art form; indigenous and rare materials such as sealskin, intestines, sea otter, and polar bear fur are essential to basic garments and pieces. But incorporating new ideas is refreshing and acknowledges the dramatic changes that have occurred from my grandparents' time to my time. My grandparents passed on to me their energy, ideas, and worldview, which have been transformed by my place in time and unusual opportunities for expression."

Messenger Bag, 2003

Young ringed seal skin, polar bear trim
28 x 12¹/₂ x 5 in. (71.1 x 31.8 x 12.7 cm)

Collection of Carla Potter

HARRIS SMITH

b. 1942, North Vancouver, British Columbia;
lives in Parksville, British Columbia

"This is a contemporary piece, inspired by
traditional feast dishes and vessels, which
were functional but also works of usable art.
With this piece, I have incorporated the use
of maple, dyed in colors of the sky and forest,
using traditional designs in an abstract way."

Out of the Blue, 2003

Maple, acrylic paint
Diam. 15 in., D. 1 ³/₄ in.
(38.1 x 4.4 cm)

Courtesy of Lattimer Gallery

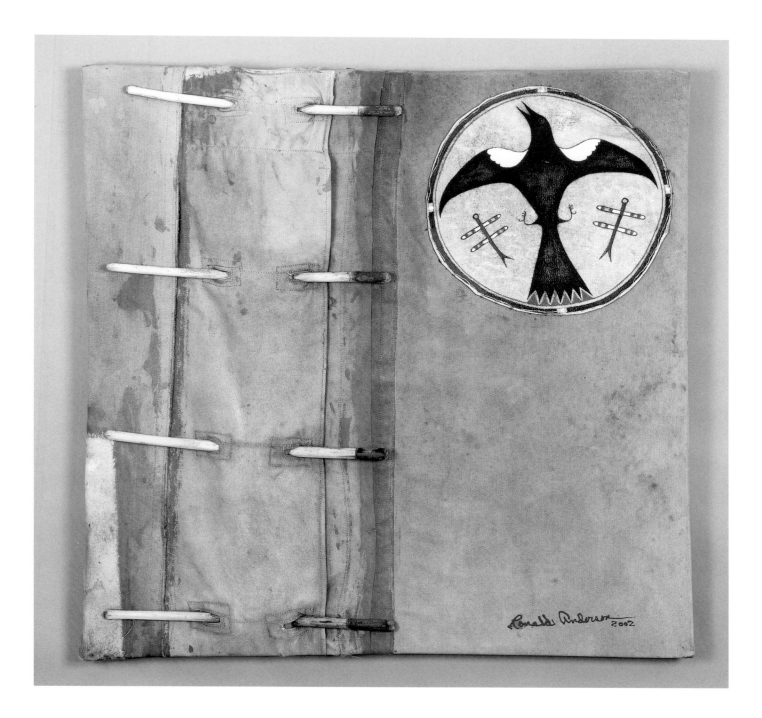

RONALD WAYNE ANDERSON

b. 1938, Buffalo Creek, Oklahoma;
lives in Gracemont, Oklahoma

"I was taught art by my German grandmother, who was affiliated with the Abstract Expressionists. I consider my art to be traditional in philosophy and symbolism, to be an intellectual stimulant for both non-Indians and Indians."

Wild Blue Yonder, 2002

Canvas and wood sticks
from a tipi, acrylic paint,
thread
29 x 28 ½ x 3 in.
(73.7 x 72.4 x 7.6 cm)

Collection of the artist

DEMOS GLASS

b. 1976, Tahlequah, Oklahoma; lives in Locust Grove, Oklahoma

"Through the relationships that I embrace between ancient America and the present, I am inspired to create contemporary forms that represent my cultural artistic identity. The technical challenges of mixed media allow me to create interaction among different mediums working together as one."

Encirclement, 2002

Pewter, walnut, poplar
11 3/4 x 8 1/4 x 6 3/4 in.
(30 x 21 x 17 cm)

Collection of Guinotte Wise

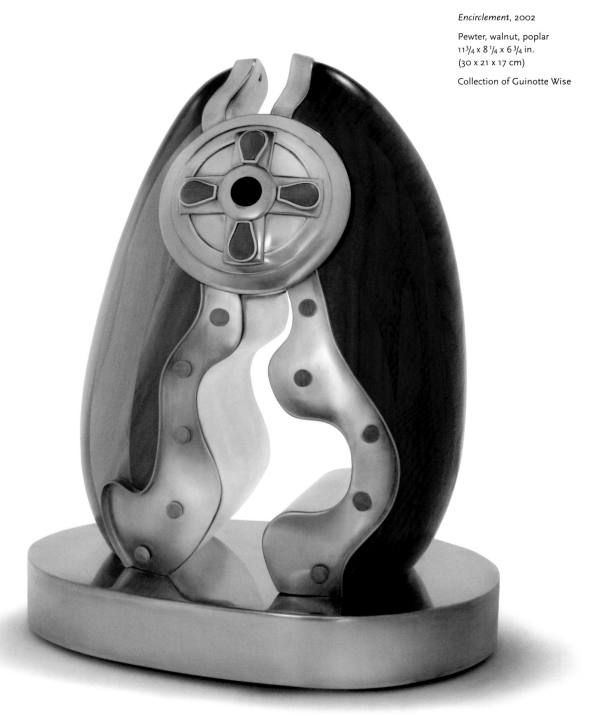

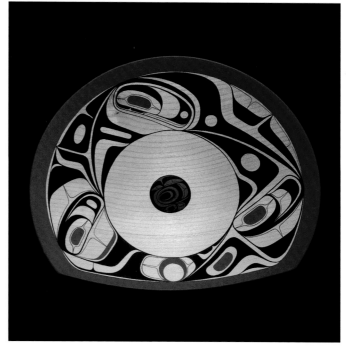

CARL STROMQUIST

b. 1969, Hope, British Columbia; lives in Hope

Wavering Wolf Clan Man, 2004

Birch, acrylic paint
Diam. 17 in., D. 2 3/4 in.
(43.2 x 7 cm)

Museum of Arts & Design;
Museum purchase with funds
provided by an anonymous
foundation

ROD SMITH

b. 1966, Vancouver, British Columbia;
lives in Parksville, British Columbia

"My goal is to create contemporary Aboriginal
art. I employ traditional Northwest Coast design
elements, colors, and techniques. My hope with
this plate was to create an abstract art piece
with its roots in the past, yet still in touch with
the twenty-first century. The truncation of the
plate is deliberate and does not interrupt the
flow in the design."

Untitled, 2004

Maple, acrylic paint
11 x 13 x 3 in. (27.9 x 33 x 7.6 cm)

Courtesy of Lattimer Gallery

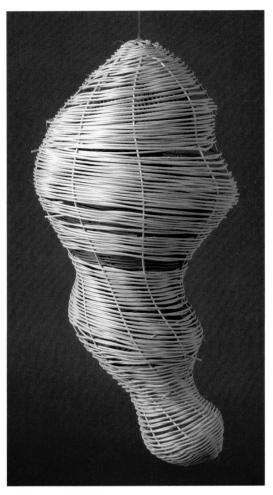

KEVIN POURIER

b. 1968, Rapid City, South Dakota; lives in Scenic, South Dakota

"In my search to learn our lifeways came an awareness of how interconnected and interdependent
we are with everything around us. My work of
making buffalo-horn spoons is steeped in tradition.
Mitakuye oyasin means 'We are all related'—this
is our first spiritual law. It is our most powerful
prayer. It is what our lifeways are centered around.
We live accordingly."

Floral Spoon, 2004

Buffalo horn, malachite,
mother-of-pearl, coral,
catlinite (pipestone),
lapis lazuli, cebu shell,
sandstone
3 x 10½ x 3 in. (7.6 x
26.7 x 7.6 cm)

Collection of the artist

NICOLE MORITA

b. 1976, Honolulu, Hawai'i; lives in Honolulu

"Oral family history and narrative play a significant
role in my work. Having been raised with both
Japanese-American and Hawaiian cultural values,
I am exploring aspects of both cultures, which
greatly influence my work. Tradition speaks of
the memory and preservation of an idea, belief,
or story. In *Wāhi*, I explore the notion of tradition
in Hawaiian culture being suppressed and
contained. Incorporating a traditional twining
technique with contemporary materials reflects
ideas of past and present. Although my work
is usually conceptually based, I find beauty in
minimal forms that simplify my concepts and
present my ideas in clear, thought-provoking
ways."

Wāhi (To Bind), 2001

Reed, natural and
synthetic dyes
16 x 7 x 6 in. (40.6 x
17.8 x 15.2 cm)

Collection of the artist

CLARISSA HUDSON

b. 1956, Juneau, Alaska; lives in Pagosa Springs, Colorado

"Dreams and visions come. Sometimes they foretell the future in symbolic forms, sometimes they tell a story long forgotten. The elders take responsibility in assisting the youth to become that in which they are naturally talented, and thus to become grounded, have a sense of well-being and purpose, and eventually share their talent in which they were guided. This perpetu-ates the continuation of customs and traditions long revered by our ancestors for the survival of our cultures. Elders of various talents taught me their art forms, and stressed the need for us to understand and acknowledge who we are and where we come from. As artists, the things we create reflect the strength of cultural traditions, values, morals, and spirituality."

Totemic Theory 2, 2001

Canvas, Masonite,
wood frame, acrylic,
gold leaf
75 1/4 x 16 x 17 in. (191.2 x
40.6 x 43.1 cm)

Private collection

YUXWELUPTUN (LAWRENCE PAUL)

b. 1957, Kamloops, British Columbia; lives in Vancouver, British Columbia

Ovoid Ground Totems, 2005 *

Wood, paint
Dimensions variable

Collection of the artist

* Only in the catalogue; another work by this artist is in the exhibition.

ROSALIE PANIYAK

b. 1934, Old Chevak, Alaska; lives in Chevak, Alaska

My Love, This Liberty, 2005

Sealskin, wolverine fur,
shredded wool blankets,
cotton cloth, electrical wire
18 x 11 x 6 in. (45.7 x 27.9 x
15.2 cm)

Private collection

PAULETTE NOHEALANI KAHALEPUNA

b. 1945, San Francisco, California; lives in Honolulu, Hawaiʻi

LEFT TO RIGHT

Hand Kāhili, 2005

Rooster hackle feathers,
wood, rope
H. 32 in., Diam. 11 in.
(81.3 x 27.9 cm)

Private collection

Hand Kāhili, 2005

Rooster hackle feathers,
wood, grosgrain ribbon
H. 50 in., Diam. 4 in.
(127 x 10.2 cm)

Private collection

Hand Kāhili, 2005

Rooster hackle feathers,
hardwood, grosgrain
ribbon
H. 39¹/₂ in., Diam. 9 in.
(100.3 x 22.9 cm)

Private collection

SEAN KEKAMAKUPA'A LEE LOY BROWNE

b. 1953, Hilo, Hawai'i; lives in Honolulu, Hawai'i

"Kamalei (which means "beloved child") refers to the life cycle of the Hawaiian *'ohana* (family unit). The circular form of *Kamalei* symbolizes the newborn and, by this act of creation, the rebirth of the *'ohana.*"

Kamalei (Beloved Child), 2003

Red granite (from India),
Belfast granite (from South
Africa)
16 1/2 x 14 x 10 1/2 in.
(41.9 x 35.6 x 26.7 cm)

Collection of the artist

RICK BARTOW

b. 1946, South Beach, Oregon; lives in South Beach

"Bears and coyotes are both inhabitants of this place that my family and I call home. The bear is a shy ghost in the brush who has been around us a number of times as we were cutting firewood for our sweat-house ceremonies.

"The berry bucket used in the piece *Bear with Humor* was my grandmother's and appears to have been used to mix plaster later in its life, prior to my utilizing it as a sculptural element. The bear piece was inspired by a blind Southern folk artist's scarecrow and Tlingit armor."

Bear with Humor, 2004

Wood, nails, metal, tar
30 x 17 x 13 in. (76.2 x
43.2 x 33 cm)

Collection of Arlene and
Harold Schnitzer

SONYA KELLIHER-COMBS

b. 1969, Bethel, Alaska; lives in Anchorage, Alaska

"*Guarded Secrets* is a series dealing with the protected secret, one shielded from the outside and one fortified from the inside."

———

"A crest, a clan, an identifier who you are

a pore
sifting, shifting
catching, releasing,
pouring

secrets
hiding, guarding
gathering
scraps
the stuff one does not talk about . . ."

— Sonya Kelliher Combs, excerpt from untitled poem

MOANA K. M. EISELE

b. 1942, Honolulu, Hawai'i; lives in Honolulu

"The continuity of the Hawaiian culture is very important to me. Making Hawaiian *kapa* provides me with an opportunity to express my Hawaiian culture, build personal character, and strengthen my Hawaiian values. Passing my experiences and appreciation for my culture to the next generation is my contribution toward continuity of the Hawaiian culture."

—from *Nā Maka Hou: New Visions— Contemporary Native Hawaiian Art* (2001)

Mohala Mau (Forever blooming forth), 2001

Kapa (mulberry bark cloth), *kauila* wood, *kua pohaku* (stone anvil)
Overall dimensions variable; *'olena*-dyed *kapa*: 80 x 15 in. (203.2 x 38.1 cm); natural *kapa*: 77 x 12 in. (195.6 x 30.5 cm); *alaea*-dyed *kapa*: 46 x 15 in. (116.8 x 38.1 cm)

Collection of the artist

PRESTON SINGLETARY

b. 1963, San Francisco, California; lives in Seattle, Washington

"When I first started working with glass, I was fascinated with the process and worked hard to master it. I was working with other glass artists and helping them execute their work. After a time, I started to think of a way of distinguishing my work from everyone else, and came up with adapting Northwest Coast designs onto glass-blown pieces. The material of glass, I feel, brings a new dimension to Native art. There is no other material that can hold the light and produce shadows in the same way."

Bentwood Chest, 2004

Glass
18 x 14 ¹/₂ x 22 ¹/₂ in.
(45.7 x 36.8 x 57.2 cm)

Collection of Daniel Greenberg and Susan Steinhauser

BERNICE A. KEOLAMAULOA OʻNALANI AKAMINE

b. 1949, Honolulu, Hawaiʻi; lives in Kaneohe, Hawaiʻi

"'Ā pele speaks of wahine akua, Pele, goddess
of the volcano. Destroyer and creator. Pele
who destroys everything in her path in order
to create anew.

   "Art making is a blessing or gift that comes
or is given."

—Bernice Akamine

———

 "He ho ike na ka po.
A revelation of the night.
A revelation from the gods in dreams, visions,
and omens."

—from 'Olelo noʻeau a ka Hawaiʻi: Folk Sayings from
the Hawaiian (1961)

ā pele, 2001

Glass, acrylic, monofilament,
volcanic cinders
glass: 5 x 6 in. (12.7 x 15.2 cm);
L. of fibers: 12 in. (30.4 cm)

Collection of the artist

RANDE COOK

b. 1977, Alert Bay, Vancouver Island, British Columbia;
lives in Victoria, British Columbia

"Native art is a continuous movement of skill
and balance. Once we as Native artists grasp
the concept of what it is to be free, in terms of
creativity, whatever the artist can conceive will
surely be achieved and will then bring us to
the next level of creation."

Ever Transforming Box, 2002

Sterling silver
4 x 2 x 2¹/₄ in. (10.2 x
5.1 x 5.7 cm)

Courtesy of Lattimer Gallery

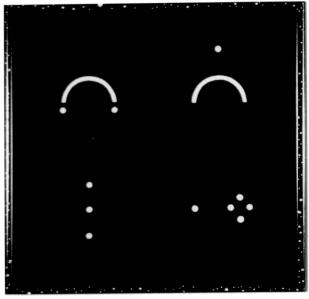

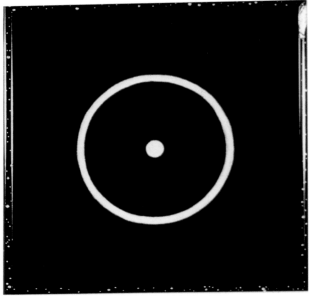

KEʻALAONAONAPUAHĪNANO CAMPTON

b. 1963, San Francisco, California; lives in Kailua, Hawaiʻi

"Traditions, whether from a Western context or Hawaiian context, have been critical to my development as an individual and an artist. Traditions are the cornerstone of my foundation, and my work reflects the ancient as well as the contemporary. Just as my ancestors continually adapted and incorporated new materials and technology, I adapt and incorporate new materials and technology. I embrace tradition, and yet I am not bound by tradition. To truly see or know beauty is not just seeing an object, place, or individual that is pleasing to the aesthetic senses, but to see and understand the essence, truth, or spirit. I am continually deconstructing my work until I find the true essence of my vision."

ʻIke Pāpālua: (clockwise from upper left) *ʻEkahi/ ʻElua/ ʻEhā/ ʻEkolu*, 2001

Acrylic, canvas, aluminum
4 panels, *each* 8 x 8 in.
(20.3 x 20.3 cm)

Collection of the artist

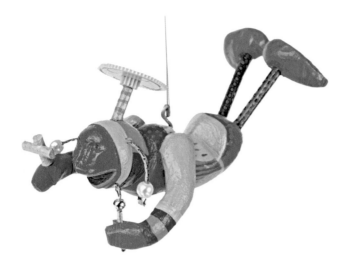

BENJAMIN HARJO, JR.

b. 1945, Clovis, New Mexico; lives in Oklahoma City, Oklahoma

"It has always been my contention that one's art speaks
from the soul of the artist and remains viable and open
to the influences of the artist's environment. Forms,
colors, and movement keep it from stagnating and allows
it to grow as the artist matures and develops. I feel that
my art covers a wide range of emotions, from serious
to humorous, and that the colors I use radiate a sense
of happiness and joy."

Untitled Ornament, 2005

Pecan wood, acrylic,
found objects (plastic,
metal, bamboo)
3¹/₂ x 1¹/₄ x 2 in.
(8.9 x 3.2 x 5.1 cm)

Private collection

DEBORAH MAGEE

b. 1955, Browning, Montana; lives in Cut Bank, Montana

"After studying art history in college, I thought
the Western tradition of fine arts had come to
an end with the ugly contemporary pieces being
produced. My Indian heritage and traditions
have given me a solid foundation of 'beauty,' as
a core value of my work, and I try to honor my
ancestors by carrying that forward."

Listening to the Ancients, 2003

Glass beads on flannel and
wool, dyed porcupine quills,
brain-tanned deerskin
5¹/₂ x 7¹/₂ in. (14 x 19.1 cm)

Collection of Adam and Kyle Canepa

RONALD SENUNGETUK

b. 1933, *Wales, Alaska; lives in Homer, Alaska*

"In order for traditions to remain traditional, they must always change and adapt to present ways. Otherwise, they become part of dead cultures.

"Beauty is also timeless. It is a will to express and it is partly a connection to who one is. I think this basic concept works everywhere on earth. In my work, I first understood 'beauty' from Western art definitions. After preferring Western art for a while, I started to concentrate on various art forms of my own people to show that Inuit always portrayed life in powerful ways, most often emphasizing 'beauty.'"

—from *Looking North: Art from the University of Alaska Museum* (1998)

Columbia Glacier Left, 2002

Silver maple, colored
furniture oil stain
23 x 37 1/2 x 1 in.
(58.4 x 95.3 x 2.5 cm)

Private collection

ROBERT DAVIDSON

b. 1946, Hydaburg, Alaska; lives in Surrey, British Columbia

"A *gagiid* is a wildman who, after his canoe is capsized, survives in the cold ocean water. He swims to shore and lives out his life in the forest. My *tsinii* (grandfather) explained to me, 'A *gagiid* is a person whose spirit is too strong to die.' Haida people and many other First Nations are like *gagiid*. As we reclaim our spirit and become whole, we can become healthy, contributing people and once again take our rightful place in the world."

Meeting at the Centre, 2004

Aluminum, epoxy powder
coating
48 x 84 x 84 in. (121.9 x
213.4 x 213.4 cm)

Collection of the artist

STEVE SMITH

b. 1968, *Vancouver, British Columbia; lives in Vancouver*

"In creating art, I try to work with the positive space and negative space. The two are inseparable and, together with the right balance, can create a sense of harmony."

Pieces of the Puzzle, 2004

Maple, acrylic paint
15 x 15 ^{1}/$_2$ x 2 in. (38.1 x
39.4 x 5.1 cm)

Private collection

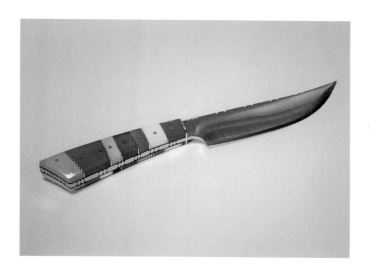

DAN WORCESTER

b. 1955, *Ardmore, Oklahoma; lives in Ardmore*

"I am constantly impressed by the people using the very basic materials and tools to create functional and artistic work. When I can blend these two elements, be it a traditional or contemporary piece, then I feel a sense of accomplishment."

Knife, 2004

Bakelite billiard balls,
sterling silver, steel,
silver coin
L. 11 in., W. 1^1/$_4$ in., H. ^{7}/$_8$ in.
(27.9 x 3.2 x 2.2 cm)

Collection of the artist

BRIAN TRIPP

b. in *Eureka, California; lives in Eureka*

Necklace, 2000

String, glass beads, stone,
coins (two U.S. quarters),
duct tape
L. 32 in. (81.3 cm)

Collection of Carla Potter

DAWN WALLACE

b. 1983, Santa Fe, New Mexico; lives in Hilo, Hawai'i

Necklace, ca. 2004

Sterling silver, 14k gold
L. 22 in. (55.9 cm)

Collection of Dolores Schapiro

JOE FEDDERSEN

b. 1953, Omak, Washington; lives in Olympia, Washington

"My work investigates signs, capitalizing on personal connections of memory interwoven in pattern as well as place. Abstract mountains, butterflies, stars, parking lots, cinder blocks, and many more patterns bring with them a saturated vocabulary based on place, some distilled through time and use within the community, while others speak of change. All portray the landscape in a visual language embedded in a simple repetitive pattern. These clearly show my interest in the zone where the signs tenuously dissolve into a modernist aesthetic while still maintaining direct ties to the Plateau designs of my ancestors."

Cul-de-sac (from the *Urban Indian Suite*), 2002

Waxed linen
H. 6 1/2 in., Diam. 3 7/8 in.
(16.5 x 9.8 cm)

Hallie Ford Museum of Art,
Willamette University

KEONE NUNES

b. 1957, Morioka, Japan; lives in Waianae, Oahu, Hawai'i

"My work with *Uhi* (Hawaiian tattoo) is a reflection of a past time of our ancestors and of the present resurgence of the intellectual realities that have sometimes been forgotten. The foundation of the work is in the power of the designs, the darkness of the night (from which all knowledge is received), and the lines of the human body—which, combined together, give a voice to our ancestors that cannot speak."

Tattoo, 1999

Tattoo ink (carbon black)
mixed with *kukui* nut soot
Dimensions variable

LEHUA DOMINGO

b. 1935, Hookena, Hawai'i; lives in Ocean View, Hawai'i

KILOHANA DOMINGO

b. 1958, Kealakekua, Hawai'i; lives in Ocean View, Hawai'i

"I think 'tradition' and 'contemporary' are relative terms. What is tradition today was probably contemporary then. They are one and the same. As a native Hawaiian, anything that I create will inherit the spirit of where I come from, whether conscious or unconscious. Sometimes we are afraid to take that leap, especially when we let our peers' opinions influence us. In my work, I always leave a piece of myself."

—Kilohana Domingo

Anoni Hats with Feather Leis,
2004

Leaves from the pandanus tree (*lauhala*), bird feathers
4 x 14 x 14$\frac{1}{2}$ in. (10.2 x 35.6 x 36.8 cm);
5 x 12 $\frac{5}{8}$ x 13 in. (12.7 x 32.1 x 33 cm);
5 x 13 x 13$\frac{1}{2}$ in. (12.7 x 33 x 34.3 cm)

Collection of the artists

JOEY LAVADOUR

b. 1954, Umatilla, Oregon; lives in Cayuse, Oregon

"My teacher was a Walla Walla tribal elder named Carrie Sampson. She was hesitant to teach a boy back in those days. I was persistent, and she agreed as long as I would agree to teach others. I've always kept my word, and to this day teach those who wish to learn. Carrie instructed me to weave the colors of my dreams. She told me, 'If you dream about a horse and he's blue, weave him blue, your baskets will be special if you weave them the colors of your dreams.' Weaving is a spiritual discipline for me. I believe that many of my designs are direct continuations of the evolution of Plateau imagery."

Bear Paws Making Scratch Marks, 2004

Pendleton blanket yarn, hemp cordage
H. 14 in., Diam. 9¹/₄ in.
(35.6 x 23.5 cm)

Collection of the artist

ALAN BELL

b. 1936, Pine Ridge Reservation, South Dakota; lives in Edgemont, South Dakota

"My mother and grandmother did quilts and beadwork; my father was a carpenter. I believe that my works reflect a blend of influences: design, on the one hand, and material and technique, on the other."

ROBERT GRESS

b. 1963, Harden, Montana; lives in Espanola, New Mexico

Rectangular Buckle,
ca. 2004

Sterling silver, oxblood coral, Cripple Creek turquoise, lapis lazuli, pink coral
2 x 3 x ¹/₂ in. (5.1 x 7.6 x 1.3 cm)

Private collection

MOLLY MURPHY

b. 1977, Great Falls, Montana; lives in Missoula, Montana

"When I was an adult in college, the art-history courses exposed me to artists I would have never known existed. I fell in love with the work of contemporary artists such as Baldessari, Oldenburg, Rothko, Hesse, and Thiebaud. I started to see a potential in taking the skills and crafts I learned very young to create beautiful objects and make critical commentary. I am not a traditional person."

Parfleche Abstraction, Cool Tones Warm Tones, 2005

Commercial woven wool, beads, satin fabric, satin ribbon
each 34 x 12 1/2 x 1/2 in.
(86.4 x 31.8 x 1.3 cm)

Collection of the artist

NATALIE MAHINA JENSEN-OOMITTUK

b. 1969, Honolulu, Hawai'i; lives in Keaau, Hawai'i

"I regard perpetuating my Kanaka Maoli culture
and the memory of my Ancestors to be my *kuleana*
(responsibility). Inspired by my father's passion
for our heritage and perseverance with the indigenous contemporary art movement, coupled with
my mother's intellectual guidance, my culture has
been my focus since childhood."

'Anakūkulukū (Kāhili), 2004

Dyed goose feathers and
hackle, cedar staff on walrus
jawbone, silk ribbon
H. 46 in., Diam. 6 in.
(116.8 x 15.2 cm)

Collection of the artist

DAVID NEEL

b. 1960, *Vancouver, British Columbia; lives in Vancouver*

Silver Box, 2002

Sterling silver, wenge wood
5 x 4 ¹/₂ x 4 ¹/₂ in. (12.7 x
11.4 x 11.4 cm)

Courtesy of Lattimer Gallery

Contemporary Native Glass:
Fusing Cultural Traditions and Individual Creativity

Carolyn Kastner and Roslyn Tunis

GLASS IS A FLUID MEDIUM that by its nature can fuse and meld disparate ideas, colors, and forms. Native American artists came to this medium one by one, but together they comprise a powerful artistic force rooted in the tradition and place of their Native cultures. As they experimented with the properties of glass—its ability to assume any form, its translucence, its permanence—each one brought something new to the medium's formal language. These Native American artists have defined an artistic movement with their generous spirit of collaboration and an aesthetic of risk. Together, they have transformed the genre of glass art.[1]

In a fitting tribute to the vitality of this movement, glass artworks by Preston Singletary (Tlingit) and Ed Archie NoiseCat (Salish) greeted visitors to the National Museum of the American Indian's inaugural exhibition, *Our Universe*, which opened in September 2004. Representing the traditional figures of ancient stories, Singletary's Raven and NoiseCat's Moon connect the oldest memories of the Tlingit and Salish peoples to living artists, who address visitors from a plasma screen. The exhibition emphatically announced the continuation of tradition, even as it recognized these contemporary artists as storytellers in a new medium. Their glass art simultaneously holds a place as a signifier of cultural continuity and of Native contributions to contemporary art. As they create new forms in glass, they extend their rich cultural traditions while at the same time expressing their individual creativity.

The Aesthetic of Collaboration

The Native American glass art movement began in 1970 at the Rhode Island School of Design, where Larry Ahvakana (Inupiaq) studied glass with Dale Chihuly. Chihuly had been present when the modern glass movement began in 1962, due entirely to an American innovation—a change in the scale of the furnaces needed to heat glass—enabling individual artists to work on their own projects outside an industrial setting. Within a decade, nearly one hundred glass programs were established in art schools and universities across the country. Ahvakana contributed to the expansion of these new glass programs after his graduation from RISD in 1972. He began his career by founding a glass studio in Barrow, Alaska, and later was the first glass instructor at the Institute of American Indian Arts (I.A.I.A.) in Santa Fe, where he met a student named Tony Jojola (Isleta Pueblo). Chihuly had contributed the necessary equipment to launch a glass program at I.A.I.A., and Jojola had been investigating the new equipment on his own until Ahvakana arrived. Encouraged by Ahvakana, Jojola immediately saw the potential of this new medium to reinvigorate ancient vessel forms created in clay and fiber by the Pueblo peoples of the Southwest.[2] He recognized the fluidity and permanence of glass: "To me, glass is like clay you can't touch. I rely on my Native American culture to create our old traditional and ceremonial forms, such as seed jars, basket forms, and ollas in glass to give my culture an even longer existence."[3]

Between 1978 and 1981, Jojola continued to expand his skill and technique as a member of Chihuly's team of glass artists at the Pilchuck Glass School near Seattle, Washington. While at Pilchuck, he was reunited with Ahvakana, who was an artist-in-residence there, and met another Native American student, Preston Singletary.[4] Both Singletary and Jojola were also working at Benjamin Moore's studio in Seattle, where they helped artists and architects learn the skills necessary to make objects in glass. Jojola continued to craft Pueblo vessel shapes in his personal work, even as he produced modern designs for Moore. However, Singletary, who grew up in Seattle, removed from his Tlingit heritage, was creating classic modern forms in his personal and professional work. He credits Jojola for encouraging him to research his own family background for the benefit of his art. By 1987, Singletary began to experiment with the Tlingit hat shape as he created bowls incised with Northwest Coast designs.[5] As he explains:

> The work that I do today is a progression of my accumulated experience, and a process of discovery. It is my attempt at transforming an ancient design style to the non-traditional medium of glass. As I have worked to understand how to approach this design system, and what these designs mean to us as Northwest Coast people, my fascination has brought a new dimension to my life.[6]

While working in glass, Ahvakana continued to work with wood and metal, but Jojola and Singletary dedicated themselves exclusively to the medium of glass. They continued to refine their techniques as they studied with and assisted the most prominent artists working in glass, including Lino Tagliapietra, Cecco Ongaro, Dorit Brand, Judy Hill, Dan Dailey, Pino Signoretto, and Stanislav Libenský. As they pursued their individual paths, studying in the United States and Europe, Jojola and Singletary began to show their work on both continents. By 2000, Jojola was honored by the Wheelwright Museum in Santa Fe with a solo exhibition entitled *Born of Fire*. In 2003, Singletary was recognized by the Seattle Art Museum in a solo exhibition entitled *Threshold*.

Singletary and Jojola define the leading edge of the Native American glass art movement. They also share a common devotion to the medium of glass, although their work looks completely dissimilar: Jojola continues to expand the size and repertoire of vessel shapes, while Singletary explores ever more elaborately carved sculptural forms. Their individual achievements are based on a deep reverence for the traditional forms of their cultures. Both were the beneficiaries and are now the benefactors of the Native American glass art movement, continuing the cooperative spirit of its artists, who encourage each other to draw from their cultural heritage to find their individual style. The collaborative nature of the hot glass process invigorates the art form, as artists assist each other in bringing personal visions to life. Cross-cultural collaboration enriches this process even further. These artists exemplify the power of an inclusive and supportive community, a celebrated tradition among Native peoples, who value relationships and connections.

FIG. 1
Ed Archie NoiseCat
Baby Frog, 2001
Glass
11^1/2 x 10 x 8 in. (29.2 x 25.4 x 20.3 cm)
Collection of the artist

A movement that has grown through trust and cooperation is expressed in its highest form in the collaboration between Singletary and Ed Archie NoiseCat, each of them contributing his specific talents and techniques to the project. Working closely together since 2002, they have created a series of highly individual masks formed from the same mold. It began when NoiseCat carved an original mask in red cedar, from which he made a two-part bronze-hinged mold. Singletary then blew glass into the mold to make identical glass forms. Although these two forms were indistinguishable when they came from the mold, the unique vision of each artist is inscribed in the finished masks, differentiated by technique, color, and design. NoiseCat's *Baby Frog* vessel, 2001 (fig. 1), and Singletary's *Killer Whale Mask*, 2004, are just two examples of the project. As these artists work from the traditional carved wooden mask to the finished glass forms, they reinvigorate and re-imagine their cultural art. NoiseCat's vessel is finished with a highly reflective surface that has been carved away to create frog motifs on a yellow/green surface. Singletary has carved away even more of the surface to reveal a ghostly white face framed in black formlines, enhanced by teeth and the sand-carved red fin projecting from the forehead. It takes more than a moment to discover the underlying shape of NoiseCat's original mask in Singletary's work.

As teachers, Jojola, Singletary, and Ahvakana set in motion a movement that continues to grow and attract younger artists. Jojola heads the Taos Glass Arts and Education Program in New Mexico,

FIG. 2
Brian Barber
The Breath of Heaven, The Vault of Heaven, 2000
Glass, oil paint
8^1/2 x 6^1/2 x 6^1/2 in. (21.6 x 16.5 x 16.5 cm)
Collection of the artist

and Singletary is now both a trustee and an instructor at the Pilchuck Glass School. Just as Singletary was once encouraged to transform his art through his cultural heritage, he now encourages his Native students to experiment and to expand their artistic and cultural horizons. He has influenced the work of two young artists, Robert Tannahill (Mohawk/Metis) and Brian Barber (Pawnee), who have broken with the functional and decorative origins of glass and with the traditional art forms of their cultures to create enigmatic and authoritative new forms.

Barber is attracted to the process of casting molten glass in sand, which leaves the visible remains of the process on the finished form. *His Breath of Heaven, Vault of Heaven*, 2000 (fig. 2), visualizes his childhood memory of his grandfather and the stories he told of a Pawnee ceremony. Barber's fascination with casting glass led him to the bust form that extends the life of his grandfather's stories and Pawnee traditions. A painted line down the nose represents the breath of heaven; a painted arc across the forehead represents the vault of heaven. His art does not follow prescribed preparations for the ceremony, nor does it visually represent the tradition, yet it reinvigorates the tradition as it literally and figuratively casts it in glass. The bust conveys solemnity by its facial expression and ceremony by the red paint. Barber has created an enigmatic portrait that is captivating, regardless of a viewer's cultural knowledge.

Similarly, Robert Tannahill's *False Face Series*, 2001 (fig. 3), reinterprets old Iroquois masks carved from living trees and used in special ceremonies. By blowing glass into a wood form, Tannahill starts a creative process that is ultimately defined by the response of the molten glass as it burns through the wood. Although his figures do not resemble the masks, they expand on the tradition of distorted representations of the face that embody supernatural beings both revered and feared. Furthermore,

FIG. 3
Robert John Tannahill
Big Mouth (from *False Faces Series*), 2001
Glass, wood
13 x 5^1/2 in. (33 x 14 cm)
Collection of Maud Hallin

like his ancestors, who had to respond to the wood they found beneath the bark, Tannahill's technique requires familiarity with the nature of his medium as well as the spontaneity to adapt to the will of the materials. Tannahill's autobiographical titles for the pieces in this series—*Four Eyes*, *Ghost in Grandma's Basement*, and *Big Mouth*—suggest the narrative of self-portraiture as well as cultural references to the past. Both Tannahill and Barber work in a cultural realm where the visible is not always legible to the uninitiated. Yet even those who have some familiarity with this tradition and its vocabulary will find these figures in glass startlingly new, a development that is shaping the future of the glass art movement.

The Aesthetic of Risk

It is easy to see the broad characteristics of Native American art in these works of contemporary glass. It is even tempting to look past the medium to see only the continuity of Native traditions. Yet the most important aspect of the entire glass art movement today is the aesthetic of risk, and it is the specificity of the risks that defines the Native American glass art movement. Singletary's *Oystercatcher Rattle*, 2005 (page 199), is a bravura performance in glass blowing, yet its remarkable resemblance to traditionally carved and painted Tlingit rattles is what first draws the viewer's attention. The risky process that brought the rattle into existence was set in motion by Singletary's keen observation of the older forms, but it is his mastery of the glass medium that brought forth this newly conceived sculptural form. Each different color of glass marks the boundary of the numerous glass elements that Singletary fused together to create the rattle, involving multiple gatherings of molten glass, blown or cast to bring life to the completed form. The process began as he placed a mass of molten glass at the end of a blowpipe, blew air into it to give it the shape of a vessel (which was barely visible by the time he finished), and then wrapped it in a second color. While the vessel was still molten, he manipulated it with tools to give form to the bird. After it cooled, Singletary took it to his studio to design the distinctive Tlingit iconography, applying rubber tape to the glass surface and then cutting away sections in the iconic shapes. The exposed glass was then sand-carved down to the primary glass body, creating the vivid contrast between the two layers of glass. The handle of the rattle was blown separately and then fused with the bird's body. The entire sculpture was returned to the fire repeatedly as each component was fused to it. Each addition, necessary for the detailed representation, presented a risk to all the work that had gone before. This serenely beautiful form was created by repeated acts of risk.

Jojola too, with twenty-nine years of experience, understands the limits of his medium, but as he works to create ever larger vessels, he pushes molten glass to the brink of disaster and beyond. Unfazed by exploding glass and encouraged by his successes, Jojola continually attempts to expand the size of his vessels. His persistence and visionary goals are evident in *Evening Colors*, 2001 (fig. 4), a vessel that began as a single gathering of molten red glass. A second color was added by wrapping the molten red glass in green near the top. Jojola then drew on the surface of the vessel with pulled glass

threads to create the designs at the base. While an assistant turned the still hot form, Jojola laid down glass thread and fused it to the surface with a blowtorch. As the vessel turned, he made hundreds of instantaneous decisions, each of which posed a risk to the design and the vessel as a whole. At the end of that series of actions, the entire vessel was sealed in a clear wrap of glass to stabilize the color and design before he began the final surface design. The bright red designs over the shoulder of the vessel were then applied to the outermost surface in the same manner. The final decorative element that he added was the series of disks that rest just below the lip of the vessel. Each of those forms was created individually by dropping a small mass of molten glass onto the surface and then pressing the glass with a silver stamp to create the pattern on the disk. During the entire process, the vessel was at the end of the lengthy blowpipe and had to be kept hot by returning it to the furnace repeatedly. Risk is inherent in any creative process, but risk is minimized as an artist works within a refined set of practices. Jojola's art demands spontaneity as each new vessel is formed, posing new risks each time.

The Aesthetic of New Traditional Forms

For centuries, in Alaska and along the Northwest Coast, carved wood totem poles were raised to honor important personages and document tribal history. In August 2001, a new kind of totem pole was carved of wood in Alaska, but was then embellished with glass inserts at the Pilchuck Glass School. This unique pole—a striking blend of materials, technologies, and cultures—was created in commemoration of the school's thirtieth anniversary to honor Chihuly, John Hauberg, and Anne Gould Hauberg, the school's founders. It is a tribute to them and a testament to the innovative fusion of traditional and contemporary Native art.

The Pilchuck Founders Pole was carved from a twenty-foot log of red cedar at Alaska Indian Arts, Inc. in Haines. Master carver John Hagen (Alaska Native) led a dedicated team of carvers including David Svenson, Wayne Price (Tlingit), and Joe David (Nuu-Chah-Nulth). Artists-in-residence at the school painted the pole and incorporated glass and neon elements. Natives and non-Natives worked on it together in a collaborative effort. At the base of the pole, shown as a high-ranking chief, is the figure of John Hauberg, who donated the land on which the Pilchuck Glass School is built. The glass dagger he holds is a replica of the one he repatriated to a Tlingit tribe. In the center of the pole is Chihuly, wearing a glass-and-neon eye patch, holding Raven with the glass Sun Disc in his beak. Just as Raven brought light to the world in Northwest legends, so Chihuly is credited with lighting the way for many glass artists. At the top of the pole is a representation of Anne Gould Hauberg, shown wearing a ceremonial Chilkat robe designed by Clarissa Hudson (Tlingit) and crowned with a spectacular glass chief's hat created by Singletary.

The pole-raising ceremony included welcoming speeches and traditional prayers, songs, and dancing, under the direction of Hagen and David. A salmon feast and potlatch followed where, as

FIG. 4
Tony Jojola
Evening Colors, 2001
Glass, stamps
H. 13 1/2 in., Diam. 9 in. (34.3 x 22.9 cm)
Collection of the artist

FIG. 5
Joe David
Spirit Wolf, 2001
Glass, cedar bark, horsehair, painted feathers
10 x 13 x 7 in. (25.4 x 33 x 17.8 cm)
Collection of John and Joyce Price

FIG. 6
John Hagen
Moonlit, 2002
Glass, red cedar, neon lighting
21 1/4 x 19 x 7 3/4 in. (54 x 48.3 x 19.7 cm)
Collection of the artist

custom dictates, guests received gifts for serving as witnesses to this historic event. This extraordinary achievement, which transformed both the traditions of wood carving and glass art, is a monument to the vigor of this artistic movement. The totem-pole project brought experienced Northwest Coast wood carvers to the Pilchuck Glass School to work with Native and non-Native glass artists. Influenced by that experience, wood carvers David, Price, and Hagen began to experiment with glass in their subsequent art. David, who is known for his carvings of wood masks, created a powerful opaque cast glass skull, *Spirit Wolf*, 2001 (fig. 5). David honored this potent spirit represented in glass with cedar bark, feathers, and the gift of tobacco. Similarly, Price began to fuse old and new as he began to add glass components to his carved and painted wood masks. Hagen used neon to backlight his house-shaped sculpture *Moonlit*, 2002 (fig. 6). The lunar image in illuminated glass at the center of his wooden sculpture is reminiscent of clan crests that were carved and painted on the front of tribal community houses.

Singletary and Marvin Oliver (Quinalt/Isleta Pueblo) also pay homage to the moon. Singletary has created several sculptural forms of Raven capturing the moon in his beak, which visualize the story of how Raven brought light to the world by releasing the sun, moon, and stars from a box in which they were hidden. Oliver represents the moon as a glowing glass orb in several of his recent works.

FIG. 7
Marvin Oliver
Facing You, 2002
Dichroic glass
28 x 13 x 6 1/2 in. (71.1 x 33 x 16.5 cm)
Collection of the artist

Oliver's *Facing You*, 2002 (fig. 7), is a masklike moon image made of dichroic glass, which manipulates light and reflects complementary colors from its surface.

Susan Point (Coast Salish) etches her culture's strong Northwest Coast imagery on glass spindle whorls, re-imagining the weaving tools of her grandmothers as sculptural forms in glass, stainless steel, and wood, as in *Return*, 2003 (page 168). Joe Fedderson (Colville) fuses basket patterns from the Inland Plateau Region of the Columbia Basin in modern glass vessels. The glass holds the memory of the basketry weave, while the bold geometric forms painted on the surface communicate the landscape and architecture of contemporary life. Cinder blocks, electrical towers, and chain-link fences are the referents for his graphic embellishments. Wrapped around the glass cylinders, the banal details of modern life create abstract designs that defy interpretation until he reveals the titles: *Parking Lot*, 2004 (page 169), *Cinder Block*, *High Power Tower*, and *Chain Link*. Each of these Native American glass artists is reinvigorating and re-imagining cultural art forms.

The works by these Native American glass artists are alive with communication between contemporary and traditional cultures, among individuals, and across generations. Each artist expands the notion of cultural heritage as he or she contributes to this artistic community. Expressing culture, community, and individual creativity, they are shaping a new language in American art.

NOTES

1. In 2002, we organized the exhibition *Fusing Traditions: Transformations in Glass by Native American Artists* for the Museum of Craft & Folk Art in San Francisco. The eighteen artists represented in the exhibition comprise the first generation of Native American glass artists.

2. Jojola's glass vessels were included in *Changing Hands 1: Contemporary Native American Art from the Southwest* in 2002, the first exhibition in the Museum of Arts & Design's three-exhibition series.

3. Tony Jojola, in a panel discussion at the Museum of Craft & Folk Art San Francisco, September 12, 2002.

4. Ahvakana, Jojola, and Singletary were at Pilchuck in 1984–85.

5. Although Singletary began working with Tlingit designs in 1987, he did not begin working in the style full-time until 1993.

6. Preston Singletary, quoted in *Fusing Traditions: Transformations in Glass by Native American Artists*, exh. cat. (San Francisco: Museum of Craft & Folk Art Catalogue, 2002), p. 83.

Native Fashion

Kimberly "Wendy" Ponca

NATIVE AMERICAN CLOTHING DESIGN is as varied as Indian tribes themselves. If I had to describe Native fashion in a single phrase, I would have to say, "Indian clothing makes the wearer feel very powerful," meaning that when you put it on, you feel comforted and you get a sense of power that makes you feel strong and healthy. You feel relaxed and centered, and you have the feeling that you could survive extreme situations.

American Indians create clothing for protection and comfort, rather than just following a trend or style. The clothing may be for ceremonial use only, or for walking down a runway, or for working or hunting. Practicality is only as important as the designer wants it to be.

In life, small things are often the most powerful awakeners of memory. A bit of color or texture can make you draw a connection to a past experience or object, and give you a physical reaction such as pleasure or warmth. These may be childhood experiences or cultural experiences—and by cultural experiences I mean everything that you are exposed to that makes you feel you are an important part of a group. Symbolism is one of the most important memory awakeners in my life.

American Indians are pros at utilizing symbolism in clothing to create a feeling, and have an inherent talent at using symbolism fluidly. For example, a designer's tribal affiliation is often apparent from a garment's silkscreened, beaded, painted, or woven symbols, or sometimes it is revealed by the garment's pattern of construction. Even in the twenty-first century, with assimilated clothing styles so prevalent, American Indians have their own unique symbolism, which may be extremely subtle or "in-your-face" crass.

American Indian artists are also as varied as their tribes, and as wild and individualistic as anything on this earth. American Indian clothing designers share the same charactersitics. Unfortunately, they are not as well known as their non-Indian peers, since the fashion world has yet to embrace an American Indian designer and give him or her the kind of respect that is deserved.

How do you define an American Indian fashion designer? When a Native American makes clothing for his family to wear in ceremonial dances, is she or he called a fashion designer? Or when a unisex corset is made by an American Indian artist as a work of art, should this person be considered an American Indian fashion designer? The lives of American Indians are still all-encompassing, in the way that there is no word for art in most Indian languages. Art, ceremony, clothing, life, and religion are all one. Maybe this is why not even one Native American designer has been dissected and transplanted into the runway world of commercial fashion. The Indian designers I have known refuse to sacrifice quality and uniqueness of design for mass product—although there are a few very popular Native American T-shirt companies that mass-produce the very symbols that help Indians feel strong. Their catchy phrases that only Indians can laugh at keep a sense of humor alive, which gives strength to all American Indians.

The saddest thing to me about American Indian clothing is that very few American Indians wear clothing made by Indian designers, their peers, as compared to the commercially made shirts and jeans they usually wear. Most American Indians have given into assimilation, an acceptance of ordinariness, and a style of clothing worn by a culture that has no culture. Dominant American culture has such a mixed-up combination of symbolism and style that the culture is virtually indiscernible.

I feel that what we call "traditional clothing" is much more comfortable and practical than what I usually wear. I would love to see my friends and family wear only American Indian–designed clothes. I wonder if they would feel different after wearing them a while—healthier, physically better. I say this because I have been amazed at the very physical feeling of strength and power I felt when wearing body painting in traditional Osage designs, in traditional placement on the body. I felt energized and strong.

Body painting has come back to the American Indians in this twenty-first-century fashion scene. More popular at one time, body painting was discouraged by the invaders from Europe. But symbolism cannot be removed from the American Indian culture, and will forever allow us to survive. We American Indians have survived the largest act of genocide in recorded history—over 90 million dead—and we owe much of the survival of our culture to our symbolism. So strong was this belief in our symbolism that cotton shirts with powerful symbolic painting (Ghost Dance shirts) were worn in the belief that they could ward off bullets.

Once, a friend of mine, someone not of Indian heritage, asked me for a shirt with my designs to give to a sick friend of his who had cancer. This friend of mine believed that my printed design on this simple shirt would help cure his friend. Surprisingly enough, the cancer went into remission. I guess he felt the power of the design the way I feel the power of American Indian art.

The Edge

Jennifer Complo McNutt

THE CUTTING EDGE IS the cool sharp line of a blade that slices through flesh to reveal the warm, red pulse of the living. For those who look, the blade will reveal what has been there all along, veiled in the soft fleshy folds of the comfortable, the predictable, the palatable. But the new edge is revealed only to those who have the courage to be humbled, and not be embarrassed by their humility.

The swift slice of the cutting edge can bring an exclamation and appreciation of beauty, stunning and unforgettable in its simplicity, a split second of intimacy and understanding between artist and viewer so alarming that it feels like an indiscretion. What follows is an abrupt laugh—and the momentary cohesion of two minds that may never really meet, yet are joined briefly in mischief and super-awareness.

This is the edge that exists in Native American art. The edge is found in installation work and the re-creation of new shapes on canvas, in new placements of indigenous design onto unexpected objects. It is a weaver, a sculptor, a photographer, and a painter.

Native artists have been operating on the edge for thousands of years. They have adapted materials and design to express and reinterpret their experience; responding to their environment, their reality—wherever the currents run at any given time. Some outside the culture expect that all Native cultures represent themselves with historical imagery and the same methods and materials that might make their work predictable. Those outsiders are afraid to admit the possibility that indigenous artists are smarter than they are, and that the strength of Native art lies in its connection to something they can neither define nor fully comprehend.

The cutting edge is the place where Native artists stand in force, looking out from their experience, their history, the realities of a global community, and the awareness that history repeats itself. And there stands the resonance of that shiny, steely line. It has the strength that resides in experience transferred from person to person, father to son, aunt to niece, and grandparent to great-grandchild,

FIG. 2
Corwin Clairmont
Turtle X's 93 (V), 2000
Monoprint
30 x 22 in. (76.2 x 55.9 cm)
Eiteljorg Museum

and from century to century. Continuity and continuum of spirit build a current that runs through a culture. Each Native artist is a part of the foundation of understanding, each experience pushing into the future and the past simultaneously, building the strength of the collective spirit and the continuum.

Native artists share this continuum and community with us by combining ancient and contemporary language and images through the dramatic, the unexpected, the humorous, and the ironic. American Indian artists working in contemporary idioms surprise the viewing public. In some ways, the public's expectation of stereotypical images of Native cultures sets indigenous artists up to deliver a hard-hitting punch line—a line that is not always funny, because the joke is on us.

Many non-Native people are eager to find mysticism in all indigenous art. They want to know the secrets of the ancient and private parts of this culture, and they openly and often offensively expose their curiosity about beliefs outside their own, maybe sensing a truth that they can't quite grasp but yearn for. Because there are definable traditions in Native culture, there is often the expectation that a work can be fully explained, interpreted—and stereotyped. Nevertheless, some elements of American Indian fine arts and traditional arts simply cannot be understood fully by those outside the culture. This is true of many works of art strongly influenced by a particular culture. That truth, however, does not leave the art unappreciable. People do, and should, bring their own experiences to each work of art they view, whether it is a landscape painting, a black-ware ceramic pot, an installation of three thousand vials of blood, or a performance of three molded chocolate kittens melting against a backdrop of the Wicked Witch of the West. However, to experience contemporary Native American art, one must not confine the experience to a pre-ordained and narrow range defined by the strict terms of a culture's past; to do so would be to reduce the art or object to a culture objectified.

Corwin Clairmont (Salish Kootenai) was part of the contemporary art scene in Los Angeles in the 1980s. He chose to leave that community to return to his own. Understanding the reason for his return is key to understanding his work. Clairmont's *Split Shield*, 2001 (page 63) refers to other work that he created during the last ten years: an installation piece, *Asphalt Storm Clouds Over the Reservation*, 1993 (fig. 1), and a print series, *Turtle X's 93*, 2000 (fig. 2), both of which document an effort to stop the enlargement from two to four lanes of Highway 93, which runs through the Salish Kootenai Reservation. The semi trailers that travel over that road barrel

FIG. 1
Corwin Clairmont
Asphalt Storm Clouds over the Reservation, 1993 (detail of installation)
Materials and dimensions variable
Eiteljorg Museum

through the reservation, splitting the reservation in two, bludgeon-
ing wildlife, spreading fumes into the air, and screaming like a
great rage-filled alien. *Split Shield*, the latest in this genre, assumes an
unconventional format of a warrior shield. Clairmont documents the
damage of the highway by means of paper cast to look like black tire
treads with small gemlike turtles embedded them, plus paper feathers printed with images of mini semi trailers, and, at the center, a
photolithograph of land, split in two by a zigzagging white line. The
shield documents efforts to modify the highway. Paper is an interesting choice of materials here, considering how the U.S. government
has used some paper documents to take the land of Native people
and destroy their communities.

In his work, Corwin Clairmont has developed a visual language
that asks viewers to consider the human condition, knowing
that it can be both ridiculous and sublime. He speaks with a
deep commitment to living in balance with everything in the
natural world and questioning everything that is harmful and
works to destroy those things that make life possible.[1]

Through his work, Clairmont's edge is revealed, his protest
registered. His work reflects and embodies his political actions, and
protects the freedom of expression that he values as an artist and
as an American Indian. The split shield serves as a symbol of the
conflict between our consumer society and Native lifeways on
the reservation, and the contrast between the dominant culture
and indigenous peoples. As Clairmont has stated,

Through contemporary Native American Art, I believe that we
have a great opportunity to bring about an awareness of our
vast cultural richness and the diversity that exists, while fostering
a better understanding of the important concerns impacting our
Indian communities.[2]

Tanis Maria S'eiltin (Tlingit) remembers a helmet of great emotional and visual intensity worn by the men in her community during
special ceremonies, and evokes her childhood memory of the helmet
in her installations, prints, and drums (see *War Head*, 2003, page 50).
She re-creates the image of the helmet as she remembers it: four
times the size of an average head, with eyes that peer from the
corners, ominous and powerful. Drawn in red, it is mesmerizing,
hypnotizing, and comforting when it is placed in the community
where it is understood. Today, the helmet, which in reality is eighteen
inches high, resides under glass in the American Museum of Natural
History, New York. But it lives in the heart of the tribe. It is a memory,
and that memory is strong enough to create a bond with its people
and its place within the community even in its absence.

I am a descendent of Tlingit lineage that can be traced back
10,000 years. Our grandmothers and great-grandmothers are
the keepers of legends that mark our migration to the icy
water's edge. Through my mother, Ldaneit, I am recognized as

a member of the Shaa Hit in Yukatat. We, as well as our progeny,
belong to the L'uknaza'di clan and the Yeil moiety. I created
this work in honor of my ancestors, my mother, my children
and grandchildren.[3]

Which edge cuts deeper—a two-hundred-year-old object honored and remembered, ferocious and commanding, or a portrait
of the object's memory the size of a stop sign, printed on the hard
flesh of rawhide? The latter, S'eiltin's drum, is played on with beaver
drumsticks by her daughter in the Tlingit and Haida celebration. At
the end of the celebration, two hundred drums beat together, and
one of them—S'eiltin's—remembers, holding the essence of the
mask itself. S'eiltin's message is unstoppable, her language emerging
from her personal history, her culture, her memory, and the honor
of bringing the memory of a helmet to its rightful place in its
community. Her edge does cut.

In his baskets of glass or of linen, Joe Feddersen (Colville
Confederated Tribes) integrates traditional and contemporary design
with humor. Many of the geometric shapes he uses have roots in
the Plateau people's traditional designs for woven baskets and bags
(see fig. 3). The genius of his work is in his translation of these

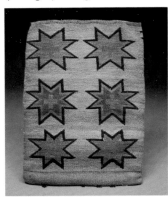

ancient designs into contemporary references to urban landscape. The combination speaks
to Feddersen's connection/
absorption in his culture and his
acute observations in the urban
environment. At first glance, his
baskets appear to be based on
traditional designs, which, in
essence, they are. Then again,
they incorporate the design of
the local supermarket parking
lot, the towering scaffolding
of monumental power lines,
and the ever popular suburban
cul-de-sac (see pages 120, 169).
Each of these illuminates vol-

FIG. 3 Nez Pierce bag, late nineteenth
century; cornhusk, natural dyes, grass,
yarn. Eiteljorg Museum, Gift of
Harrison Eiteljorg

umes about our everyday lives and choices and in many ways brings
beauty to otherwise excessive daily consumption of goods and energy
in contemporary culture. In all its elegance and simplicity, Feddersen's
work is layered with wit and irony.

Some of Feddersen's wit comes from clashing cultural icons,
paying homage to history and nudging the viewer to see our world
from a new perspective. When Native artists impose a new view, the
result is humor and pleasure, and possibly even a feeling of relief.
Humor becomes an entry point and creates a common ground, invit-
ing and invigorating the audience. Steven Deo employs that edge
of irony or humor as he illustrates the effect of "make-believe"
and play, with a message that delivers a thoughtful blow.

Deo's installations *America's Child*, 2004 (detail, page 65), and
Knowledge Transformed address the "education" or indoctrination of

individuals. In *America's Child*, the children, made of toy soldiers, amuse themselves with the helicopters and other war paraphernalia. Deo's grave concern is that innocent children become desensitized to the realities of war through this kind of make-believe. "I also played with these toys, as did many other generations of children, thus becoming part of the continuum."[4] This type of exposure can create an atmosphere that produces ambivalence to the consequences of war. In *Knowledge Transformed*, Deo molds papier-mâché brains from encyclopedias and installs them on bookshelves. This creation of the brain through encyclopedic knowledge may also be interpreted as homogenizing and desensitizing education. Deo may be encouraging us to transform knowledge from the dusty shelves of conventional learning, with its often-narrow scope, to a greater and more evolving understanding and wisdom.

Martha Gradolf's *Made in Japan*, 2002 (page 70), like Deo's re-contextualization of toy soldiers, takes a commonplace object—salt shakers, literally made in Japan—and examines their deeper meaning or consequences. Gradolf, struck by the ironies of one culture taking ideas or images from another and using them for profit, combines boldly colored feathers and wool with kitsch salt shakers, perhaps playing to aesthetic stereotypes generated by the consumer culture and passively absorbed by the mainstream. Not only do American Indians have to protect themselves from the misuse of their image in their own country, they are also challenged by other cultures' exploitation as well. The brass bells that dangle at the bottom of the weaving may be Gradolf's effort to protect the authenticity of the representation of Native American culture by sounding a warning.

Just as Gradolf uses the tradition of weaving to create a contemporary comment on our culture, so does Marcus Amerman (Choctaw) use the tradition of beadwork in his *Postcard* from "Indian Country" (page 56). Amerman is well known for his application of beadwork on objects usually associated with mainstream popular culture. A portrait of singer Janet Jackson based on a cover of *Rolling Stone* magazine and a beaded baby carrier are, for him, two icons representing a combination of Native tradition with contemporary culture. His embellished items create such a stimulating image as to strike the viewer as beautiful and clearly Indian at the same time. Amerman's work, both serious and playful, deftly illustrates that the cutting edge often has more to do with the mundane and the everyday than with the unknown.

Rick Bartow (Wiyot) expresses in his work an achingly personal combination of his unshakable commitment to his family and to the Indian community. Bartow's life manifests in the spirit of animals and dancing figures throughout his drawings and sculpture. His strength and spirit are as playful as *Bear with Humor*, 2004 (page 107), and as ferocious as his *Dog Pack Series*, 2003 (page 213). Surrounded by dogs and dog lovers, he likens them to the coyote, teaching lessons by what they respond to and what they ignore. Like coyote, Bartow teases us. Fiery creatures with nasty expressions sing out his music. They bark and growl and burn their beady eyes into

us. They can lead us down the path behind the pied piper, while the trickster coyote is filled with mischief and revels in our mishaps. Bartow exercises the cutting edge in tandem with ancient memory. There is a universal understanding to his wink and grin, alerting us to look beyond the obvious. It is humbling at first and then amusing, forcing us to laugh at our own seriousness. Bartow gets a real kick out of leading us there.

Through celebration, mourning, or other personal history, these and other Native artists draw a thread through their individual lives to today's world. The strength of their creations is not in their clearly discernible connection to recognizable symbols of Indian culture, but in the strength of their visions, each made unique by the language created from their experiences and their connection to all that has come before them, drawn together on a continuum.

Memory Prom Dress, 2005 (page 24), by C. Maxx Stevens (Seminole), is a self-portrait about transition, symbolizing the stepping stones, the markers that denote important changes in our lives. Stevens makes dresses such as this one—essentially baskets turned upside down—to communicate and document her own experience in her family and her place in time. The dresses have an elegant presence, the feeling of a whimsical and wonderful hoop skirt. They are mischievous and playful, giving glimpses of Stevens's life as they mark transitions to her future.

> Stories are the major source of my inspiration. My dad was always telling stories over and over to my sister and me when we were young. Today when I think of those stories I can still see the many images that he put in my head along with a feeling of connection to my history as a Seminole woman. My installations carry on this storytelling tradition but in a visual language. Each installation is based on my journey in life, my experience as a native person, my motivation and beliefs, and my family. That connection to history within my work is what is important to me.[5]

Arising from rich, robust stories that are thousands of years old, the art of Native artists on the edge is layered with the infinite experience and memories of their own lives and their peoples' history—a humbling prospect. And the power of that humility is in the appreciation of Native artists who have nurtured the cutting edge for centuries. Thanks to their cunning and creativity, the edge is as sharp today as it was ten thousand years ago, morphing their experience of being engaged with the natural environment—or with the modern energy of suburbs and cities—into undeniably fresh perspectives on the world. It is the translation of the urban within the indigenous crucible, interpreted into universal language, that is beautiful, sometimes painful, and always unique. The edge rages and pulses with truth, shining with such strength that one must watch out of the corners of one's eyes, smiling and, hopefully, nodding with some small measure of new understanding.

NOTES

1. Gail Tremblay (Onadaga/Micmac), "Corwin 'Corky' Clairmont," in *Pathbreakers: The Eiteljorg Fellowship for Native American Fine Art,* 2003 (Indianapolis: Eiteljorg Museum, 2003), pp. 45–46.

2. Corwin Clairmont, artist's statement for the Eiteljorg Fellowship for Native American Fine Art, 2003, on file at the Eiteljorg Museum.

3. Tanis Maria S'eiltin (Tlingit), artist's statement for the Eiteljorg Fellowship for Native American Fine Art, 2005, on file at the Eiteljorg Museum.

4. Steven Deo, telephone interview with the author, February 2005.

5. C. Maxx Stevens, artist's statement for the Eiteljorg Fellowship for Native American Fine Art, 2005.

2 Be(ad) or Not 2 Be(ad), That Is the Question

Tom Haukaas

THE TITLE OF THIS ESSAY alludes to continuity and creativity in contemporary Native beadwork. More specifically, it presages some of the important themes addressed in current art production, the three most prominent being identity issues, the cross-fertilizing influences of the multicultural environment in which we live, and the maintenance of our traditions.

Beadwork is one of the oldest forms of decoration, found in almost every culture and historical period. Archeologists have discovered evidence of beads used to adorn the body or clothing as far back as the Paleolithic period, made from materials such as bone, shells, stone, seeds, horn, and ivory, and, in later periods, more refined beads made from metal and glass (the earliest examples of the latter are from about 2000 B.C.E.), with an increase in the range of colors and styles.

Most beads used in older Native beadwork were products of trade during the eighteenth century, and some even before that, although it is likely that there has always been substantial Native production of beads made of shell, bone, and seeds. "From the earliest days of European contact with the Americas, glass beads became an essential trade commodity.... In order to supply the burgeoning demand for them, glass works in several European centers manufactured many millions of beads from the sixteenth through the nineteenth centuries."[1] However, a small amount of glass bead production by the Fort Berthold people in what is now North Dakota was recently noted. In fact, it is not yet clear that all the sources for the Natives' glass beads are known. The latest scholarship in this field includes the possibility that there may have been other sources for trade beads in addition to the documented European centers of glass production such as Italy; new research suggests that Chinese glass beads may have arrived in North America via Russia and the Northwest Coast. Whatever the sources, glass beads "made it possible to expand and enhance art using beadwork, because of the variety of sizes and colors, uniform manufacture, and ready accessibility," although they never entirely displaced Native-made beads: large numbers of eighteenth-century marine shell beads have been found in excavations of Native sites, indicating that "the trade in marine shell from the Atlantic and Gulf coasts survived well into the historical period."[2] A cape worn by Powhatan (d. 1618; leader of a confederacy of some thirty tribes of Native peoples in the Chesapeake Bay region) includes excellent examples of handmade Native shell beads from the early contact period.

Plains Natives obtained glass beads in small amounts in the late eighteenth century to decorate their clothing and other objects, and, starting with the early nineteenth century, when supplies increased, a greater number of Plains objects were decorated with beads. Of the five colors available, there was a distinct preference for blue, with some white, black, red, and, occasionally, yellow or a golden color. Blue beads were therefore a highly valued trade commodity. At first, we favored the larger beads known as "Crow" beads, along with a somewhat smaller version called "pony" or "pound" beads.

Beadwork, hide painting, and quillwork were the preferred forms of decoration. By about 1855, even smaller beads known as "seed" beads became available (often the size of a pinhead), in a wider range of colors. Using beads of this size, Natives could purchase more beads per weight unit, enabling them to decorate a larger area for the same price; and even though they were now sewing more beads onto each individual object, the decorated piece that resulted was not as heavy. Moreover, beads were not as fragile as quills, nor did they fade easily. The use of smaller beads and the increase in the number of colors led to the development of distinct tribal styles of beadwork during the last quarter of the nineteenth century.

During that last quarter century, the reliance on beadwork as a means of sustenance reflected the demise of the buffalo and thus a decrease in our opportunities to leave the reservations for hunting. The planned near-extinction of the buffalo meant that we no longer had a "one-stop shopping" resource for both food and home materials, but instead had to buy food and other staples for our daily needs. Treaty-based dependence on the government did not provide us with the degree of sustenance our families needed, leading periodically to apocalyptic announcements of our demise—which, although it never occurred, created an expectation of a sudden scarcity of Native-made objects and produced a big art market for such items. The heavy tourist trade that resulted saved us during the terrible economic depressions and severe droughts of the 1890s.

By the early twentieth century, however, the "dead-as-the-dodo" marketing strategy no longer worked with the general public. They knew we were out there and didn't want to hear about our problems. That is, all except for one subculture who institutionalized our supposed disappearance: museums and other forms of repositories for the remnants of our race, including philosophical societies, some secret men's societies, church organizations, and the Department of the Army. Many of them were now collecting fast and furiously. Eventually, they too thought we became passé, and little mention was made of us. In fact, from the first quarter to the third quarter of the twentieth century, we became invisible. During that time, our cultural material production largely centered around familial needs.

The drop in tourist trade, coupled with continued enforced constraints on practicing Native cultural rituals, made our production of quality objects increasingly unnecessary. Perhaps the most insidious form of censorship came from the adoption of the Pan-Indian style of decoration, in which all pride in preserving the distinctions of individual tribal cultures was actively surrendered. However, we can be thankful that this was just a phase. In tandem with the social changes that took place during the last quarter of the twentieth century, several federal laws were passed enabling us to maintain and promote our cultural heritage. As a result of these Congressional acts, our ceremonial and religious institutions could now come out of hiding and become revitalized, and the arts started to flourish again in Native communities.

Renewed production fostered a greater appreciation of our art forms and materials. In turn, we changed our thinking toward economic development while maintaining cultural continuity. Native arts, including beadwork, became an ever-growing cottage industry. The emergence of various Native art shows and competitions brought us a wider audience and, with it, a new appreciation of our work as art, a development that has paralleled the rise of postmodern art criticism. The art we create in some mediums has moved faster than others along the "Native-arts-as-Art" continuum. For example, the public now regards good pottery, well-made dolls, and various permutations of Northwest Coast art forms as legitimate artistic expressions, while other Native art forms and genres have lagged behind. Traditional drawing and painting by Native artists have only recently begun to undergo the same kind of transformation, and I have great hopes for the positive changes this will bring. As the public and critics become more familiar with the new forms and styles, I expect an even greater appreciation.

So, how is today's beadwork different from classic late-nineteenth-century pieces? By and large, earlier Native beadwork is characterized by compositions that lack a baseline, with specific icons or motifs emphasized instead of the overall composition, and using contrasts in scale for various elements in order to convey their relative importance. There was a different standard of beauty then. In contemporary beadwork, one is more likely to find centrality in composition, an imagined baseline, and elements in consistent scale with one another. Furthermore, much of the work is now strongly or even exclusively narrative, featuring icons and motifs in styles ranging from an updated silhouette form to a contemporary hyperrealism derived from photographic imagery; and most current artists opt for a broad range of colors, which in some (but not all) cases reflects tribal notions of color theory. In addition, these are objects made for displaying as art, and are imbued with layers of cultural meaning. They are not meant to be looked at solely in terms of aesthetics or art history but also as statements addressing the Native experience in today's milieu. They celebrate both context and content, whether by inclusion—such as those that contain references to Sacred Narrative and other reminders of long-held values—or by purposeful omission. In many ways, the type of art made is less important than the underlying narrative.

My discussion of the artists and their work is very different from the usual methods of contemporary art criticism. It is not a descriptive approach; labels do that efficiently. Instead, I address at least one theme salient to each artist's work and where the artist stands on a continuum of positions relative to that theme, reflecting the presence or absence of some quality. It is important to note that the themes discussed are not mutually exclusive, and that there is almost always some degree of overlap. (For example, you can't discuss women's lives without also discussing children and societal roles.)

The work of two artists—Deborah Magee and Susan Peebles—frames the middle ground for this essay. Magee's work, which exemplifies production within our tribal communities, consists mainly of large ceremonial pieces based on historical production tenets, such as war shirts and pipe bags. Her piece in this show is a quilled and beaded tableau of women looking at a mountain, *Listening to the Ancients*, 2003 (page 113). This is not an extension of the European woman-at-the-window motif. Rather, it is a depiction of women facing and celebrating the wonders of the world outside: women filled with agency—that is, the capacity to determine one's destiny. Still, one can easily see in this work a reflection of the romance with tribal history.

Peebles's work, conversely, is more in line with Clement Greenberg's notion of "painterly abstraction." Instead of exploring the formal possibilities of paint, though, she explores the formal potential of beads, as in her prayer bag, 2004 (page 175). Her work is sensual, sculptural, exploiting the play of light over the surface of the colored beads without apology. This is a creative use of the medium unfettered by traditional ideas of how it should be employed. I can almost hear her say, "I'm Indian, this is what I like, end of story." She's right, but so is Magee. Each of them attempts to balance tribal artistic tradition with contemporary adaptation, producing a tension that enriches their works.

The work of Jackie Larson Bread is enriched by a different tension, that between romantic imagery and the reality of native life, which she evokes in a painterly, photo-based realistic style, as does Marcus Amerman. They also both favor the color blue in their compositions, including skin tones, which, for her, reflects her tribe's partiality to various shades of blue. She is best known for boxes that unfold to convey a specific message, inspired by traditional material culture, as in *Untitled Hanging*, 2005 (page 158). Her boxes refer to Native boxes made of parfleche (hide with the hair removed) and used to house sacred material or personal items. *Untitled Hanging* is typical of her work but further along in terms of social commentary. Note that the outside of the box is festive and colorful, and the inside is painted with muted earth pigments and punctuated with beaded words that function as postmodern "signifiers"—as valid a decorative element as any other. Here, the words are epithets and proscriptions encountered in our tribal histories, past and present.

Judy Chartrand takes a more urban approach, using modern art and culture as a starting point, and humor as an antidote to despair. For well-socialized Native folks, humor is the preferred form of dealing with life's vagaries. Most do that verbally, whereas Chartrand does it visually, usually through the medium of clay, as in her *Metis Soup Cans*, 2004 (page 54). Another work by Chartrand in the current exhibition is *Buffalo Soldiers*, 2003 (page 151), a soft sculptural form that addresses the topic of gender in art—more specifically, the ubiquitous images of women as sexual objects, as a reflection of male desire. Depictions of the "Other" in Western art are usually female, often shown as a blatant temptress whose actions have dire consequences. Think of the moral turpitude implicit in all those images of Turkish harems and tropical native girls, Delacroix's oriental paintings and Gauguin's Tahitian works being the paragons for this genre. There are far fewer works in the history of art that provide an unabashedly sensual look at men. Native male imagery most often takes the form of either the Noble Savage or the Murderous Savage, two stereotypes, neither of which is true. For Native folks, sexuality, like death, is a part of the complexity of adulthood, an undeniable fact in one's journey through life.

Gender-based humor is frequently found in our narratives, in part because they are used to teach proper behavior by ridiculing unacceptable or taboo relationships. On a deeper level, though, such humor is about intimacy and personal boundaries, which is the context in which I experience such works. Chartrand presents viewers with a colorful, suggestive exterior image that belies the true nature of men in relationships. Chartrand's work also addresses another aspect of Native art and its relation to the art world—the issue of censorship, by which I mean both outwardly imposed and self-imposed censorship. The latter is most evident when there is an inequality of power and privilege: fear keeps many people quiet. To fully appreciate the pervasiveness of outwardly imposed censorship, one must consider what kinds of art and anthropological material were favored by collectors: not surprisingly, the great majority of these items might be said to project a high level of testosterone, such as Native war materials and heraldic imagery. Images of women, family, and domestic life were of no interest to them, and, consequently, were rarely made—an insidious form of self-censorship.

Emil Her Many Horses' tipi and toy soldiers speak on both a forthright and an ironic level. His 9/11 Tipi, 2002 (page 76), a conceptual piece, addresses a horrific national tragedy without trivializing the event, and evokes the subsequent cohesion and resolution our nation has experienced. An unspoken aspect of this issue is the high number of Native men and women who fill the U.S. armed services. They are an extension of our warrior-based culture. The 9/11 Tipi is symbolic of our homes and our nation. It is decorated in a very traditional manner in that it has no centrality, features individual icons, and uses silhouettes to depict contemporary imagery. Note the groupings of four and six icons, signifying the presence of the Creator throughout. On a more ironic level, the item utilized is a toy tipi in the service of very adult issue: extreme violence. This is unnerving to some, including me. However, the fact remains that children learn to handle aggression through both regular play and role playing. The question is actually about control of these impulses. Still, the adult in me thinks about the multigenerational consequences inherent in acts of enormous aggression. This is true whether the issue is 9/11, the Battle of Wounded Knee, the Holocaust, or smaller events with similarly monstrous consequences. Not many artists address these dark issues. Goya did it well, and there are some contemporary artists who confront these issues on a subtler, more personal level. Their work, like that of Her Many Horses, is neither exploitive nor immoral.

Teri Greeves's work addresses a theme common to contemporary art—the interplay between the iconic and the banal, originating with Marcel Duchamp's everyday objects reconfigured into art, taken up and made monumental by Claes Oldenburg in his gigantic sculptures of a clothespin or baseball bat, and extended in the work of Jeff Koons and other contemporary artists who take icons of pop culture as their subject. Who can forget Koons's sculpture of Michael

Jackson and his pet chimpanzee? Clearly, the banal is fodder for artistic statement.

Greeves took these as her artistic precedents, but based the specific form and content of her work on historical precedents from her Native culture. Due to the severe drought and poverty of the 1920s and '30s, many Indians during that period made moccasins out of canvas and rawhide. My own family used to wear them, decorated or not. The idea of decorated footwear was reworked on boots during the heyday of the American Indian Movement (AIM) in the 1970s and early '80s, although not many people made them because of the time and expense involved. Greeves took that tradition, transposed the form to sneakers, and added beaded imagery that sometimes reflects the trickster role. Her *Khoiye-Goo Mah*, 2004 (page 149), is about women—specifically, walking in the shoes of women and fighting for their rights (in Plains iconography, the red hand symbolizes battle).

Marcus Amerman explores postmodern issues of identity from an Indian perspective, combining the personal and the political, Native culture and American pop culture. He filters these with his healthy sense of irony. Amerman's works, ranging from beadwork sculptures to performance art, focus on reinterpreting artifacts of the two cultures and the ways in which the mix of the two has shaped his identity (and the identity of most Natives in present-day America). His less politically committed works depict mainstream iconic figures such as rock stars and Hollywood actors. Some of his beadwork pieces also occupy a middle ground, involving the iconic imagery of Native luminaries. At the more profound end of the spectrum is his work dealing with social issues, a particularly good example of which is Amerman's *Postcard*, 2002 (page 56), which examines the multivalent influences that define Native life today. We do not live in a vacuum, nor are we ensconced in some idyllic setting inside a tipi. Amerman chose the tourist postcard motif for its cheesy quality; in the message "Greetings from the INDIAN COUNTRY of the Great Southwest" and the images with which he has filled each big letter of the two main words, he conveys his mixed feelings of dismay and pride. Each image is a statement in itself. My own favorites are his bearded self-portrait and the view of this planet from the stratosphere—not typical Native imagery, but definitely a slice of our lives. One of Amerman's passions is providing correctives to the pervasive negative imagery of Native people in commercial entertainment and marketing campaigns—you know, the ones that use stereotypical images of our people to promote some sports team or product, which are insensitive at best, and ultimately damaging.

The careful navigation of the space between dependency and agency is explored by Donald Tenoso in his witty version of a chess set. *One Bull's Chess Set*, ca. 1997 (page 49), is unquestionably a social satire of colonialism and the inequities of power, though mindful that lack of agency and lack of power are not grievances limited to Native peoples in their relationship to state and federal governments. Feeling powerless is an experience that everyone goes through many times throughout life, beginning in childhood and adolescence. In such situations, one does not know whether to move forward in a direct attack, proceed obliquely, or jump over or around the particular obstacle or affront. On one level, all players are equal, because they all have the potential to diffuse a threat in most situations; but within the system, some figures have more power and can cover more ground more swiftly. In life, we all have to negotiate who is going to take care of us, to what degree, and how much of our own future we can determine. Leon Golub's powerful paintings about power address these same kinds of issues. Many artists have done so; it is an eternal question. Tenoso has done it using Native imagery and sculptural form. By the way, Tenoso is a descendant of Sitting Bull. That should go a long way in explaining my take on his work.

On the continuum from the historical (the glorification of some luminary or event) to the metaphysical or visionary in art, Todd Lonedog Bordeaux's work is more concerned with historical experience. He makes wonderfully creative memory sticks that detail the tribal events recorded by his great-grandfather in a work known as the Lone Dog Winter Count. Bordeaux utilizes a different form, borrowing the idea of the memory stick from other tribes, and then beading various images from the winter count onto the stick to represent a particular period of time, as in *Wakan Tanka: The Great Mystery*, 2002 (page 158), which shows his masterful command of color and technique. Bordeaux infuses these images with a sense of wonder (after all, *wakan* means "mysterious"), inspired by unconscious images, sometimes provided by dreams, as the Surrealists often did. Bordeaux once had a dream that reminded him of a narrative his grandmother used to relate to him when he was a child, a tribal story concerning the origin of butterflies, and he has used that dream imagery to make beaded renditions of his grandmother's narrative as objects for personal adornment.

Maynard White Owl Lavadour's body of work is concerned entirely with his local environs in northeast Oregon. But his work differs from most artists who depict the world around them in that he is the receptacle of many generations of artistic knowledge, giving him an exceptional understanding of tribal art and its long-established rules of color and composition. This multigenerational level of knowledge can only be learned on a one-to-one basis, a continuous education process that includes the nurturance of many people over a long period of time. Among Native artists, his exacting eye for color is matched only by Todd Bordeaux. *Purse*, 2003 (page 219), is an eloquent example of White Owl Lavadour's masterful technique and exceptional facility with color. The form is traditional, as is the use of food imagery—more typically plants or animals, but here it is salmon. Some viewers will interpret the composition in art-historical terms (since the repetition of the motif and the exuberant coloration carry a hint of Pop art), while others might read it as a statement about the pollution of tribal fishing waters with uranium and the implication for the food chain. For Native people, thinking about our interdependence with the world around us is second nature. The land is part of us, and we are part of the land.

Now, for my own work: Like most of the artists discussed here, beadwork was in my background throughout my life. My great-

grandmother lost her husband early and supported her family by making pictographic and Lakota abstract floral beadwork. Some of her work remained with us—a fully beaded dress, leggings, moccasins, and many smaller items—and were a source of family pride. When I was older, I wanted my own traditional attire so that I could learn to dance, and I tried to make it myself. This was the beginning of my education in the traditional arts. Like most Native practitioners, I did not have formal training. Rather, my skills are a result of the kindness and thoughtfulness of many generations of Lakota people. Learning beadwork often allows time for passing on family histories and myths as well as transmitting tribal values and narratives. One does not learn beadwork without a social context. These narratives, and more modern ones, inform our art at a deeper level, imbued with notions of tribe and spirituality.

All of that provides some context for my *Special Boy's Shirt*, 2004, and *Special Girl's Dress*, 2005 (both on page 147). The tension here is between anomie—the feeling of being without direction—versus uplifting hope. I made the boy's shirt after the tragic demise of my teenage niece, as an indirect memorial to her. The beaded surface design is our Creation Narrative, which stands as a reminder of who we are, where we came from, and what we value. This composition has centrality, but the iconography both honors and departs from tradition. It is filled with the hope that we will all turn around the violence so prevalent among young people growing up in today's world. After completing the shirt, which had helped lift some of my grief, I wanted to make a female counterpart that directly addressed the beauty and joy of my niece. However, before I had finished the dress, we lost one of her sisters, too, and the dress became a memorial for both of them.

There is one other piece of mine in this exhibition—*Beaded Purse*, 2002, the beaded, pictographic section of which is round. For Lakota arts, that shape is rare, although we have a long and strong tradition of beading purses and other items used for carrying personal materials. My motivation for making it was to take on the difficult challenge of executing circular images. Some of my favorite examples are classical Greek ceramic vessels, Mimbres pottery, and Renaissance ceramic sculpture from the workshop of Luca Della Robbia. All of this is great stuff. I don't pretend that my own example is at their level, but the challenge intrigued me. Because I like the visual flow of the circular Yin-Yang symbol of Asian art, I chose to make a male figure with hair flowing in the wind, a depiction that makes manifest the constant tension between reality and fantasy. The hills in the background are the buttes visible from my grandparents' kitchen window, the view that we saw while we ate or just visited. Those were the best years of my life, and I often like to go there.

Another work of mine, an installation from my *Tribal Member Stereotyping* series (not in the show), is meant to be both humorous and poignant. The individual figures are boringly faithful renditions of tribal technique and color theories, but the overall message is unrelated to aesthetics or tribal art history. My intent here was to address the stereotyping of Native people as embodying unbridled aggression or passion for what it is—misperception and exaggeration—and, second, the tendency of all humans to consistently attribute to others those fantasies we would want to act out if there were no social consequences. Hence, I would say that these pieces traverse the area between prohibition and desire.

Regarding the presence or absence of beadwork: In this essay, I have discussed beadwork both as a medium and as a cultural signifier of today's Native arts. The latter premise is a slippery slope. We are not defined by material culture, but vice versa. Identity as a Native person is first dependent on biological relationship: if you don't have Indian blood, you're not Indian—period. Second, and equally as important, is enculturation. The shared histories and shared values of Native groups are what define us. No amount of beadwork or any other traditional art form can make up for that. However, the absence of beadwork is irrelevant to a Native artist's identity or the authenticity of his or her work. Among the exemplars of such beadless art in this exhibition are the works of Bently Spang (a mix of traditional and modern materials, but no beadwork), Susan Point (wood and glass), Preston Singletary (glass), and Anita Fields (clay). *Ohan.*

NOTES

1. John R. Grimes and Karen Kramer, cat. no. 114 in *Uncommon Legacies: Native American Art from the Peabody Essex Museum* (New York: American Federation of Arts, in association with University of Washington Press, 2002), p. 242.

2. Duane H. King, "Art of the American Southeast," in ibid., p. 115.

BEYOND FUNCTION

The paraphernalia of daily life often function on two or more levels simultaneously. These everyday objects—clothing, tools and implements, recreational devices—are necessary adjuncts for contemporary life. At the same time, they may also be imbued in their making and use with cultural signifiers that give them a position and importance far beyond that of the merely practical. The differences may range from the choice of materials from which they are made (whether local or imported, rare or commonplace), the specialized and often virtuoso skills needed to transform these materials into recognizable forms, and the diversity of visual and symbolic colors, patterns, and textures with which they are embellished.

TOM HAUKAAS

b. 1950, San Juan, Puerto Rico; lives in Lutz, Florida

"Making art is one of the most fundamental aspects of my spirit. Each project makes fresh commentary on issues of aesthetics, identity, tradition, voice, creativity, and, ultimately, self-expression. The pieces are purposely designed to engage the viewer in romantic notions of Native peoples and our histories. It is hoped that the aesthetic seduction fosters interest and begins a dialogue about the concepts driving each object, the ultimate aim being a reflection on the commonality of humanity."

OPPOSITE TOP
Special Boy's Shirt, 2004

Deerskin, glass beads, cotton cloth, wool cloth, thread, ink
19 1/4 x 28 3/4 in. (48.9 x 73 cm)

Collection of Frances Marton

OPPOSITE BOTTOM
Special Girl's Dress, 2005

Deerskin, glass beads, cotton cloth, wool cloth, thread, ink
22 3/4 x 25 1/2 in. (57.8 x 64.8 cm)

Collection of Mr. and Mrs. Michael Wahlig

PHILLIP CHARETTE (AARNAQUQ)

b. 1962, Little Rock, Arkansas; lives in Portland, Oregon

"Most of my work is contemporary in nature, reflecting traditional ideas and themes; my newer works relate to themes in today's rapidly changing multicultural society. I remain open-minded, allowing the past, present, and future to speak through my work. My goals are achieved through a constant exploration and discovery of new methodologies, utilizing new materials, exploring new art forms, overcoming technical challenges, and addressing cultural issues as my body of work evolves."

Negaqvaq (North Wind Spirits), 2003

Low-fired clay, porcelain, wild turkey feathers, handmade glass beads, rawhide, synthetic sinew, red oak
each 43 x 31 x 19 in. (109.2 x 78.7 x 48.3 cm)

Collection of the artist

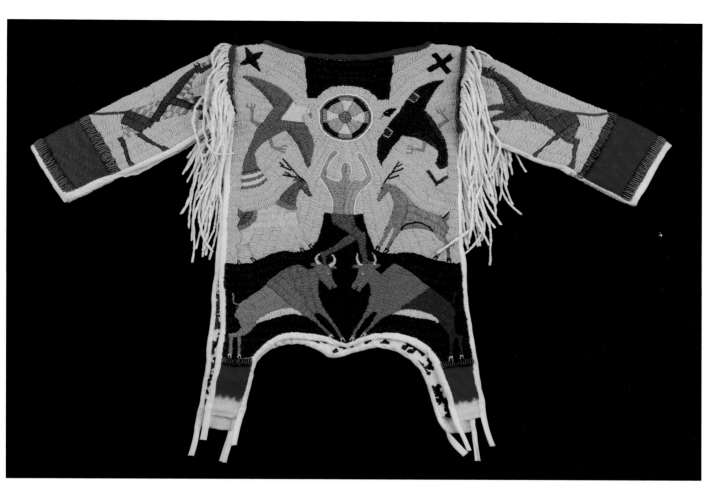

GLEN WOOD

b. 1951, Prince Rupert, British Columbia; lives in Vancouver, British Columbia

CLOCKWISE FROM UPPER LEFT

Spiritual Whorl, ca. 1996

Spiritual Whorl, ca. 1996

Redface Whorl, ca. 1996

Blackface Whorl, ca. 1996

Wood, hide, antler, acrylic paint
Diams. 17 in. to 17 3/4 in.
(43.8 to 45.1 cm), D. 2 1/2 in. (7 cm)

Collection of the artist

TERI GREEVES

b. 1970, *Wind River Reservation, Wyoming; lives in Santa Fe, New Mexico*

Khoiye-Goo Mah, 2004

Glass beads, silver-lined
glass beads, commercially
manufactured tennis shoes
each shoe 6 x 12 x 4 in.
(15.2 x 30.5 x 10.2 cm)

Museum of Arts & Design;
Museum purchase with funds
provided by the Collections
Committee, 2004

ARTHUR AMIOTTE

b. 1942, Pine Ridge, South Dakota; lives in Custer, South Dakota

OPPOSITE
Woman's Dress: An Impressionistic Sketch in Fiber, 2005

Cotton, wool, synthetic yarns, glass trade beads, tin cones, brass hawk bells, "giant" dentalium seashells, Indian hand-tanned elk hide, elk tooth
78 x 68 in. (198.1 x 172.7 cm)

Collection of the artist

"I purposefully decided to treat Sioux life from approximately 1880 to 1930, a period when cultural change and adaptation were drastically taking place in the areas of technology; printed media and language; fashion; social and sacred traditions; education; and, for Sioux people, an entirely different worldview."

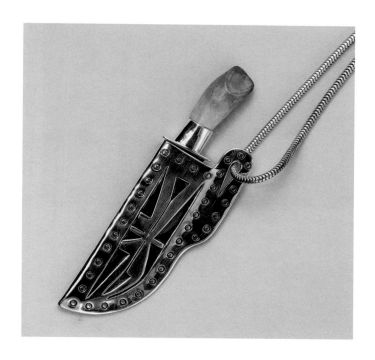

TCHIN

b. in Norfolk, Virginia; lives in New Jersey

"Inspiration for my work simply comes from living with my senses and trying to be aware of the magnificence of the everyday natural world. Tradition is the way the people of the near and far past thought and did things. Tradition is the starting point of being creative."

Knife and Sheath Set, 2004

Sheath: sterling silver; knife: brass, fossilized walrus tooth
as shown L. 4 3/4 in., W. 1 3/4 in. (12.1 x 4.4 cm)

Collection of the artist

JUDY CHARTRAND

b. 1959, Kamloops, British Columbia; lives in Coquitlam, British Columbia

Buffalo Soldiers, 2003
(one of four thongs shown)

Chamois, red satin, beads, porcupine quills, buffalo hair, wood-and-Plexiglas frame, velvet backing
13 x 18 1/4 x 4 in. (with frame)
(33 x 46.4 x 10.2 cm)

Collection of the artist

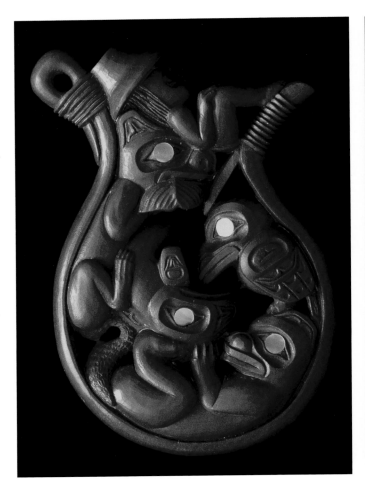 

GARY OLVER

b. 1966, The Pas, Manitoba; lives in Vancouver, British Columbia

Halibut Hook, 2003
(two views)

Catlinite, abalone
2 3/8 x 1 1/2 in. (6 x 3.8 cm)

Courtesy of Douglas Reynolds Gallery

KAREN BEAVER

b. 1972, Bethel, Alaska; lives in White River, South Dakota

"I see tribal art as coming from within the individual. Not only that—the works represent ancient life and life today. They give insight to our culture and the spiritual way we refer to the earth and all living beings."

"The Wind" Yup'ik Mask, 2004

Glass seed beads, feathers, leather, arctic fox fur, felt, gold, brass, wood
4 1/2 x 3 3/4 x 1/8 in. (11.4 x 9.5 x 0.3 cm)

Collection of the artist

NELDA SCHRUPP

b. 1952, Arcola, Saskatchewan, Canada; lives in Lakota, North Dakota

"I incorporate cultural influences with abstract modern designs to create art with a futuristic appeal. Much of my work revolves around the 'rattle,' a sacred object used in spiritual ceremonies. I call my art pieces 'amuletic forms with audio aesthetics,' referring to the sacredness of the rattle and the sound (voice) that emanates from the pieces. The colors of semi-precious stones that I use are significant, and so are the shapes—hard-edged geometric forms mixed with soft, hollow 'pillow-like' forms representing how the spirit of Native people could not be harmed or tied down."

Rattle, 2004

Copper, sterling silver, carnelian, deer antler, horsehair
H. 9 1/2 in., Diam. 3 3/4 in. (24.1 x 9.5 cm)

Collection of the artist

REBECCA LYON

b. 1955, Cordova, Alaska; lives in Anchorage, Alaska

"Nothing is as personal as the clothing we wear. Clothing can be seen as a vessel or chalice that holds the human spirit, and I have created these copper women's dresses to represent a gathering of women's spirit that is housed inside the most feminine of metals—copper. Clothing of metal representing strength and longevity; the use of nontraditional materials moves the visual dialogue into the present. This is my way of honoring the women of the North for their ability to survive natural and cultural adversity, and for their artistry. I wish to dedicate these four pieces from the series *Women of the North* to my mother, Joan Elva Corliss, to commemorate her love and strength."

LEFT TO RIGHT

Aleut Woman (from *Women of the North* series), 2004

Copper, glass, patinas 70 x 40 x 8 in. (177.8 x 101.6 x 20.3 cm)

Collection of the artist

Athabascan Woman (from *Women of the North* series), 2004

Copper, glass and copper beads, dentalium shells, moosehide 68 x 39 x 8 in. (172.7 x 99.1 x 20.3 cm)

Collection of the artist

Yup'ik Woman (from *Women of the North* series), 2004

Copper, patinas 68 x 40 x 8 in. (172.7 x 99.1 x 20.3 cm)

Collection of the artist

PETER LIND, SR.

b. 1930, *Chignik Lagoon, Alaska; lives in Homer, Alaska*

Aleut Chief's Hat, 2004

Sitka spruce, ptarmigan feathers,
fur-seal whiskers, glass beads, Russian
trading beads, ivory, imitation sinew,
acrylic paint, ocher
26 x 8 x 13 in. (plus 16-in. tie strings)
(66 x 20.3 x 33 cm, plus 40.6-cm tie
strings)

Collection of Dr. James and
Diana Zirul

KERI-LYNN DICK

b. 1982, *Burnaby, British Columbia; lives in Queen Charlotte
Islands (Haida Gwaii), British Columbia*

Pair of Shoes, 2003

Red cedar, red cedar bark, leather
each shoe H. 6 in., W. 3 ¹/₂ in.,
L. 9¹/₂ in. (15.2 x 8.9 x 24.1 cm)

Private collection

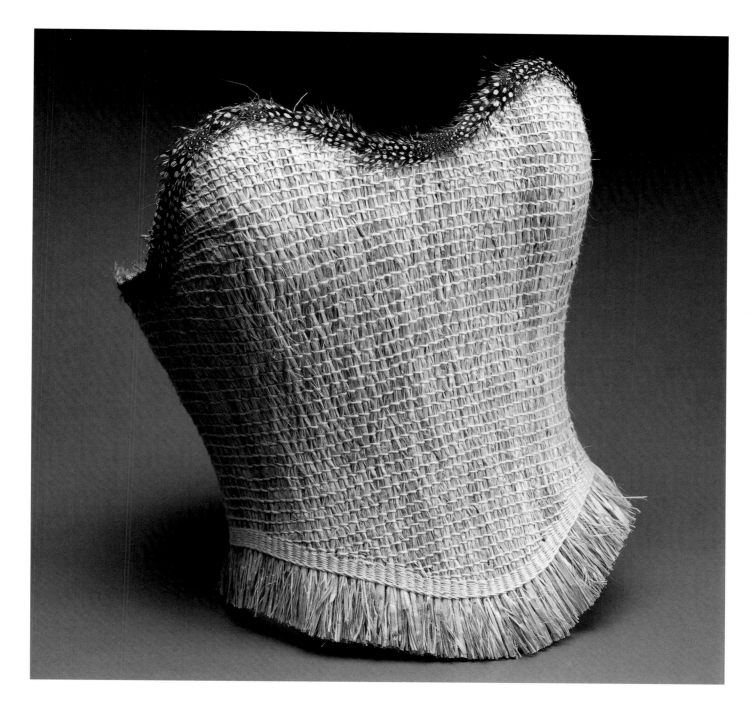

LISA TELFORD

b. 1957, Ketchikan, Alaska; lives in Everett, Washington

"I grew up around art and took it for granted until I moved to Washington. There, 'urban Indians' made me realize how important basketry was to our culture. I was inspired to continue."

A Night on the Village, 2004
Red cedar bark, guinea feathers, cotton cordage, leather, ivory buttons
15 1/2 x 11 1/2 x 11 in.
(39.4 x 29.2 x 27.9 cm)

Heard Museum

JACKIE LARSON BREAD

b. 1960, Conrad, Montana; lives in Great Falls, Montana

Untitled Hanging, 2005

Wool cloth, rawhide, smoked
buckskin, deerhide, glass beads,
nylon thread, brass hawk bells
16 x 18 x 3 in. (40.6 x 45.7 x 7.6 cm)

Private collection

TODD LONEDOG BORDEAUX

*b. 1967, Minneapolis, Minnesota;
lives in White River, South Dakota*

Wakan Tanka: The Great Mystery,
2002

Glass beads, cedar, quartz,
turquoise, crystal, mink, leather,
horsehair, brass bullet, deer
antler, antique ledger key, thread
H. 20 3/4 in. Diam. 3 3/8 in.
(50.7 x 8.6 cm); length of
horsehair braid: 14 in. (35.6 cm)

Collection of Bruce and
Kristine Yerigan

PRESTON SINGLETARY

b. 1963, San Francisco, California; lives in Seattle, Washington

"Glass is not a material traditional to Native art, but has a defining historical connection to the material through trade beads, which were incorporated into ornamentation of clothing and other sacred objects. I see working with glass as a progression of that tradition. It is important to realize that Native cultures are alive, and it is we who are declaring who we are and what new traditions are developing."

Shaman's Amulet, 2001

Glass
9 x 19 x 3 ½ in. (22.9 x 48.3 x 8.9 cm)

Collection of John and Joyce Price

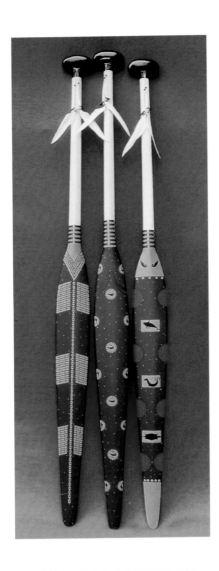

JERRY JACOB LAKTONEN

b. 1951, Kodiak Island, Alaska;
lives in Granite Falls, Washington

"I have taken on a responsibility to decipher what were traditions and what were not. One thing I dread is to create a melting pot of Native American artistic vision that adds only mud to the water, and helps us lose our individuality. I have created contemporary pieces and brought together life experiences up in the village. My art has the power to answer many questions—personal, family, community, and maybe universal. Cross-cultural communication is one of my interests, to express the beauty of my culture and to foster mutual respect."

Dream Paddles (3), 2004

Cottonwood, paint, glass beads, dentalium, feathers
each 60 x 4 x 1 in. (152.4 x 10.2 x 2.5 cm)

Collection of the artist

DEAN KAAHANUI

b. 1957, Honolulu, Hawai'i; lives in Kamuela, Hawai'i

"The carving on the board, inspired by another Marquesas carver, Joseph Kimitete, is from a legend of Honu'akea (White Turtleback Island). Honu'akea carries the spirit of the ancestors, which one day will re-awaken all Natives, that we may perpetuate our culture through our art and carry the spirit to the next generation so that the legacy may live on."

Surfboard, 2004

Pine, mother-of-pearl, cow bone
72 x 17 x 1 in. (182.9 x 43.2 x 2.5 cm)

Collection of the artist

SUSAN POINT

b. 1952, Musqueam Indian Reserve, Vancouver, British Columbia;
lives on Musqueam Indian Reserve

"In creating a visual piece of art, it is my hands,
my heart, and my soul that is involved, all working
together within a language that knows no words."

A Gift for Qulqulil, 2004

Red cedar, acrylic paint, copper
82 x 31 x 4 in. (208.3 x 78.7 x
10.2 cm)

Collection of Donald E. and
Robert C. Bergstrom

GEOFF GREENE

b. 1959, Skidegate, Queen Charlotte Islands (Haida Gwaii), British Columbia; lives in Vancouver, British Columbia

Wasgo, 2005

Glass sphere (found Japanese fishing float), acrylic paint, fixative
Diam. 12 in. (30.5 cm)

Courtesy of The Legacy Ltd.

PHILIP GRAY

b. 1983, Vancouver, British Columbia; lives in Vancouver

"I never saw a good reason to start carving but now that I am doing it, I could not see myself doing anything else. My only hope is to continue to progress in my work and to bring Tshimshian art to another level."

Killer Whale House Drum, 2004

Elk hide, acrylic paint, red cedar, elk antler
Diam. 17 in., D. 5 in. (43.2 x 12.7 cm)

Courtesy of Douglas Reynolds Gallery

lessLIE (LESLIE ROBERT SAM)

b. 1973, Duncan, British Columbia; lives in Duncan

"I generally don't draw a dichotomy between traditional/contemporary. As long as I perpetuate the traditional design elements and iconography of Coast Salish art with integrity, I believe that I am reflecting my contemporary cultural reality. Coast Salish art revolves around positive and negative design principles. I believe it is graceful and beautiful to transform the negative elements of my reality (racism, oppression, colonialism, prejudice, etc.) into positive paintings."

Salish Symbiosis, 2005

Cowhide, acrylic paint, wood
Diam. 16 in., D. 3¹/₄ in. (40.6 x 8.3 cm)

Courtesy of Alcheringa Gallery

SHAUN PETERSON

b. 1975, Puyallup, Washington; lives in Tacoma, Washington

"My grandmother has been an ever-present source of inspiration to me. It has become important to me to understand the roots of my people's art and help make it appealing as well as relevant to our people today. There seems to be this void in Native America today for what was taken from our grandparents' generation. This void has left the following generations with poor self-esteem and confusion. There are those of us who feel that the very art itself helped to signify who we were/are in the world. Without that, we sit as a blank canvas to the world, without definition or reason."

Life Cycle One, 2000

Deerskin, maple, acrylic paint
Diam. 15¹/₂ in., D. 2¹/₂ in.
(39.4 x 39.4 x 6.4 cm)

Collection of Andy Benjamin

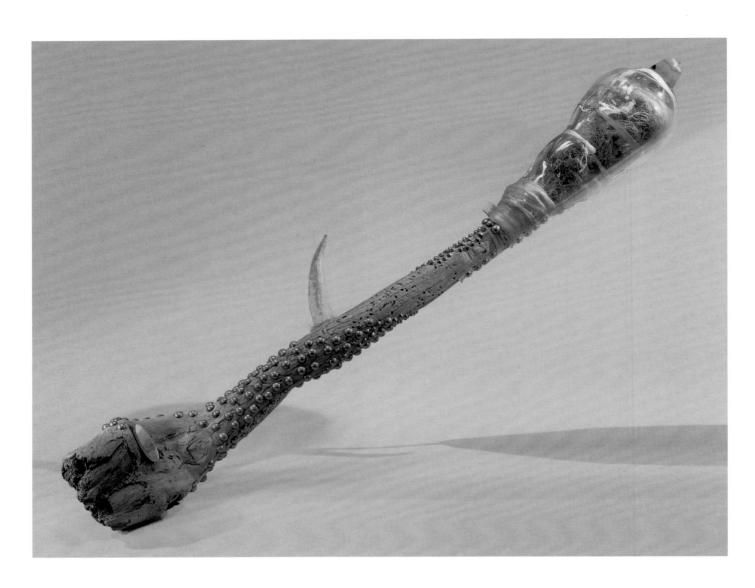

BENTLY SPANG

b. 1960, Crow Agency, Montana; lives in Billings, Montana

War Club #1 (from *Modern Warrior* series), 1998

Glass, moss, wood, brass, mirror, hot glue, rawhide 37 ¹/₂ x 7 x 5 in. (95.3 x 17.8 x 12.7 cm)

Collection of the artist

KIM KNIFE CHIEF

b. 1957, Pawnee, Oklahoma; lives in Pawnee

"I think being raised poor (although I never knew it until much later) and making our own toys and clothes, I used my imagination to create what I couldn't buy. Museums and galleries, and also studying the work and lives of artists (past and present), have had an impact on how I feel. It motivates me and drives me to create. When Native people first traded with Europeans, traditions changed and it was reflected in their art. I work with metals, clay, leather, and beads. My work is always evolving and changing."

Pawnee Cradleboard Pendant,
2002

Sterling silver, 14k gold,
semi-precious stones
2^1/$_4$ x 2 x ^{1}/$_2$ in. (5.7 x 5.1 x 1.3 cm)

Collection of the artist

MARQUES HANALEI MARZAN

b. 1979, Honolulu, Hawai'i; lives in Kaneohe, Hawai'i

"Fiber work is one of the first skills that developed in our heritage. It has persisted through time by the perpetual passing down of knowledge from one generation to the next. Without this constant cycle, this skill would be lost and forgotten. This piece was made to forever remind us of this gift our *kūpuna* (ancestors) gave us. They taught us the way to weave together individual elements, to form a stronger whole. The test of fire and molten metal proves that we lose something along the way, but we retain enough to see the whole."

Contemporary Artifact, 2001

Bronze
12 x 4 x 4^3/$_4$ in. (30.5 x 10.2 x 12 cm)

Collection of the artist

YÁYA (CHARLES PETER HEIT)

b. in Hazelton, British Columbia;
lives in Kispiox, British Columbia

"I think tradition is continually in a state of change, or innovation, constantly being altered to reflect the artists' life experiences. Sometimes I think I have a duty to show the world something. Our art and our culture and our language have always been changing. Innovation is the second-oldest form of tradition."

Tele Box, 1999

Birch, mahogany, ebony, bird's-eye maple, curly maple, abalone, argillite, brass, telephone
10 x 16 x 13 ½ in. (25.4 x 40.6 x 34.3 cm)

Collection of the artist; courtesy of Spirit Wrestler Gallery

TODD DEFOE

b. 1970, Fond du Lac, Minnesota; lives in Cloquet, Minnesota

Improvisation #5, 2004

Red catlinite (pipestone),
silver, oboe reed
8 3/8 x 13 1/2 x 7 7/8 in.
(21.3 x 34.3 x 20 cm)

Collection of Jean Mulder

SUSAN POINT

b. 1952, Musqueam Indian Reserve, Vancouver, British Columbia;
lives on Musqueam Indian Reserve

"Salish tradition is the root of my inspiration. My
love for Salish design is infinite and has inspired
me to create a visual language that both honors
the traditions of my ancestors and reflects my own
personal style."

Return, 2003

Glass, red cedar, stainless steel
29 x 32 x 36 in. (73.7 x 81.3 x
91.4 cm)

Museum of Arts & Design;
Museum purchase with funds
provided by an anonymous
foundation

JOE FEDDERSEN

b. 1953, Omak, Washington; lives in Olympia, Washington

Parking Lot, 2004

Glass
H. 14 in., Diam. 10 3/4 in.
(35.6 x 27.3 cm)

Collection of the artist;
courtesy of Froelick Gallery

PRIMROSE ADAMS

b. 1926, Queen Charlotte Islands (Haida Gwaii),
British Columbia; lives in Duncan, British Columbia

ALFRED ADAMS

b. 1958, Massett, Queen Charlotte Islands (Haida Gwaii),
British Columbia; lives in Duncan, British Columbia

> "To me, beauty is nature. I have lived my whole life
> on Haida Gwaii (Queen Charlotte Islands), so I
> have been lucky in the sense that I can dig my
> own roots and truly appreciate my surroundings."
>
> —Primrose Adams

CLOCKWISE FROM UPPER LEFT

*Miniature Woven Hat Pendant
with Black Fish Design*, 2005

*Miniature Woven Hat Pendant
with Octopus Design*, 2002

*Miniature Woven Hat Pendant
with Butterfly Design*, 2002

Spruce root, acrylic paint,
black onyx beads, string
each Diam. 3 in., D. 1^1/$_2$ in.,
L. (with string) 13 in.
(7.6 x 3.8 x 33 cm)

Collection of Robert G. Argall

LAWRENCE "LARRY" AHVAKANA

b. 1946, Fairbanks, Alaska; lives in Suquamish, Washington

"Through my work, I can express my ideas of tradition, those feelings of being part of a society that's thousands of years old, with contemporary artistic influences and a variety of materials, including non-traditional ones. I continually gain insight, direction, and psychic or emotional strength through the stories of how the Inupiat defined their total subsistence lifestyle with the shamanism, ceremony, and natural cycles of Arctic living. Within my designs, I incorporate the sense of my culture, but the interpretation is very personal, and the conceptual format, I hope, will give the viewer an idea of the tradition."

LEFT
Qatluaqaq Tim-Inua, Spirit of the Box Drum, 2004

Old-growth red cedar, red oak, yellow cedar, glass, acrylic, neon lights, horsehair, walrus membrane, ivory, trade beads
4 panels (one shown above), *each panel* 62 x 30 in. (157.5 x 76.2 cm)

Collection of the artist

RIGHT
Open Lead, 2005

Glass
30 x 15 x 1 1/4 in. (76.2 x 38.1 x 3.2 cm)

Collection of the artist

MARVIN OLIVER

b. 1946, Seattle, Washington; lives in Seattle

Transporter, 2005
Glass, steel
49 x 14 x 5 in. (124.5 x
35.6 x 12.7 cm)
Collection of the artist

WHITE BUFFALO

b. 1946, Gallup, New Mexico; lives in Sedona, Arizona

Candelabrum, 2003

Elk antler, sterling silver
16 x 40 x 8 ½ in. (40.6 x
101.6 x 21.6 cm)

Courtesy of Lovena Ohl Gallery

PAULA RASMUS DEDE

b. 1946, in *Aberdeen, Washington; lives in Chugiak, Alaska*

"Everyday objects (shoes, toys, necklaces) not only have utilitarian function but a strong form and design as well. I try to create an object with exaggerated architecture—one that forces the viewer to reconsider their basic utility. I enhance this object with beads, wire, and found objects to further redefine them as vessels of culture, transcending utility to become art. Using a palette of colors and textures, I try to force reconsideration on the basic form and function. By reinforcing stereotypes or developing my own cultural connections, I seek to create surprising visual references."

Not Your Mama's Mary Janes, 2003

Glass beads, aluminum, wire, commercially manufactured shoes covered in patent leather and fabric pair of shoes (one shown above) *each* 19 7/8 x 7 7/8 x 10 5/8 in. (50.5 x 20 x 27 cm)

Anchorage Museum of History and Art

GEORGE NIXON BLAKE

b. 1944, *Hoopa, California; lives in Hoopa*

"As you grow up here, the culture just becomes a part of you, and it often spills over into my work. Tradition is what is in the heart and soul of your home, your land, country, and social environment. Tradition evolves, and it changes regardless of what you do to maintain it. I consider myself more of a traditional artist than a contemporary artist. I don't exploit tradition for the market but focus more on my artistic abilities to uphold traditions."

Boot, 2003

Elk antler, silver
8 1/2 x 2 x 10 in. (21.6 x 5.1 x 25.4 cm)

Collection of the artist

SUSAN LAURE PEEBLES

b. 1957, Grand Forks, North Dakota; lives in Beaverton, Oregon

"Growing up on the prairie, with its wide expanse of sky and open land, I have always felt a deep, spiritual connection to my humanity and my place on earth. I draw inspiration from my memories of this connection, and attempt to express that connection through my beadwork.

Additionally, I am deeply moved by the stories of those who came before me. Understanding traditional techniques and methods of creation is a foundation. The knowledge of the 'old' ways of doing things is empowering and freeing. I believe that tradition has enough elasticity to include change. Artistically, I don't feel the need to re-create what has been done in the past."

Prayer Bag: Touch the Sky, 2004

Glass seed beads (some antique), silk, balsa wood, deerskin, nylon thread
8½ x 10 x 3 in. (21.6 x 25.4 x 7.6 cm); length of strap: 14 in. (35.6 cm)

Collection of the artist

It's Art:
"Keep talking while we keep working, but hold it down so I can hear myself think"[1]

Bruce Bernstein

WITHIN THE AFFAIRS BETWEEN the Native and non-Native worlds,[2] art has remained a negotiated space, where Native people can tell their own stories in their own ways. Although many lament the changes in designs, tools, materials, and forms brought to Native art by the non-Indian world, we have only to look to the Native world to understand how these new ideas have continued to keep Native peoples and their traditions vital. Fortunately, because Native cultures require a moral and cultural context to make art, American Indian art—whether made for home use or for sale, or with indigenous or introduced materials—must place these and other new ideas into their own vast cultural reservoir. Ultimately, because of these contexts, Native arts persist as windows into their world.

For Indian art, the world of scholarship and collecting is often divided between old and new art. Older Indian art is most often considered more authentically Indian, or, if you will, of the culture—representing an Indian past unadulterated by outside influences. This purer art is thought to be more beautiful in its authenticity and its unchanged nature. If possible, this authentic art is more Indian than contemporary art. Such a dichotomy between old and new suggests more about the non-Indian viewer than about Native people as art makers. This insidious argument also reveals deeply held cultural attitudes about primitivism and the associated belief that tribal cultures are less advanced and more likely to be absorbed by stronger cultures. Measuring authenticity in this way sucks the agency out of Native people by negating their voice and replacing it with the category of "tradition," or a wholly freestanding one of "Indian art." Unfortunately, as art critic Paul Chaat Smith (Comanche) suggests, this same "ideological prison is capable of becoming an elixir that [we] Indian people ourselves find irresistible."[3]

It is a culture trap as real as the piece of art we admire. We must ask ourselves whether each work is a stand-alone piece, or if it is a reference to culture—can we read it as art, or must we always see it from the perspective of Indian culture and lifeways? Authenticity and tradition used in this way create a time warp in which Indian artists' thoughts, and consequently their art, are placed and appreciated, further isolating them far beyond the boundaries of what others might say or think about them. Such art made today is as Indian as such art made at any other time in history, for no other reason than that it is made by a Native person. Art was and remains, in its most fundamental sense, a direct reflection of the artist's own perspectives and understandings of the world around him or her. Authenticity is truth to self.

While an artist never sheds his or her identity, do we as viewers appreciate the art because it is Indian, or because it is art, or both? Rick Hill, a Tuscarora colleague, once described to me something he called "genetic memory"—in essence, that "Indians [regardless of the hardships] are not through being Indians yet, so we can't stop time, there can't be an ahistoric time, or a real versus authentic Indian; because everything and anything is who we are."

Artist Truman Lowe (Ho-Chunk) told me that there exists an incontrovertible part of Native people, and therefore of the art they create. He defines four aspects of this: "origin," a knowledge of the past; "vision," in particular, a continuing newness; "local," reflecting upon the natural and cultural landscapes; and "voice," an expression of the individual's personality. For both Hill and Lowe, this is not a biological argument centered on genetics, but rather one of consciousness and worldview.

Indian art is sometimes wedged in between the dichotomies of high and low art, relegating Indian art to categories of craft because it comes from societies that some perceive as "less advanced" than European, or European-based, societies. As craft, Indian-made art is interpreted as a replication of existing forms, rather than the celebration of creativity, change, and continuity that it presents. Contemporary art made by Native people deserves to be considered on its own merits, and not against chimerical standards of imposed and imagined tradition and authenticity. Without a doubt, Indian-made art, whether it introduces something new or is a continuation of established forms, whether it uses new or traditional mediums, is always fresh and reflective of the world in which the artist lives. In the stereotyping of Indian people, we arrive at an erroneous conclusion that all Indians are artists; but Indian-made art, like all art, has its innovators, geniuses, and followers.

Why is change usually considered such a bad idea? We don't berate ourselves for no longer living in a subsistence economy, or being landless and futureless in a class-bound guild system working for the right to remain alive. The Indian people I know enjoy automobiles, cell phones, Internet, travel, restaurants, and shopping for clothes (rather than making their own). To the American public at large, Indians and Indian arts and crafts represent an anti-modernism and environmentalism that pre-dates industrial America. Ironically, the social movements of the 1920s and 1930s that advocated for the continuance of Indian art did so on the basis of economic need, so that Indian people could afford to purchase the very modern conveniences and necessities—to which their art production served, and today continues to serve, as an antithesis and antidote to industrial society. Why, at such a late date as the twenty-first century, should we worry about whether something is traditional or not? Is it not enough to establish that it is Native-made? Indian people have survived, thrived, and flourished; and we can also say that Indian people have, for the most part, survived with style and grace because their culture and traditions are so dynamic. In short, we should understand that the strength of Native culture is change. Saying that art has evolved over the centuries is a truism—trite and meaningless. Moreover, as much as this is not a genetic argument, all of the above also assumes that artists and their work are not equal. Again, in the interest of revealing insidious assumptions, Indian-made art is more often than not viewed as an undifferentiated mass of work, rather than work of variable skill and vision. Developing an art history of American Indian art that includes the old and new—and, even more important, includes Indian-made art in the canon of American art—will begin to create the contexts necessary for this differentiation and better understanding.

The Museum World and Indian Art

Indian art expresses the ongoing shaping of Native identities, but museum displays of Indian art and culture often reflect an idealized Native past. Compounding this problem are visitors' expectations that Indians are themselves artifacts of the past—a historical anachronism to be examined in the safety of a museum. Visitors and users of a museum expect it to be filled with older, historical objects, which they believe to be more authentically Native.

Art is made to bridge the boundaries of different worlds. Indian art must be confronted and challenged with what we know, or believe that we know. We need to seek clarification as to its meanings and associations beyond the normative museological taxonomies. We have sought to begin to present viewpoints that provide contextualization not only for traditional museum subject matter—objects—but also for the cultural systems that produced these items. Native cultures are experienced holistically, an experience that is not covered by the disarticulated way they are presented in most museums.

Museums need not and should not rest on earlier interpretations of their collections and subject matter, but rather should encourage everyone, including scholars and public audiences, to continue to question what is in the collection and how it is presented and interpreted, both as individual objects and included in groups of objects. All museums must continue to grow, not necessarily by increasing the size of their collections, but rather through the growth of the collections' intellectual potential and value by applying layered knowledge—especially, composite forms of interpretation and knowledge that encourage understanding of the simultaneous validity of multiple interpretations.

Although these objects might be old and long removed from their makers, museums can inform visitors that they remain part of the current heritage of Native communities, contributing to their conscious identity—and thus continue to be a vital part of their lives, a part of continual becoming. As one Native friend says, "Once we use the past tense, we admit to these objects being lost."

Even older objects, removed generations ago and now often thousands of miles from their homes, continue to shape Native thought because there is knowledge encoded into them by their makers and original users. Native cultures are this unbroken cultural chain. A museum collection containing such objects demonstrates that we more than likely have inherited a partial system of knowledge that can only be made whole through their explication by Native peoples, or at least by including Native peoples in the process. Indigenous peoples have a living heritage, which is not something that can be collected and/or removed to museums. Their cultures are in a constant state of becoming, being shaped by today's circumstances.

Thus, exhibitions need to express the ongoing shaping of Native identities. These installations should challenge the conventions that currently govern the display of indigenous cultures—certainly by presenting historical art differently, but even more so by unabashedly including contemporary Native art. The usual design of indigenous exhibitions is determined by an assumed division between art and science ("natural history"), as well as between aesthetic experiences and the study of ethnographic objects. Cultural and aesthetic experience and the idea of beauty are not co-joined with ethnographic evidence and social curiosity, but opposed to them. Rather than cram objects and their wall labels into congested ethnographic displays, museums might arrange the pieces to provide the visitor with an aesthetically pleasing and memorable experience. Released from the clutter, these objects would move beyond their roles as icons of cultural differences to engender a new definition of art. I want to emphasize that this view is not a replacement for existing systems and appreciations, but rather a call for an inclusive understanding, which can only be achieved by incorporating the words of the people who created the art, and by properly reflecting their cultures.

Through these changes in the contexts of presenting and viewing Native art, deeper understandings and associations can be made and absorbed. This approach brings to the forefront indigenous conceptions of the world, one of relationships and interdependency, a worldview that is unique to Indian art, whether the art is newly made or old.

The Artists

Native art is about change, about absorbing and incorporating new ideas and materials, as much as it is about sustaining traditional values, materials, and iconography. Whenever Native artists work, and whatever they create, they work within a world filled with meanings and encoded choices. This genetic memory is as much manifest as enviable. These deep philosophical underpinnings are what have sustained Native art for millennia. One way to reflect on this phenomenon is to view art as having both inside and outside features. Those outside features are what are constantly evolving to acquire and adapt to the ever-changing world, while the inner features are the intensely held values and understandings that continue to tell Indian people who they are, thus assisting them in making sense of being a part of the world.

Consider that Indian art is made from the very substance from which the First Peoples are made, either in its material or ideational form. Thus, art sustains people through use and incorporation of the Earth and its materials. Understood within the contexts of the Native world, Creation is ongoing and is not something that happened long ago or someplace else. Today's artists, as much as any other generation, are part of a continuous state of creation, an ever-changing state of becoming; and therefore, as part of this immutable world, Native art is about that ever-changing being and becoming. In this regard, the most significant context for thinking about the making of an object is its imperative, rather than the viewers' admiration or even the finished piece itself.

The visibility of American Indian art has increased as the non-Native world of Euro-American cultures closed in and forced changes on Native people. Art became one of the few Native expressions allowed, even as the U.S. government's prohibitions on Native peoples' religious ceremonies continued through the early 1930s, and as children were taken off to boarding schools, away from their families, and punished for speaking their own language or showing any other outward sign that they were thinking of home. During the nineteenth century, as Native groups' land and water rights disappeared, Native artists began the practice of incorporating religious iconography into their works, or making religious objects for the non-Native world to remind Indian people who they are, as well as to tell non-Natives, "We are still here."

Today in North America, Native societies and artists use the arts to continue to express their resolve to survive—what one Pueblo friend describes as "persistence and insistence." How many stories do we know and hear about someone who "returned home" to make art and to "learn more about my culture and self"? The non-Indian world surrounds Native cultures and can entice their members away, but the arts have served as a buffer as well as a shield against the outside world. At first contact, Native artists were undoubtedly energized by new materials and ideas, as is evident from the rapid absorption and integration of these new influences. There is nothing more quintessentially "Indian" than beadwork or silver-and-turquoise jewelry made by Native hands and the minds that guided them. But as Northwest Coast art clearly demonstrates to us, new influences could enhance artists' work, and strengthen and stretch their abilities; and new tools could propel the evolution of their art forms. The introduction of metal knives along the Northwest Coast and metal awls in California—tools that stay sharper longer—helped artists bring their materials and visions to new levels of refinement.

New styles of Indian art emerged throughout the twentieth century, particularly through the fine-arts movement, but also through the continuation of the making of button blankets, carving of argillite, beading, and the use of metal tools, to list but a few. Each new style and innovation has built upon traditional styles and designs, but there are other changes that are wholly new. Innovation requires artists to integrate new influences into the wellsprings of their own world. Even when Indian art is made for the non-Indian world, it is still of the Indian world. Artists work within the boundaries of their world to make art; therefore it is as pure and aboriginal as their ancestors' art has always been.

Indian art has survived because its inner features or core values have remained in continuous use. While we might see new designs depicting flowers, baseballs, or cars on a canvas, necklace, or carving, we should understand that ephemeral aspects of our societies will no more become Indian history than what we ate for dinner last night. What we do know from the history of Indian art is that it is enduring because it continues to mitigate and reflect the broader world and continues to be autobiographical.

Contemporary Art and Artists

What about the contemporary artists? What is their role in the above scenario? Is art made by Indian people considered art, or is it something different, to be considered within its own classification and only within its own boundaries? Fortunately, while we talk and fret

about definitions, artists continue to make art, allowing their work to speak for whatever needs saying, demonstrating the simultaneous interrelatedness and newness of cultural production, including continuity and innovation in ideas and materials.

What do I mean? Well, Indian artists are dealt with as—well, as Indian artists, rather than as artists with an Indian birthright. A European painter paints from his or her personal and cultural background, and the audience—mostly within European-based populations—knows and understands the references in the work. An Indian person paints from her or his perspective as well; it might be most likely what they know and understand best, or what they are interested in knowing better. But the reference points for viewers might not be as accessible. In addition, images of Indians might be viewed as "Indians" and nothing more, rather than as culturally relevant identity, icons, stereotypes, or whatever. Viewing Indians as "just Indians" creates the problems of Indians having no relevancy outside of their cultures. Certainly, Indians make sense to Indians, but then what does the French countryside have to do with a man born in California some fifty years ago? Nothing, I think; however, I am open to considering the notion that the interstices of emotion and landscape have formed and continue to create human consciousness. Are we ready to consider that Indian lives and stories can be and are relevant to our non-Indian lives? And, that we have lessons to learn as well as visions to luxuriate in from the Native perspective? What do we in the dominant society learn from Indian peoples, whom European and American governments tried to destroy and then dispossessed for centuries? Can Indians from the fringes of our society paint us, while they seem to be painting themselves? It should be clear from the above that Indian people are as sentient and captured in modernity as any one of us.

American Indian art systems are about beauty—not just skin deep, but, at a profound level, as measurement of a holistic world and as a carrier of the continued vitalities of Native cultures. The use and meaning of American Indian art can be tied to both the beautiful and the good, because it is intended to please the eye and the spirits by upholding moral values—a proposition requiring that the creation of beauty is about integrating one's self into larger social and cultural systems. In Native cultures, beauty ultimately derives its meanings from a collective sense of societal responsibility. This is not just of the present, but is "timeless" in that artistic creation and consumption, like life itself, are fully dependent on continuing to create a world for past, present, and future ancestors.

To be blunt, people see art made by Indians and they classify it as Indian art—art made by the Other, and not to be confused with or considered together with American art. Funny thing, without due consideration of Indian art, we are missing the vast majority of American art history—thousands of years of the development of ideas about the American landscape and peoples that have shaped, and continue to shape, American populations and identities. Art of Native people is excluded because Indian histories are left out of American histories, in an act of what Chaat Smith says "is a constructed amnesia."[4]

Change Is Not Cultural Death

Unfortunately, definitions of "traditional" and "non-traditional" continue to permeate the Indian art market and the Indian world, originating from both artist and consumer, most flagrantly in the standards and judging of experts who bemuse us with pontifications on the art's authenticity, age, and aesthetic quality. If we were to read an indigenously authentic history of Indian art history, we would immediately understand that the tradition of all Indian art is change itself, rather than the way the market and museums have promulgated traditional Indian art as unchanged. Ultimately, these distinctions can only deny Indian people their own agency in the production of art, and, furthermore, diminish necessary discussions about the inherently indigenous aesthetic systems and histories molded into their art.

Tradition has come to be synonymous with "unchanged." Beadwork as a traditional art form presents an interesting paradox, in that the small glass beads so identified with Indian people are manufactured in Europe and became part of the lexicon of Indian art only in the middle-to-late nineteenth century. Such a spurious definition of tradition, together with the rewriting of Indian history, sought to create a baseline for Indian art that separates it from all other art. However, in tying the definition of authenticity for non-Western arts to these arts' putative, pre-industrial quality, museum curators, collectors, artists, and scholars have denied Indian people their place in modernity.[5]

Indian art has changed, but we cannot assume that change means cultural death. Rather, we might acknowledge that the only thing we know for certain about tradition is that it continues to change. Change is best understood in the context of Indian art as strength, because it produces a vibrancy that, in turn, creates survival. The artists of the past, as do today's artists, understand—whether consciously or unconsciously—the necessity of the simultaneous nurturing of continuity and change to sustain themselves.

Nonetheless, even with vibrant Indian cultures surrounding us, we tend to think that Indian art is decontextualized as a result of museums, collectors, and consumerism.

Ultimately, Indian art enters within our own ethos, influenced, of course, by our own perceptions. Indian art can be as liberating as it is restrictive. Some artists might feel bounded by a set of standards and techniques that are believed to be historical and culturally accurate, while others use those as borders beyond which they do not wish to venture. Design repertoires might be severely limited both as personal choice and as a matter to maintain their community and cultural ties. While there are complaints about the numerous successful artists who live off the reservation or outside the villages but still have the audacity to call themselves "Indian," there is the understanding that at least by making art, they are keeping their connection to their own people alive, and that they could at some point return. Artists can also be highly criticized in their own village for their successes, for their changes, and for their choices of lifestyle, among other things. Art without doubt has facilitated change as much as it guards against it. It must certainly speed the acculturation process forward, providing an entrance into the cash economy and enabling Indian artists to work at home and continue to be part of their village and its activities. Modernity and attendant cultural changes in Indian communities would have happened anyway, but art provided them with the means to change more upon their own terms. Using art to earn money allowed people to stay within their own cultural boundaries while participating in the broader world, a practice that continues today. Art has helped sustain people over difficult periods, and often was one of the only indigenous forms of knowledge and practice that Indian people were overtly allowed to continue. Today, there is a multitude of voices openly singing for all of us. We have only to listen to hear the hearts and minds of Native peoples and know that they are still here, unchanged but changing—as Native as they have ever been.

NOTES

1. Anonymous Indian artist commenting on pesky questions from a friendly ethnographer.

2. My interchangeable use of the terms "Native peoples" and "Indian peoples" (and "Native art" and "Indian art") follows the non-linear conventions one hears and uses in conversation and discourse. These are understandably broad and rather unspecific categories, and are used here as conveniences.

3. Paul Chaat Smith, "Luna Remembers," in *Emendatio* (Washington, D.C.: National Museum of the American Indian, 2005). James Luna's performance and installation work *Emendatio*, curated by National Museum of the American Indian curators Truman Lowe and Paul Chaat Smith, was presented at the Fondazione Querini Stampalia in Venice as part of the 51st Venice *Biennale*.

4. Ibid.

5. Ruth Phillips and Christopher Steiner, *Unpacking Culture: Art and Commodity in Colonial and Postcolonial Worlds* (Berkeley: University of California Press, 1999), p. 10.

The I.A.I.A. and the New Frontier

John Richard Grimes

IN ITS MOST CONDENSED FORM, the pattern of Euro-American colonization of North America is a simple but still sobering narrative, chronicling a cascade of cause and effect that could serve as a perverse parody of the "Jack's House" nursery rhyme: here is the explorer that drew the map, that attracted the traders (nowadays "entrepreneurs"), who built the outposts, that enlisted the military (to protect the new economic interests), who enabled the missionaries (who lived in the protective shadow of the forts), who preached the Gospel, that attracted the pilgrims, who took the land, etc., etc.

The process didn't take long, contrary to the depictions by the popular media, which often seem to portray a cavalry-and-Indian contest for the American West that persisted, nip and tuck, through the late 1800s. In reality, within the span of two or three generations following the first trading posts, many Native communities found themselves living as a marginalized, dependent, and nearly decimated underclass in a radically altered world. The rapid progress of colonization is an important factor in understanding the early (1849) shift of U.S. Indian administration from the War Department to the Department of the Interior. Over the ensuing century-plus, federal Indian policy—administered by the Bureau of Indian Affairs (B.I.A.)—is usually characterized as one of paternalism and forced assimilation. Although the B.I.A. mission is now to "fulfill . . . trust responsibilities and promote self-determination on behalf of Tribal Governments, American Indians, and Alaska Natives,"[1] this earlier legacy is still frequently invoked as evidence of a tragically flawed federal Indian policy.

It may be surprising to the B.I.A.'s critics that it can count among its accomplishments the creation of the Institute of American Indian Arts (I.A.I.A.), an institution dedicated to deconstructing stereotypes and promoting self-determined concepts of Indian identity, art, and culture. The I.A.I.A. was a bold B.I.A. experiment, inspired by earlier Native education initiatives in the Southwest between about 1930 and 1960. One such strand is the Indian arts program established in 1932 by Dorothy Dunn at the Santa Fe Indian School. Dunn's premise was that encouraging Indian art fostered student self-esteem, self-sufficiency, and increased English proficiency. Dunn's Studio School and its graduates became widely known. While it succeeded for a time, the school eventually sowed the seeds of its own demise, as graduates such as Allan Houser began to react against

FIG. 1. Lloyd Kiva New, ca. 1966

Dunn's view that Indian art, to be genuine, should adhere to "traditional" styles.

More direct precedents for the I.A.I.A. can be traced to the University of Arizona's Southwest Indian Arts Project (1958–61) and the Directions in Indian Art conference (1959), both funded by the Rockefeller Foundation, and both seminal to the beginning of the modern history of Native American art. At the formative center of this activity was the Cherokee-Irish designer and artist Lloyd Kiva New (1916–2002), who served as

FIG. 2. I.A.I.A. faculty, ca. 1965–66: left to right (first row) Terry Schubert, Seymour Tubis, Jim McGrath; (second row) Lloyd Kiva New, Fritz Scholder, Otellie Loloma, Josephine Wapp; (third row) Kay Wiest, Allan Houser, Michael McCormick, T. D. Allen, Rolland Meinholtz; (back row) Neil Parsons, Leo N. Bushman, Ralph Pardington, Louis Ballard

director of the Southwest Indian Arts Project from its inception (fig. 1). Breaking with the notion that Native art and culture are static entities, New championed a radically different vision. Instead, he argued that contemporary Indian art should be inspired by the past but grounded in the demands of the present; and, moreover, that Indian art should be individual, that it should be expressive, and should utilize the full range of available mediums, "traditional" or otherwise. In 1962, when President John F. Kennedy issued an executive order creating a new Indian arts high school—the Institute of American Indian and Alaska Native Arts Development (later shortened to I.A.I.A.)—under the auspices of the B.I.A., it was this modern doctrine that became its driving influence. Headed by George A. Boyce, a B.I.A. educator, with Lloyd New as artistic director, the institute was initially situated on the grounds of the Santa Fe Indian School, displacing the Studio program. In the fall of 1962, 130 students representing 69 tribes entered the school, and the first class graduated in 1963.

Lloyd New is most strongly identified as I.A.I.A.'s founding visionary. The power of New's vision, together with his personal charisma, became a magnet for attracting such highly talented teachers as Allan Houser and Fritz Scholder to its faculty (fig. 2). Through the 1960s and '70s, the school's reputation grew rapidly, and it garnered national and international attention. These early successes gave way, in the 1980s and '90s, to a period of consolidation as the school shifted from its experimental footing to a more durable foundation. In 1988, as part of this change, the U.S. Congress reorganized the school, removing it from B.I.A. administration and establishing it as a congressionally chartered institution of higher education—one of only three congressionally chartered colleges in the nation. In 1992, the I.A.I.A opened a new museum in downtown Santa Fe (fig. 3), enabling the institute to showcase its acclaimed collection of contemporary Indian art, and offering its visitors glimpses of the student talent that is continually emerging from the school. Since 1997, the institute has been led by Della Warrior,

180

FIG. 3. I.A.I.A. Museum, downtown Santa Fe
(after 1992)

FIG. 4. The Library and Technology Center on
the new I.A.I.A. campus in southwest Santa Fe

FIG. 5. Group photo of I.A.I.A.'s Class of 2004

whose national standing has galvanized the support of tribal leaders, government officials, and educators. A new, strikingly designed academic campus (fig. 4), which opened in 2000 on a 140-acre site in southwest Santa Fe, is a dramatic expression of the I.A.I.A.'s new growth and stability under President Warrior.

Within Indian country, the I.A.I.A.'s influence can be measured by the number of students (nearly four thousand) and communities (almost every federally recognized tribe) that it has served since its founding, a breadth that may be evident in a photo of a recent graduating class (fig. 5). Beyond Indian country, there are few exhibitions of contemporary Indian art in which the I.A.I.A.'s influence is not strongly evident, and whose artists are not directly or indirectly linked to the school. The I.A.I.A.'s presence, for example, is readily felt at the new National Museum of the American Indian (N.M.A.I.) in Washington, D.C., where inaugural installations included a survey of works by former I.A.I.A. instructor Allan Houser.

The I.A.I.A. has influenced the landscape of Indian art. But there are still many challenges. It is still too true that many Americans (and Europeans) want to be told the familiar Indian Story, in which genuine Indians only exist in a romantic past; this seems to have

been the subtext of some of the initial reviews of the N.M.A.I., which lamented a lack of context (ethnography?) or history (the familiar one?). Sadly, Native Americans, and the museums that showcase their art, are still expected to deliver stereotypes and stick to the past—or be prepared for disappointed visitors and snippy critics. Sometimes, the process of change is very, very slow.

The I.A.I.A. has never wavered from its commitment to promote Indian art that addresses the contemporary world. For all its students, this means finding the freedom to express, in their own way as individuals, in any medium, the values and knowledge of their cultures. For others, this means accepting the right of Native people to redefine themselves, and their arts, as they believe the changing world requires. Indeed, in this work, the I.A.I.A. is part of an American counter-colonization, its campus the antithesis of the frontier outposts of earlier times: in the midst of the Euro-American majority, in the heartland of the mythic American West, surrounded by homogenizing consumerism, the I.A.I.A. shelters an Alternate Destiny for Indian art, and casts a protective shadow over Indian artists.

NOTES

1. Web site of the U.S. Department of the Interior University; http://www.doiu.nbc.gov/orientation/bia2.cfm (as of February 27, 2005).

A Postcard from the Edge of Contemporary Native Art

David M. Roche

DAMIEN HIRST, A HIP BRITISH ARTIST of the moment, was quoted in the New York Times as saying, "I prefer to be seduced by an image than presented with a real person. It's kind of a Warhol thing." Andy Warhol, along with his Pop contemporaries, created works characterized by stylized, emblematic imagery that are not in any sense realistic. As unlikely as it might seem, the work of Marcus Amerman and other artists featured in Changing Hands 2 has a great deal in common with the work of Warhol and other contemporary twentieth-century artists—perhaps more than with the art created by their tribal ancestors.

Like Warhol, Amerman—a contemporary Indian artist of Choctaw descent—has developed a strong reputation for his portraits, which raise questions regarding identity and have ranged in subject matter from Janet Jackson to Wonder Woman. (His work has graced the cover of Rolling Stone Magazine.) His work possesses a distinctly "Pop" feeling reminiscent of Warhol, and—through the appropriation of certain graphic techniques and content found in comic strips, to which beadwork effectively lends itself—of Roy Lichtenstein, too.

The evidence of popular visual culture is clear in Amerman's Postcard, 2002 (page 56). This beaded panel recalls advertising art or popular illustrations on billboards or postcards from the mid-twentieth century, perhaps something that one might have found along the old U.S. Route 66, which went through the Southwest all the way to Los Angeles.

A striking art-historical precedent for this type of work can be found in the paintings of Ed Ruscha, particularly in his works of the 1960s and '70s. Ruscha was born and raised in Omaha, Nebraska and was heavily influenced by the aesthetic language of billboards, corporate and commercial signage, and Hollywood Westerns from the 1940s and '50s. "He dedicated himself to illustrating contemporary, prosaic subject matter like gas stations, brand-name logos, and everyday words and subject matter."[1] Like Ruscha's iconic word paintings, Amerman has taken a simple but loaded phrase, "Indian Country," and has made it the subject of his work. By isolating the phrase and putting it into the context of a postcard, Amerman seems to be almost literally sending a message to viewers asking them to reconsider its meaning. The words "Indian Country" therefore function as both a visual subject and abstract signifier of meaning, and, like Amerman's other works, moves beyond the tenets of the Pop movement. Warhol and artists of similar temperament explored surface and helped shape popular opinion, whereas Amerman seems to implore the viewer to look beyond the surface and, in the process, deconstruct popular opinion. By juxtaposing images that both conform to and contradict popular notions of Native America, Amerman comments on the past and present reality of Native Americans.

One past reality to consider is that Amerman's ancestors suffered terribly under the restrictive and punishing policies of the United States government during the nineteenth century. The Choctaw were originally a Southeastern tribe that was displaced—and disenfranchised—by the U.S. government, which moved them

and approximately 84,000 other Indians to the lands beyond the 95th meridian. They were one of the five so-called "Civilized Tribes," the other four being the Cherokee, Chickasaw, Creek, and Seminole—"Civilized" because they adopted ways of living that resembled the whites. Despite this tragedy and the passing of almost two centuries, when considering tribes from this region that include the Choctaw, Cheyenne, Arapaho, Blackfoot and Sioux, it's easy to summon up some of the idealized images presented in Amerman's Postcard, such as the dancing Indians in feather bonnets or the roaming buffalo. It's safe to say that since the expansion of the whites into the territories west of the Mississippi during the nineteenth century, the Plains Indian, more than any other, has shaped the popular notions of Native America and has created a sort of "Pan-Indian" ideal.

The befeathered image of Indians, made popular through a variety of sources, has become a stereotype that undermines all Native people, as well as the integrity of the individual Indian artist working today.

> Today, when many Native Americans live and work in urban environments while others still struggle to emerge from the poverty and oppression of the reservations, the commercial advertising stereotypes . . . persist. . . . The continuation of these stereotypes and the scarcity of urban images of Native Americans in all forms of popular cultures maintain the fiction that Native Americans still remain primitive, with no place in modern society.[2]

The struggle for authentic identity is the present reality with which Amerman and other artists featured in Changing Hands 2 must contend, and that some tackle in their work.

The idea of identity in any work by an artist of Native descent is enormously loaded. In historical tribal communities, individual identity was expected to be sacrificed for the greater identity of the tribe. That changed over the course of the twentieth Century as tribes disbanded, became acculturated, and, in some cases, disappeared. Amerman's tribe was displaced almost two hundred years ago, and he grew up in Portland Oregon, half a continent away from the current home of the Choctaw tribe, and studied art at the I.A.I.A. in Santa Fe. How does his experience inform his identity? And how does this information influence the public's perception of his identity? Following the 1970s boom in the American Indian art market, Fritz Scholder, a high-profile artist of that era whose work featured substantial Native content, suffered when his authenticity as an artist was challenged because, by some arbitrary measure of his genetic makeup, he was deemed by some to be insufficiently Luiseño. This is a clear case of the Native artist being caught between two worlds. Amerman makes an interesting counterpoint to this in the following statement: "If you (a Native artist) do a painting or a sculpture, say of Janet Jackson, then it's like you're going over into Western culture. With beadwork, you're taking it back. It becomes

Indian. Janet Jackson becomes Indian." This remark reveals Amerman's savvy and his command of Western culture, and is representative of a new generation of Native artists who won't be subjugated or allow their identity to be overtaken or denied by mainstream Western culture.

Among the mosaic of images in Amerman's *Postcard* is his self-portrait, the presence of which suggests that he is coming to terms with the many social and cultural components that inform his identity. His "postcard" shows the viewer stark differences that exist within his reality, ranging from popular notions of being American Indian to current societal issues.

Other artists whose works are presented in *Changing Hands 2* also explore their identity by leveraging popular culture. David Bradley provides a provocative commentary on the exploitation and commercialization of Native America by Madison Avenue in *Land O Bucks, Land O Fakes, Land O Lakes*, 2003 (page 59), his spoof of the branding strategy that Land O'Lakes, Inc. uses for its Land O Lakes butter package and advertising. Another example is Judy Chartrand, who pays a backhanded homage to Warhol in her ceramic work *Metis Soup Cans*, 2004 (page 54).

The use of appropriated popular images from mainstream Western culture in works by these artists represents a leap from content to commentary. Historically, there were uniform standards for excellence and aesthetics in hand-crafted items that existed within most of the tribes of North America. With reference to nineteenth-century Plains Indian art in particular, "most objects made and owned . . . had some purpose to serve," and "the culture's artistic inclinations were directed toward beautifying and improving functional objects."[3] There was little or no room for commentary as we think of it today.

For this reason, and due to the apparent influence of work by several twentieth-century masters, many artists who have participated in *Changing Hands 2* fall more comfortably into the continuum of twentieth-century Western art than of Native American art. Indeed, certain tribal traditions *have* changed hands. Amerman's use of glass beads, for example, significantly ties him to the tradition of his tribal ancestors—a distinct difference from the work of such artists as Warhol, Ruscha, and Lichtenstein. However, by drawing on a broad range of cultural resources, from Warhol's art to commercial packaging, and fusing those elements with their own experience and unique set of skills, these artists make more of a statement about twenty-first-century art in general than about Native art in particular.

In the last letter of the word "Country," Amerman encloses an image of the Earth. Perhaps this is a fitting symbol of unity, suggesting that we are each a sum of all our experiences, and, together, greater than the whole.

NOTES

1. Sarah Louise Eckhardt, quoted in Josef Helfenstein and Jonathan Fineberg, eds., *Drawings of Choice from a New York Collection*, exh. cat. (Champaign, Ill.: Krannert Art Museum, 2002), p. 126.

2. Zena Pearlstone, "Native American Images in Advertising," *American Indian Art* (Phoenix) 20, no. 3 (1995), p. 39.

3. Richard Conn, *Circles of the World: Traditional Art of the Plains Indians* (Denver, Colo.: Denver Art Museum, 1982), p. 12.

NATURE AS SUBJECT

The works presented in "Nature as Subject" refer to the primary elements of air, earth, and water, but from diverse, subjective points of view. Native art celebrates the full range of the natural world, from prairie flora to coastal fauna, evoking universal themes that have been explored by all cultures. The personal and spiritual relationships that Native peoples have had with the land—despite the social disruptions they have endured and, in many cases, their forced isolation—cannot be underestimated as a special source of inspiration for Native artists.

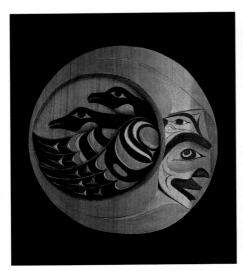

TIM PAUL

b. 1950, Esperanza Inlet, Vancouver Island, British Columbia;
lives in Port Alberni, British Columbia

TOP, LEFT TO RIGHT

April Moon Mask, 1999
Red cedar, acrylic paint
16 x 15 1/2 x 2 1/4 in.
(40.6 x 39.4 x 5.7 cm)

Collection of Chris Bredt
and Jamie Cameron

*May Moon: The Month the
Fur Seal Is Hunted*, 1999

Red cedar, cedar bark,
acrylic paint, cedar rope
15 1/2 x 15 1/2 x 5 in.
(39.4 x 39.4 x 12.7 cm)

Private collection

Huckleberry Moon, 2000

Red cedar, acrylic paint,
cedar rope, artificial flora
(huckleberry)
18 x 14 x 6 in. (45.7 x
35.6 x 15.2 cm)

Private collection

OPPOSITE

The Rainbow People, ca. 1999

Red cedar, cedar bark, acrylic
paint, cedar rope
78 x 32 x 16 in. (198.1 x 81.3 x
40.6 cm)

Collection of Russell and
Suzy Campbell

BOTTOM, LEFT TO RIGHT

December Moon, 2000

Red cedar, acrylic paint
28 x 27 x 7 in. (7.1 x
68.6 x 17.8 cm)

Collection of Dr. and
Mrs. Mark R. Olsen

Winter Seasonal Moon #17, 1999

Red cedar, acrylic paint
15 x 13 x 5 in. (38.1 x
33 x 12.7 cm)

Collection of Jim and
Todd Cowart

Fall Seasonal Moon, 2000
Red cedar, acrylic paint
22 x 18 x 7 1/2 in. (55.9 x
45.7 x 19.1 cm)

Collection of Stephen and
Jazmin Signer

PAULA RASMUS DEDE

b. 1946, *Aberdeen, Washington; lives in Chugiak, Alaska*

Shadows on Chugach Moon, 2005

Brushed aluminum, chrome
hubcaps, glass beads, thread,
double-sided tape
overall 12 x 40 x 6 in. (30.5 x
101.6 x 15.2 cm)

Collection of the artist

KIM KNIFE CHIEF

b. 1957, Pawnee, Oklahoma; lives in Pawnee

Pleiades Ring, 2003

Sterling silver, 14k gold
3 x 2 ¹/₂ x 2 in. (7.6 x 6.4 x 5.1 cm)

Collection of the artist

HAROLD ALFRED

b. 1953, Cormorant Island, Alert Bay, Vancouver Island, British Columbia;
lives in Victoria, British Columbia

"The four phases of the moon represent the circle of life. One starts out small, then slowly becomes larger, eventually fading away at the end, only to be reborn again with the next generation. The children are represented by the abalone and symbolize the treasure of the new generation."

Phases of the Moon Necklace, 2003

Sterling silver, abalone
L. 18 in. (45.7 cm)

Courtesy of The Legacy Ltd.

GLEN NIPSHANK

b. 1961, *Athabasca, Alberta, Canada; lives in Santa Fe, New Mexico*

"My career began with traditional symbolic imagery from geographic areas, and spiritual themes. The clay will work with you if you respect it. The pieces are traditionally made, but are contemporary in form, structure, and texture. I never lost my painting techniques, and, to this day, I continue to paint contemporary images on clay. In the work I do, I create images and ideas—playful imagery and form, and serious monumental pieces."

OPPOSITE
Large Vessel, 2004

Ceramic, glazes
23 x 16 x 16 ¹/₂ in. (58.4 x 40.6 x 41.9 cm)

Museum of Arts & Design; Museum purchase with funds provided by the Horace W. Goldsmith Foundation, 2004

DAVID RUBEN PIQTOUKUN

b. 1950, *Paulatuk, Northwest Territories; lives on southeast shore of Lake Simcoe, Ontario*

"Our survival customs and traditions revolved around the 'creative imagination' and the skills of creating objects for practical use or for elaborate ceremonies. We can never go back in time physically; but as artists, we are capable of transforming those traditions into contemporary visual formats. I take the 'old' and give it new light for this generation of people to grasp. Hopefully, future generations will understand and comprehend the continual change of lifestyles, which has the greatest influence to motivate and generate changes in 'modern traditions.'"

Shaman Returns from the Moon, 2004

Italian alabaster, soapstone, artificial sinew
9 x 16 ¹/₂ x 8 in. (22.9 x 41.9 x 20.3 cm)

Collection of Dr. Elizabeth McLean

KLATLE-BHI (CHUCK SAM)

b. 1966, Alert Bay, Vancouver Island, British Columbia;
lives in North Vancouver, British Columbia

Moon Mask, 2005 *

Red cedar, acrylic paint
Diam. 21 in., D. 6 ½ in. (53.3 x 16.5 cm)

Courtesy of Douglas Reynolds Gallery

MAYNARD JOHNNY, JR.

b. 1973, Campbell River, British Columbia;
lives in Duncan, British Columbia

"I have been inspired by contemporary artists
such as Robert Davidson and Susan Point, and
also my father, who carved in wood. Tradition
to me is like expression, and it tells our history.
Tradition reflects who we are. I believe that art is
a reflection of who I am and where I come from."

Soaring Moon Drum Pendant,
2002

Deerskin, acrylic paint
Diam. 3 in. (7.6 cm)

Courtesy of Alcheringa Gallery

*Only in the catalogue; another work by this artist is in the exhibition.

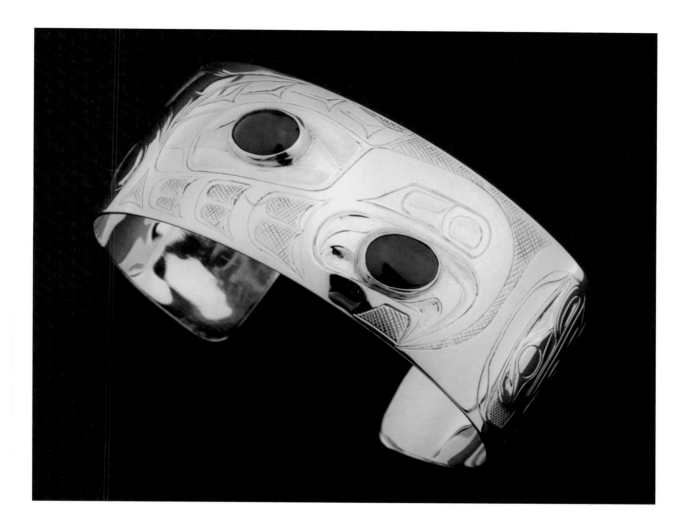

CHRIS COOK

b. 1971, Alert Bay, Vancouver Island, British Columbia;
lives in Victoria, British Columbia

"When I began making art, I chose not to work with ceremonial objects. The figures that I have chosen to create within my artwork do not contain ancient demons. My ongoing goal is to draw on symbols of balance, peace, and humor from my traditions so that those who wear my artwork will be positively affected."

Thunderbird Bracelet, 2001

14k gold, garnet
1 x 2¹/₂ x 2 in.
(2.5 x 6.4 x 5.1 cm)

National Museum of
the American Indian—
Smithsonian Institution

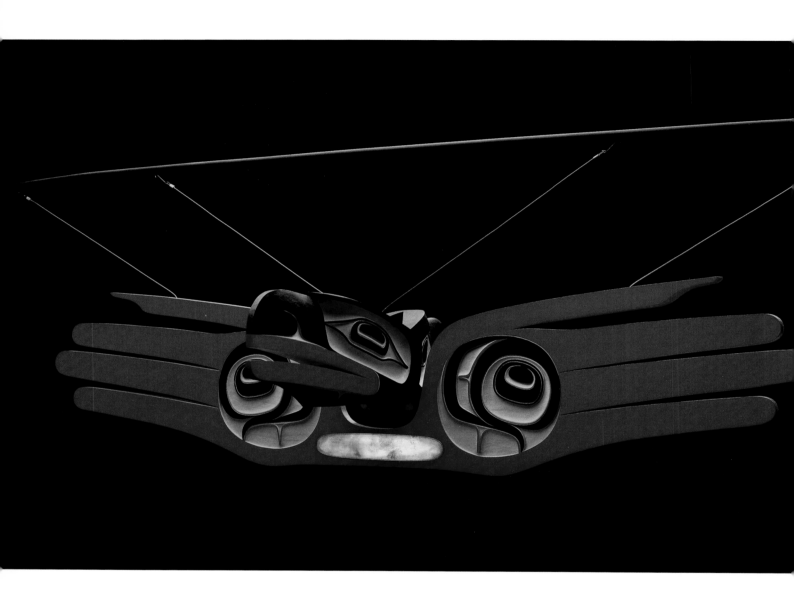

ROBERT DAVIDSON

b. 1946, Hydaburg, Alaska; lives in Surrey, British Columbia

"Haida ideas had been developing for millennia, until the process came abruptly to almost a complete stop after contact with the *yaatz xaa.adee* (the iron people). Since that time, the thread that has kept us linked to our cultural past is nature. But now nature is being destroyed by deforestation of the land and by the destruction of life in the ocean. What will be the long-term consequences of razing the land so it lies barren? What will be the long-term consequences of plundering the ocean so it is empty of all life?"

Hugging the World, 1999

Yellow cedar, copper inlay, acrylic paint
H. 7 1/2 in., W. 17 1/4 in.,
L. 38 3/4 in. (19 x 43.8 x 98.4 cm)

Collection of the artist

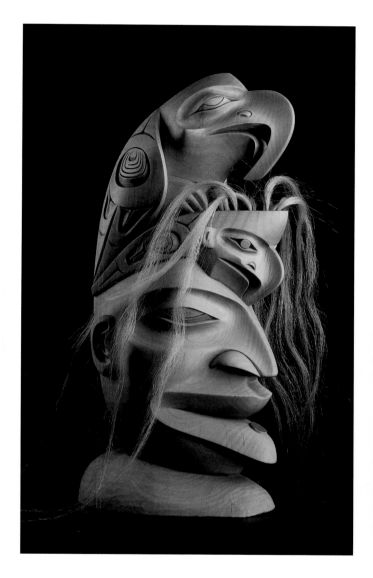

DEMPSEY BOB

b. 1948, Telegraph Creek, British Columbia;
lives in Terrace, British Columbia

"Our art has to evolve, otherwise it will die. The old master artists carved bone, copper, gold, horn, ivory, silver, stone, and wood. My great-grandfather was a carver, and if he were carving today he would have 'gone to town' with all the new tools and materials. I often wonder where the art would be today if our people did not do carving for all those years."

LEFT
Eagles, 2003

Alder wood, horsehair
21 x 8 x 9 in. (53.3 x
20.3 x 22.9 cm)

Private collection

RIGHT
Eagles Bronze, 2003

Bronze, horsehair
21 x 8 x 9 in. (53.3 x
20.3 x 22.9 cm)

Private collection

KEN MOWATT

b. 1944, Hazelton, British Columbia; lives in Hazelton

"Sophie Mowatt, my grandmother, was my inspiration, not only by her incredible talent for storytelling but also by her ability to survive an overwhelming non-Native culture. Tradition is a journey, it does not change who you are. The old traditions, protocols, legacies, oral teachings, and language are slowly disappearing today. I find it very important for the younger artists to be diligent and investigate the visions of our elders who are still with us. Let art express the universality of our culture."

Egret Sculpture, 2002

Red cedar, yellow cedar, birch, copper, abalone, glass beads, acrylic paint
18 x 18 x 9 in. (45.7 x 45.7 x 22.9 cm)

Collection of Dr. M. Jane Smith, Gitxsan Nation

DENNIS ALLEN

b. 1935, Shelton, Washington;
lives on Skokomish Reservation, Washington

"I like walking and hiking in the woods here,
and I have seen birds pretend to be injured and
drag their wings on the ground in an attempt
to distract me from their nearby young. Ravens
are especially protective of the young birds.
In this design, inspired by my son Andy Wilbur
Peterson, the young ravens' eyes peer out at
the tail and wings of the parent."

Raven Panel, 2003

Red cedar, acrylic paint
Diam. 26 in., D. 1 in.
(66 cm x 2.5 cm)

Courtesy of The Legacy Ltd.

BRADLEY HUNT

b. 1946, Bella Bella, British Columbia;
lives in Gibsons, British Columbia

"A long time ago, my people believed that to live
on earth was to live in harmony with nature. Like
strips of cedar woven together in a basket, my
people understood the interconnection of all life.
They knew that if even one strand was allowed
to unravel, the whole creation would fall apart.
My elders in Bella Bella have taught me that it is
paramount to our survival to protect our natural
environment and respect the lives of the animals
that share it with us. My art serves as a reminder
of the significant role these animals played in
the everyday lives of my people and that the
connection between us has not yet been lost."

Heiltsuk Butterfly, 2004

Red cedar, acrylic paint
Diam. 21 in., D. 2 in.
(53.3 x 5.1 cm)

Collection of the artist

PRESTON SINGLETARY

b. 1963, San Francisco, California; lives in Seattle, Washington

"My definition of beauty in the context of this show is the codes and symbols that have survived the generations at great odds. They are the forms and shapes of this continent. They represent the people and the great care and love that they create in their work. Each piece will represent tribe, family, and history, on a deeply personal level."

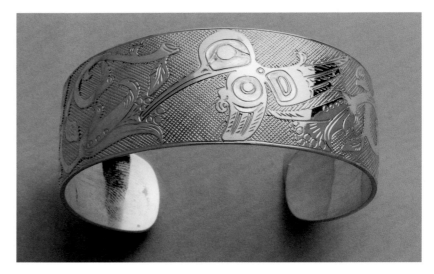

VALERIE MALESKU

b. 1953, Williams Lake, British Columbia; lives in Queen Charlotte Islands (Haida Gwaii), British Columbia

Raven Earrings, 2004

14k gold
each 1 x 1/2 in. (2.5 x 1.3 cm)

Courtesy of Douglas Reynolds Gallery

NORMAN TAIT

b. 1941, Kincolith, British Columbia;
lives in Surrey, British Columbia

Bracelet, 2004

Sterling silver
1 1/8 x 2 1/2 x 2 in.
(2.9 x 6.4 x 5.1 cm)

Private collection

JOHN MARSTON

b. 1978, Duncan, British Columbia;
lives in Ladysmith, British Columbia

"The thought of my ancestors living day-to-day
life for thousands of years on the same beach I
now walk inspires me to continue our traditions.
Carving has always been around me, since I can
remember. The most familiar smell? Cedar in
the morning! My art is based on nature, but
the main imagery comes from tradition. Basic
shapes, cuts, relief, and sculpture—this is all
based on carving techniques that have been
taught to me. Clean, soft, flowing shapes,
relative elements brought together to form
one piece—to me, this is beauty."

Creation Story Bentwood Chest,
2003

Yellow cedar, abalone
17 x 26 x 15 in. (43.2 x
66 x 38.1 cm)

Private collection

JERRY JACOB LAKTONEN

b. 1951, Kodiak Island, Alaska;
lives in Granite Falls, Washington

Puffin Man, 2004

Red cedar, red cedar bark (cape
by Lisa Telford), maple, abalone,
dentalium shells, feathers, glass
beads, horsehair, fiber-optic glass
overall 59 x 58 x 8 ¹/₂ in.
(149.9 x 147.3 x 21.6 cm);

Courtesy of Home & Away Gallery

KERI ATAUMBI

b. 1971, Lander, Wyoming; lives in Santa Fe, New Mexico

"My work is the meeting ground for my inner and outer worlds. The content directly relates to the progression of realizing myself. Our experience as human beings is conveyed through the equivalent use of content and form. Perhaps the part of us that is human responds to the content or images of the work, while it is the part of us that we refer to as 'being' that responds to the form. It is the place between 'human' and 'being' that interests me."

Tah'lee's Parents, 2004

Sterling silver, 24k gold, peridot stones
L. 22 in. (55.9 cm)

Heard Museum

RICHARD HUNT

b. 1951, Alert Bay, Vancouver Island, British Columbia; lives in Victoria, British Columbia

Flower Blowing in the Wind on Box Lid, 2003

Yellow cedar, red cedar, abalone, operculum shells, acrylic paint
22 x 21 x 7 in. (55.9 x 53.3 x 17.8 cm)

Private collection

MARY LONGMAN

b. on Gordon Reserve, Saskatchewan; lives in Merritt, British Columbia

"The subject matter of my work is always evolving as I evolve; it is contextual to the influences in my life, as a First Nations person, whether it is political or personal. It is my belief that the human story of life is what connects hearts and people. I see my exhibitions as an opportunity for the viewer to bear witness to my story directly and perhaps make meaning in their own lives.

"At the same time, my work is a continuation of the creative expressions of my ancestors whose work reflected their time and place, their current realities, from within their cultural context of beliefs, values, philosophy and customs. My work reflects this perpetual continuum of artistic practice. Today my work will be defined as contemporary. Tomorrow, when my life has passed, my work will be defined as traditional and another contemporary artist will have taken my place, with new creative expressions."

Thunderbird Nest, 1999–2005 *

Wood, stones, Matrix G
(gypsum casting material),
willow branches
29 7/8 x 28 3/8 x 23 5/8 in.
(75.9 x 72.1 x 60 cm)

Collection of the artist

*Only in the catalogue; another work by this artist is in the exhibition.

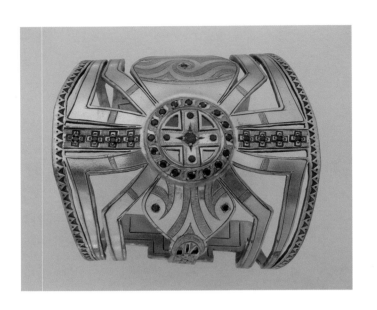

KENNETH JOHNSON

b. 1967, Lubbock, Texas; lives in Santa Fe, New Mexico

Spider Cuff Bracelet, 2003

Copper, black diamonds, ruby
3 x 2 ¹/₈ x 2 in.
(7.6 x 5.4 x 5.1 cm)

Collection of Janice Moody

KERI ATAUMBI

b. 1971, Lander, Wyoming; lives in Santa Fe, New Mexico

Martini Purse, 2004

Sterling silver, 14k gold,
diamonds, smoked buckskin,
beads
3 ¹/₂ x 5 ¹/₂ x 1 ¹/₂ in.
(8.9 x 14 x 3.8 cm)

Collection of the artist

FRANZ KAHALE

b. 1959, Honolulu, Hawai'i; lives in Mount View, Hawai'i

"Although I am not fluent in my native tongue and did not practice Hawaiian religion growing up, my household's atmosphere was definitely Hawaiian. At present, you might say that I am on a path of self-rediscovery that is making its way into my artwork. When I hear the term 'traditional art,' I automatically think of deities, tiki carving, jewelry, tattoo, weaponry, functional craft, and work on natural fiber. Although I do incorporate the use of natural fiber at times and use traditional characters from Hawaiian legends in my subject matter, the mediums I use are generally non-traditional."

Lauhala, 2004
Ceramic, glaze
13 x 15 x 14 in. (33 x 38.1 x 35.6 cm)
Collection of the artist

VICTORIA ADAMS

b. 1950, Oakland, California; lives in Santa Fe, New Mexico

*Red Bird and Morning Star
Hunt for Horses*, 2004

Sterling silver, 18k gold, spiny oyster, Carrico Lake turquoise, fossil palm wood, red coral, mother-of-pearl
L. of necklace: 13 in. (33 cm);
L. of each earring: 2 3/4 in. (7 cm)

Collection of the artist

LUKE MARSTON

b. 1976, Duncan, British Columbia;
lives in Ladysmith, British Columbia

"I define tradition as a way of life, a certain way that things should be done. This plays a big role in my art. There are traditional shapes and forms that make up Salish art, and after these are understood they can be arranged in different patterns to create feathers, scales, eyes, etc. This tells who I am and where my family comes from."

Bentwood Box with Butterfly Design, 2003

Red cedar, acrylic paint
20 x 14 1/2 x 14 1/2 in. (50.8 x 36.8 x 36.8 cm)

Courtesy of Alcheringa Gallery

KEVIN POURIER

b. 1968, Rapid City, South Dakota; lives in Scenic, South Dakota

Butterfly Spoon, 2002

Buffalo horn, mother-of-pearl,
earth pigment
3 1/2 x 12 x 2 1/2 in. (8.9 x 30.5 x
6.4 cm)

Private collection

PAHPONEE

b. 1958, Rural Prairie, Missouri; lives in Elizabeth, Colorado

Pretty Pond, 2004

White natural clay
Diam. 23 1/2 in., D. 2 3/4 in.
(55.9 cm x 7 cm)

Collection of the artist

NATHAN HART

b. 1961, Marion, Kansas; lives in Oklahoma City, Oklahoma

"We have the work of four generations of Cheyenne bead workers in my family. My decision to become an artist was influenced by their creativity and cultural preservation. I also envisioned the traditions and lifestyles of earlier generations and sought a way to renew their cultural expression. The origins of my Cheyenne heritage suggest a culture whose everyday life utilized the materials of wood and clay. I want to embrace these pre-migration traditions, yet move the medium of wood beyond utilitarian origins and into the realm of contemporary art."

Turned and Inlaid Bowl, 2005

Red maple burl, catlinite, rosewood
H. 7 1/2 in., Diam. 12 1/4 in.
(19.1 x 31.1 cm)

Private collection

PAHPONEE

b. 1958, Rural Prairie, Missouri; lives in Elizabeth, Colorado

"Each pottery vessel I make is designed to tell a story. Using clay minerals and pigments from many geographical locations allows me to create a variety of different clay mixtures. Each time I carve the 'white buffalo,' I remember the actual physical beauty of this animal. For me, the spiritual qualities of this animal are numerous, but one in particular that stands out is the feeling I wanted to convey in *New Age* (a time of transformation)."

OPPOSITE
New Age, 2003

White natural clay
H. 26 in., Diam. 16 in.
(66 x 40.6 cm); H. of lid: 8 in.,
Diam. of lid: 11 in. (20.3 x
27.9 cm)

Collection of the artist

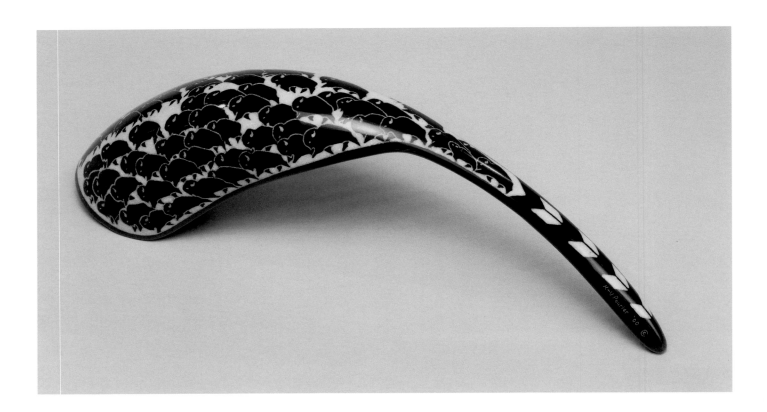

KEVIN POURIER

b. 1968, Rapid City, South Dakota; lives in Scenic, South Dakota

White Buffalo Spoon, 2003

Buffalo horn, mother-of-pearl
9 x 11 x 3 in. (22.9 x 27.9 x 7.6 cm)

Collection of Gloria Ury

CAROL EMARTHLE DOUGLAS

b. 1959, Oklahoma City, Oklahoma; lives in Seattle, Washington

"My baskets are what I call contemporary/traditional. Using non-traditional materials while using time-honored techniques, I began to develop my own style by using non-traditional colors along with unusual shapes to create baskets that are 'art objects' rather than being strictly utilitarian."

The Hunt, 2003

Hemp, Irish waxed linen thread
H. 4^1/2 in., Diam. 13 in.
(11.4 x 33 cm)

Collection of Lynn and
Marc Appelbaum

RICK BARTOW

b. 1946, South Beach, Oregon; lives in South Beach

Dog Pack Series (#1, 2, and 3), 2003
#1: Mixed woods, nails, screws, paint,
17 x 23 x 7 in. (43.2 x 58.4 x 47.8 cm)

#2: Mixed woods, nails, screws,
21 x 27 x 9 in. (53.3 x 68.6 x 23 cm)

#3: Mixed woods, nails, lead mask, tar
27 x 40 x 13 in. (68.6 x 101.6 x 33 cm)

Private collection

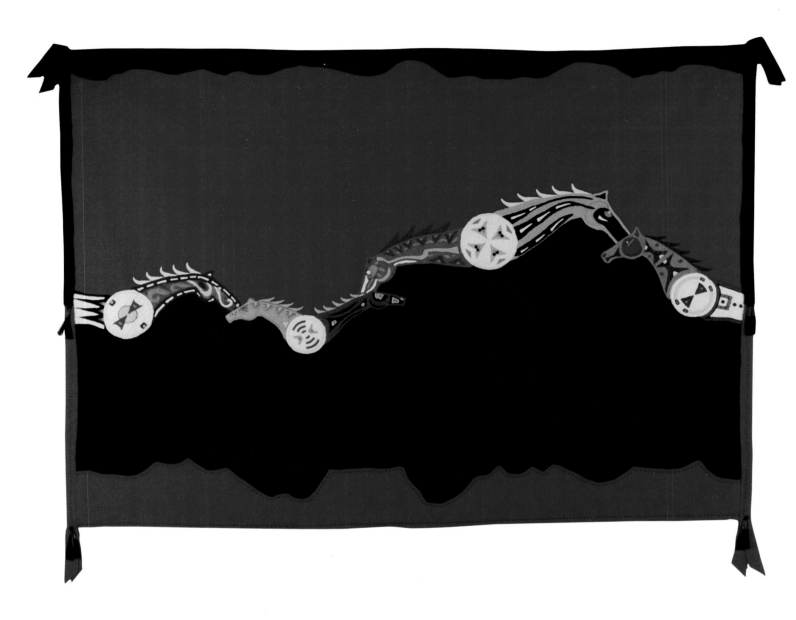

MOLLY MURPHY

b. 1977, Great Falls, Montana; lives in Missoula, Montana

Six Horses Courting Blanket,
2005

Commercial woven wool, glass
beads, horsehair, store-bought
trim, brass cones
50 x 80 x 1 in. (127 x 203.2 x
2.5 cm)

Collection of the artist

MARGARET ROACH WHEELER

b. 1943, Sisseton, South Dakota; lives in Joplin, Missouri

"My heritage is an integral part of my artistry. Incorporating traditional weaving techniques with my fine-arts training, I create contemporary garments, 'art for the body,' that are a fusion of past and present. My work is a new interpretation of ancient traditions and recognizes clothing as an expressive cultural art form.

"I am a very unconventional weaver. I approach my weavings as an artist approaches a canvas. I lay several colors in my warps and let the eye mix them together, as the Impressionists did with their paint. I have always used my heritage as a subject matter for my artwork. It has been my identity."

Forest Dweller: The Bear, 1998

Silk/wool yarn, copper, sterling silver, deer antler, deer teeth, gray goose feathers
72 x 20 in. (182.9 x 50.8 cm)

Collection of the artist

SUSIE SILOOK

b. 1960, Gambell, St. Lawrence Island, Alaska;
lives in Anchorage, Alaska

Sedna with Mask, 1999

Ivory, seal whiskers, baleen,
whalebone
13 x 1 1/2 x 3 1/2 in. (33 x 3.8 x 8.9 cm)

Collection of Thomas G. Fowler

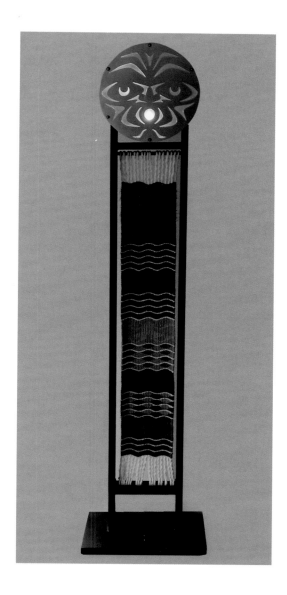

BILL GLASS, JR.

b. 1950, Tahlequah, Oklahoma; lives in Locust Grove, Oklahoma

"I'm having fun with my work, doing things that I enjoy, working with ideas that I can relate to, with as much quality and craftsmanship that I can muster. My work is created from red Georgia clay, using contemporary and traditional techniques. Along with all the demanding aspects of working with the clay, I have continued to research the Southeast Woodland culture through the historic and prehistoric Temple Mound period. These ancient motifs provide an art basis from which the Cherokee people are culturally related. Through the study of this art, we can retain our rich and colorful tribal heritage, knowledge, and worldviews. My tribe's southeast roots will continue to influence my work and life."

ED ARCHIE NOiSECAT

b. 1958, Canim Lake, British Columbia; lives in Santa Fe, New Mexico

SUSAN PAVEL

b. 1968, Milwaukee, Wisconsin; lives on Skokomish Nation, Washington

"I love that I get to resurrect and strengthen the indigenous weaving style among our people. I love being moved by the spirit of weaving. It is my hope that my love of weaving will touch and inspire you as well."

—Susan Pavel

Winter Moon, 2004

Wool, copper, steel, lightbulb,
lighting apparatus
72 x 15 x 15 in. (182.9 x 38.1 x 38.1 cm)

Collection of Sonosky, Chambers,
Sachse, Endreson & Perry, LLP

Flying Canoe, 2001

Alluvial clay, glaze
H. 14⅛ in., Diam. 9½ in.
(35.9 x 24 cm)

Collection of Barry Coffin

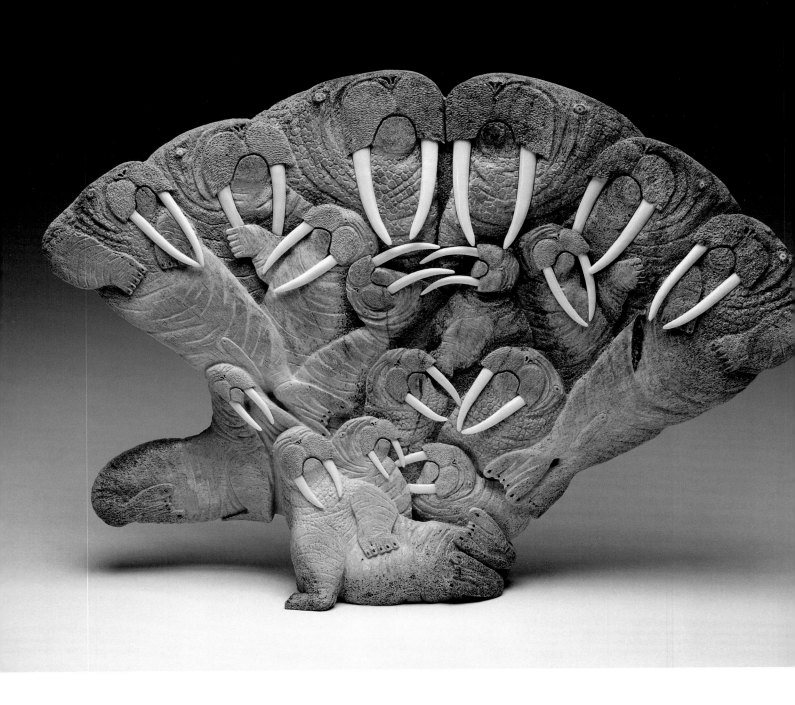

FREDERICK KINGEEKUK

b. in Savoonga, St. Lawrence Island, Alaska; lives in Savoonga

Untitled (Group of Walrus),
2001

Whale scapula, walrus ivory
16 3/4 x 23 7/8 x 5 1/8 in.
(42.5 x 60.6 x 13 cm)

Anchorage Museum of
History and Art

MAYNARD WHITE OWL LAVADOUR

b. on Umatilla Indian Reservation, Oregon;
lives in Pendleton, Oregon

Purse, 2003

Glass beads, metallic beads,
tanned hide
10¹/₄ x 6¹/₂ in. (38.1 x 16.5 cm);
L. of strap: 10 in. (25.4 cm)

Private collection

LILLIAN PITT

b. 1943, Warm Springs, Oregon; lives in Portland, Oregon

"I love the challenge of creating new works,
always with my culture in mind, as in the salmon
rattle. I love copper, grids, and salmon."

Fish Rattle, 2003

Copper, aluminum, paint
10 x 8 x 5 in. (25.4 x
20.3 x 12.7 cm)

Collection of the artist

LISA MARIE DAVID

b. 1969, *Seattle, Washington; lives in Bremerton, Washington*

"Back in my childhood, I remember being in all the great carvers' workshops, watching and listening to all the different master carvers of that time. I grew up rich in the cultures of both of my parents. They are artists, perfectionists, the best at whatever it is they put their hands to. I grew up at the powwows listening to the heart of the drums and the pride of the Plains people. Both of my parents inspire me, Sandra Lee Tuifua and Hyacinth Joe David."

Sea Devil Design Button Blanket, 2001

Melton wool, mother-of-pearl buttons
47 x 59 in. (119.4 x 150 cm)

Collection of the artist; courtesy of Inuit Gallery of Vancouver

KEN McNEIL

b. 1961, Prince Rupert, British Columbia;
lives in Terrace, British Columbia

"After learning the basics of technique and form,
I was inspired by how superior our forefathers
were, taking the art form from primitive forms to
technical wonders. This achievement has helped
me to strive for my own idea of perfection in my
work. Anyone who studies our traditional art
will see that it has evolved through innovation.
If I can put honor and respect into each piece I
create, the beauty will follow."

Octopus Mask, 2004

Alder, horsehair, acrylic paint
14 x 10 x 6 in. (35.6 x 25.4 x 15.2 cm)

Collection of Court and Meg Clara, in
memory of Courtney and Ellamay Clara;
courtesy of Inuit Gallery of Vancouver

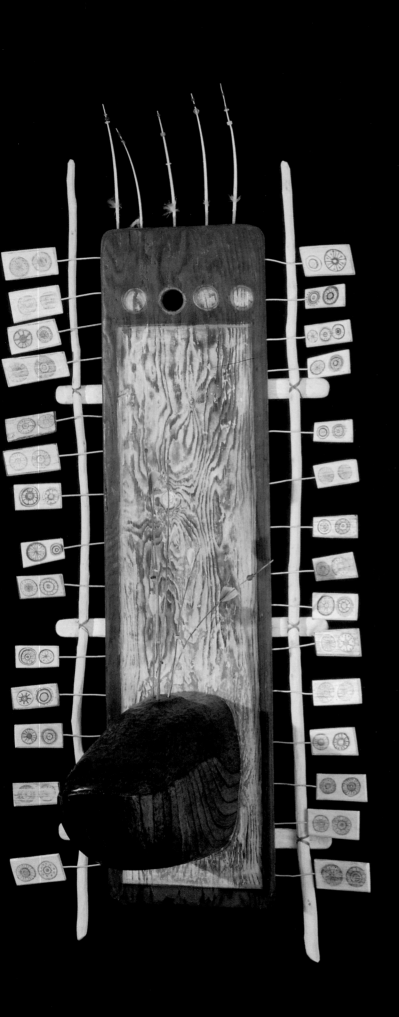

LENA AMASON

b. 1976, Kodiak Island, Alaska; lives in Old Harbor, Alaska

"The materials and imagery that I use relate to my objective of making a connection between the past and present cultures of the people of Kodiak."

Whale, 2003

Wood, baleen, electrical wire, acrylic, feathers

55 x 14 x 25 in. (139.7 x 35.6 x 63.5 cm)

Collection of the artist

DENISE WALLACE

b. 1957, Seattle, Washington; lives in Hilo, Hawai'i

Transformation Seal with Removable Baby brooch, 2004

Silver, fossilized walrus tusks
open 4¼ x 5⅛ x 1⅜ in. (10.8 x 3.5 x 13 cm)

Collection of Dolores Schapiro

SYLVESTER AYEK

b. 1940, King Island, Alaska; lives in Anchorage, Alaska

"I think we are in a generation where we have a lot to do with preserving, teaching and sharing our traditional ways with the young people in our respected villages not only as hunters and gatherers but as visual artists while at the same time getting into contemporary forms, showing the young people that it is possible to be an artist in any generation rather than becoming too repetitious in traditional forms. It is only appropriate to experiment with traditional forms in times of using modern materials and tools."

Seal's Breath, 2004

Walrus ivory, baleen, fossil ivory
6 x 4 x 4¼ in. (15.2 x 10.2 x 10.8 cm)

Collection of Alice Rogoff Rubenstein

VALERIE MORGAN

b. 1961, *Alert Bay, Vancouver Island, British Columbia;*
lives in Kitwanga, British Columbia

"What I've come to realize more and more, when studying art, creating art, or just thinking about art, is the importance of legends. Legends convey from my past a close relationship of our people with their environment and the animal kingdom."

Crest: Frog Design, 2001

Melton wool, spandex, buttons
as shown 50 x 59 in. (127 x
149.9 cm)

Collection of the artist

JESSE BRILLON

b. 1972, *Prince Rupert, British Columbia; lives in*
Skidegate, Queen Charlotte Islands (Haida Gwaii),
and in Hazelton, British Columbia

"Each piece that I create is imbued with feelings and power released during the creative process. My sentiment offers the carved item the power to protect its owner and shine a bright light toward good luck and fortune."

Eagle, 2004

20k gold
Diam. 2 in., D. $\frac{1}{4}$ in.
(5.1 x 0.6 cm)

Courtesy of Coastal Peoples Fine Arts Gallery

SHAWN HUNT

b. 1975, *Vancouver, British Columbia;*
lives in Gibsons, British Columbia

"I am inspired by life and the world around me.
Becoming an artist was not a conscious decision
for me. The choice was not whether or not I
would become an artist, but in what way would
I choose to express myself. I would not say that
my work is 'traditional'; however, tradition is the
origin, it is the foundation that creation is built
on. Although my work does not appear to be
traditional, without it my work would be without
context. I could not create new forms and
express new ideas without first studying what
has already been done."

The Gathering, 2005

Sterling silver
2 7/8 x 1 5/8 x 2 in.
(7.3 x 4.1 x 5.1 cm)

Collection of the artist

MARCEL RUSS

b. 1973, *Queen Charlotte Islands (Haida Gwaii),*
British Columbia; lives in Vancouver, British Columbia

Wasco Pendant, 2004

Argillite, yew wood, sterling
silver, abalone
4 1/2 x 2 1/4 x 2 in.
(114 x 5.7 x 5.1 cm)

Collection of John and Joyce Price;
courtesy of Inuit Gallery of Vancouver

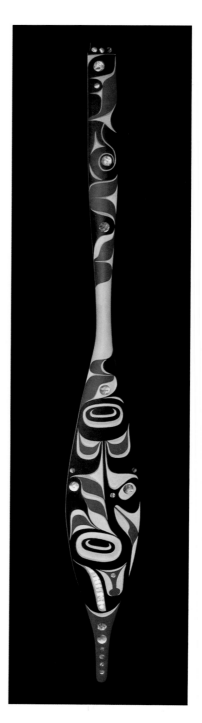

JOHN MARSTON

b. 1978, Duncan, British Columbia;
lives in Ladysmith, British Columbia

Salmon Cycle Storage Box, 2003

Red cedar, abalone, operculum,
acrylic paint
24 x 13 1/2 x 13 1/2 in. (61 x
34.3 x 34.3 cm)

Private collection

MORRIS "MOY" SUTHERLAND

b. 1974, *Ahousaht, Vancouver Island, British Columbia;*
lives in Victoria, Vancouver Island

Grey Whale Paddle, 2004

Yellow cedar, abalone,
acrylic paint
66 x 7 in. (167.6 x 17.8 cm)

Courtesy of Douglas Reynolds Gallery

ED ARCHIE NoiseCat

b. 1958, Canim Lake, British Columbia;
lives in Santa Fe, New Mexico

"I think tradition is everything that is established
and viable to a community. As creative and
innovative people move forward and seek out
new and exciting ways, we establish new traditions."

Spirit of the Salmon I, 2002

Salvaged red cedar, walnut,
salvaged oak, glass, river rocks
40 x 70 x 23 in. (101.6 x 177.8 x
58.4 cm)

Courtesy of John and Tawna Farmer

OTHNIEL KAʻIOULIOKAHIHIKOLOʻEHU OOMITTUK, JR.

b. 1963, Point Hope, Alaska; lives in Honolulu, Hawaiʻi

OPPOSITE
Walrus Inua, 2001–04

Oak burl, walrus ivory, baleen
8 x 9 x 18 in. (20.3 x 22.9 x 45.7 cm)

Collection of Helene Singer and Seymour Merrin

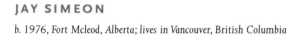

JAY SIMEON

b. 1976, Fort Mcleod, Alberta; lives in Vancouver, British Columbia

Wasco Battling Killer Whale, 2004
(profile view and front view)

22k gold, abalone
Diam. 2 in., D. 1³/₄ in. (5.1 x 4.4 cm)

Courtesy of Douglas Reynolds Gallery

RICHARD "RICK" ADKINS

b. 1955, Prince Rupert, British Columbia; lives in Vancouver, British Columbia

Frog Ring, 2004

Gold, pearl
1 x ³/₄ in. (2.5 x 1.9 cm)

Courtesy of Douglas Reynolds Gallery

ERIC ROBERTSON

b. 1959, Vancouver, British Columbia; lives in Vancouver

"[*The Hub* was made] in celebration of the eulachon. Eulachon are small fish that reproduce in the major river systems on the West Coast. Their use has maintained a substantial role in cultural exchange, trade, and commerce. This cultural exchange continues above the old intersecting travel routes known as 'Great Trails,' which are today the foundations of the provinces' major transportation highways."

—Artist's statement in brochure for exhibition at Kelowna Art Gallery, Kelowna, British Columbia, 2001

The Hub, 2001

Aluminum, copper, stainless steel
3 panels, *each* Diam. 96 ⅛ in., D. 3 ⅛ in. (244 x 8 cm)
Department of Indian and Northern Affairs Canada

Tracing Raven: A Few Fleeting Thoughts on Transformation in Contemporary Northwest Coast Art

Allan J. Ryan

The Northwest Coast of North America is a place of unparalleled beauty, where snow-covered mountains merge with dense cedar forests, and surging rivers flow down to the Pacific Ocean. According to oral tradition, indigenous peoples have inhabited the coastal inlets and islands for countless millenia, living off the bounty of the sea. In their world, the waters are sacred, and the Creator a most generous provider. Salmon, in all its many shades and varieties, is the ultimate gift of spiritual and physical sustenance. In addition to salmon, numerous other species of fish and seafood can be found in coastal waters. Traditionally, all that was required of indigenous people to maintain this constant supply of riches was a commitment to respect the strength and spirit of the rivers, and practice communal sharing and conservation.[1]

IN A RICH AND ABIDING COLLECTIVE MEMORY that stretches back some ten thousand years on the Northwest Coast, the androgynous trickster-transformer, Raven, looms larger than life. It is an imposing presence befitting a cultural hero, which in fact he/she is. Raven's pivotal place in the communal consciousness of coastal peoples cannot be overstated. His mythical exploits are legendary, preserved in a variety of local languages and passed down through generations in wondrous tales of stealing the sun, scattering the stars, and satiating a sexual appetite. In many of these tales, mischief is tempered with accidental beneficence, accounting for Raven's reputation as reluctant creator.

Raven's transformative powers contribute to his continuing appeal; his uncanny ability to alter his appearance to accommodate new circumstances and surroundings is a source of endless fascination. Even in disguise, or in new guise, Raven's restless spirit remains vigorous. This is reassuring to contemporary artists who look to Raven for inspiration and seek to stabilize cultural beliefs and values while infusing them with new life and vision. Maintaining a balance is a constant challenge.

Traditionally, the arts were given their fullest expression at great potlatch celebrations that were hosted by a prominent village family and spread out over several days during the long gray winters. On such occasions, invited guests would come from near and far in large painted dugout canoes to affirm kinship ties, exchange gifts, and witness claims to hereditary names, titles, songs, dances, stories, and economic resources such as fishing grounds and hunting territories. Feasting and grand theatrical performances were integral to such events, as ancestral encounters with supernatural beings were recounted and re-enacted in comic and dramatic presentations staged in the smoky firelight of the great cedar longhouses. In the months leading up to the potlatch, the most accomplished artists and artisans were commissioned to produce an array of ceremonial items and regalia for distribution and display. These included: painted panels, carved masks, articulated headdresses, woven garments, musical instruments, eating utensils, and bentwood storage boxes, all adorned with the anthropomorphic crests of the host family. In some villages, great totem poles of cedar were raised at this time to honor an esteemed individual. These were all made according to a strict set of iconographic rules and design principles that has evolved on the Northwest Coast over several centuries.

At the heart of this sophisticated system of heraldic representation is the free-flowing formline, an elegant and sinuous two-dimensional design element that can swell, stretch, bend, and curl back on itself, and, without warning, spring into three dimensions and dart back into two. This seemingly infinite capacity for elasticity is part of the formline's enduring appeal; it can circumscribe any shape, fill any void, cover any surface, from paddle to rattle, to mask or pole. More important, the formline can visualize and animate the mythic narratives and oral histories of the ancestors and their animal relations. In many ways, the constantly moving formline embodies Raven's adventurous and playful spirit, teasing borders, testing boundaries, and ultimately acknowledging limitations, much like the practice of Native artists.

It has been little more than two centuries since European explorers such as Captains James Cook and George Vancouver first visited the Northwest Coast and marveled at the elaborate ceremonial creations made by the local indigenous population. Interest in the socio-political function of such items was limited. Nevertheless a brisk trade soon followed, as broadcloth, metal utensils, and other European trade goods were exchanged for sea-otter pelts and a variety of ceremonial paraphernalia, which were eventually taken back to Europe for display as primitive exotica in the well-known "cabinets of curiosities." As contact and trade increased over the following decades, the broadcloth blankets were transformed into sumptuous ceremonial garments, the metal chisels and axes gave added dimension to the great poles and masks, and the bright commercial paints added greater vibrancy to ancestral forms and figures. From the early nineteenth century onward, the Haida took a leading role in the development of a market for souvenirs and cultural collectibles, fashioning an assortment of ornamental pipes, plates, poles, and small figures from argillite, a soft black slate native to their homeland of Haida Gwaii (Queen Charlotte Islands). These were embellished with a mix of hereditary crests and, in later years, Anglo-inspired designs. The art forms and regalia produced during this period of relative material affluence have come to symbolize the "pure" and "authentic" in Northwest Coast indigenous art.

By the end of the nineteenth century, Aboriginal peoples across North America were experiencing severe cultural trauma and social upheaval, and those living on the Northwest Coast were not exempt. With no immunity to European diseases, the populations of many communities suffered drastic decline, while the number of settlers encroaching on Native lands increased. Moreover, political pressure to accelerate Aboriginal assimilation into the cultural mainstream led to legislation prohibiting indigenous religious ceremonies. This shook the potlatching system to its core, as many people sold or gave away their ritual belongings or in some cases had them confiscated. Throughout those dark days, which lasted well into the twentieth century, it fell to a few individuals to preserve cultural knowledge and carving skills, among them Charles Edenshaw, Charlie James, and Mungo Martin. An untold number of now anonymous Native women also kept the textile arts alive. It was not until the mid-twentieth century, when ceremonial sanctions were lifted and cultural celebrations encouraged, that the arts began to flourish once more on the coast. Even then, the work of the nineteenth-century masters, now housed in museums, set the standards and parameters for artistic revitalization. After all, there was a "look" to authentic Northwest Coast Native art that had to be maintained. One of the people who helped transform that look—if not in form, at least in material and scale—was Haida artist Bill Reid (1920–1998). Reid inspired a generation of contemporary artists through his bold sculptural interpretations of Haida mythology in gold and silver jewelry, and large wooden carvings and bronze castings. Two of his best-known pieces are reproduced on the Canadian twenty-dollar bill: *Raven and the First Men* and *The Spirit of Haida Gwaii*. The latter, an enormous bronze boat filled with mythical figures, is set in a reflecting pool in front of the Canadian Embassy in Washington, D.C. It is polished black to resemble a giant argillite carving. Raven is steering the craft into uncharted waters.

Material Transformations

In *Changing Hands* 2, material transformations abound, and two-dimensional figures achieve three-dimensional realization in surprising new ways. For example, Reid's foremost student, Robert Davidson, now a renowned artist in his own right, isolates familiar graphic formline elements and recasts them as freestanding aluminum sculptures, such as *Meeting at the Centre* (page 117) and *Raven Calling*, both 2004. Painted red and black, respectively, in traditional Haida fashion, the thin metal sculptures allow viewers to appreciate the subtly shifting relationships of line and light from a variety of angles and changing perspectives. Benjamin Davidson, like his father, Robert, with whom he apprenticed for four years, also shows a fondness for isolating design elements and employing verbal/visual punning. Both these characteristics are evident in his carved wooden panel whimsically titled *Two U's Don't Always Make a Double-U*. However, his *Killer Whale* crest, 2004 (page 90), is playful in a different manner. With its dark patina and distinctive iconography—heavy eyebrows, thick lips, and signature dorsal fin—it has the weighty appearance of bronze but is in fact made of cast resin. On the Northwest Coast, transformations can be deceiving; they can also be transparent, as with Dempsey Bob's twin sculptures, both 2003 (pages 195). This Tahltan artist provides a double vision of the same eagle mask: *Eagles*, a sumptuously carved composite figure highlighting the alder wood's

warm golden grain, and *Eagles Bronze*, a polished bronze casting of the same figure, here recalling the argillite carvings from the nineteenth century as well as ebony figurines and Benin dynasty bronzes from Africa. In each version, thin strands of white hair flow down from the crown of a tiny forehead masquette, contrasting with the sculpture's fixed, more formal facial features. Larry Rosso is also represented in the exhibition by a cast crest mask, *Grizzly Bear*, 2002 (page 91), but unlike Davidson and Bob, he has shaped his mask from paper, a medium generally reserved for two-dimensional depictions. It is a dramatic image both firm and fragile, portraying a mythic animal caught in the act of transformation. The bear is not so much emerging from as climbing through the white paper panel from another temporal dimension, like a ghostly apparition.

Perhaps the most surprising transformative medium to be explored by coastal artists in recent years is glass—cut, cast, sandblasted, fused, and even painted. On reflection, this development should not seem so surprising. The Northwest Coast potlatch has long been home to visual artists who skillfully manipulate light and shadow to create the illusion of presence, the appearance of substance. Is this not what glass artists strive to do? Surely, their work extends the historic theatrical tradition as much as it perpetuates and reinvigorates the graphic and plastic arts. Still, the artists seem to have only scratched the surface.

Two individuals at the forefront of the new art glass movement are Preston Singletary and Marvin Oliver. At times, Singletary's fused and sandblasted pieces seem to be more about material transference than transformation, so closely do they replicate the shapes and patterns of traditional objects, as in his *Shaman's Amulet*, 2001, *Bentwood Chest*, 2004, and *Oystercatcher Rattle*, 2005 (pages 159, 110, 199). Still, there is no denying their visual and tactile appeal, and the inner light and life they seem to reveal. In this case, material transference proves an effective metaphor for cultural revitalization and regeneration. Singletary's glass objects seem quietly refined when seen alongside Oliver's wildly exuberant *Raven Kachina*, 2004, a seven-foot-high sentinel fashioned from fused and cast glass that is barely contained within its rigid steel frame. It is an alien vision pulsing with restless energy and richly patterned in colors reminiscent of the brash, surrealist palette of Coast Salish artist Yuxweluptun (Lawrence Paul). As the title suggests, *Raven Kachina* is a hybrid vision, reflecting Oliver's cultural ties to both the Northwest Coast and the American Southwest. In this piece, Oliver fuses formline patterns in a manner that suggests the intricate stone-and-shell inlay found in the jewelry and freestanding kachina figures made by Pueblo silversmiths.

Transformations in Scale

Like Oliver, Coast Salish artist Susan Point incorporates a life-size portrait mask into an object perhaps more familiar to viewers on a smaller scale. Her sculpture *A Gift for Qulqulil*, 2004 (page 161), is a giant comb fashioned from red cedar and painted in the traditional manner. Like the oversize spindle whorl sculptures for which Point has become especially well-known, this piece elevates to the level of fine art the ordinary and the overlooked in traditional Salish culture. It makes monumental what was once deemed insignificant, and respectfully recognizes the cultural contributions of indigenous women. In the past, combs were often decorated with family crests and given as ceremonial gifts, to be valued and appreciated for both their symbolic and artistic merit. Point continues to work in this tradition. Arguably, just as effective a strategy for acknowledging the arts of Aboriginal women is the process of miniaturization. Following in the footsteps of Charles and Isabella Edenshaw, from whom she is descended, Primrose Adams weaves miniature spruce root hats, which are then meticulously painted with Haida crest designs by her son Alfred, and sold as pendants to both Native and non-Native consumers (page 170). As "wearable art," such creations keep alive traditional basket making and decorative techniques for a transformed and greatly expanded contemporary community.

Transformations in Communal Context

Keri-Lynn Dick, like Primrose Adams, also strives to keep traditional textiles relevant to the present through the production of her own wearable art. However, she does this by acknowledging non-tribal influences directly, embracing the mainstream with an infectious playful spirit. Nowhere is this more evident than in the pair of open-toed, high-heeled, leather shoes that she embellished with woven cedar bark and pendant miniature masks in 2003 (page 156). The shoes may not resemble traditional ceremonial footwear, but they are surely made for dancing. An equally enthusiastic engagement with popular culture can be seen in the drawings and textile arts of Sonny Assu—such as *When Raven Becomes Spider Embrace (Blanket Series #2)*, 2003 (page 44)—which draw inspiration from comic books and other forms of mass media, as well as from his Kwagiulth heritage. Assu's youthful confidence and bravado, along with several examples of his artwork, are much in evidence on his personal Web site. Like many other Web-savvy artists, his concept of community is both local and global, and he uses the Internet to build a global audience for his work.

The responsibilities that come with global citizenship are addressed by fellow Kwagiulth artist David Neel, in a series of compelling masks that treat such issues as racism, injustice, over-population, environmental abuse, and, in the *International Mask of Commerce*, 1999 (page 58), the accumulation of wealth and power by transnational corporations. Neel brings both a personal and a tribal perspective to this unsettling and highly original series, insisting that these are "traditional" masks, since innovation is part of Kwagiulth tradition. In giving the issues a human face, Neel emphasizes our common humanity and conveys the idea that, in terms of the issues symbolized, we are all implicated, Native and non-Native communities alike.

———

Nothing is more transformational than the birth of a child, and nothing more intimate, or universal, than the image of a mother and child. For Nuu-chah-nulth artist Joe David, the birth of his daughter, Marika, to him and his New Zealand-born Maori wife, Paula Swan, in 1982 was both personally and artistically transforming. The event is wonderfully commemorated in his sculpture *Mother and Child*, 2003 (page 37), which honors his daughter's dual heritage, through the Maori tribal designs painted on the pregnant mother's torso and the distinctive Nuu-chah-nulth mask, representing the face of the child about to be born. From the comfort and security of her mother's womb, the child peers out with wonder into a world full of promise and possibility. The face not only represents Marika but her father as well. For David, life is a series of continual transformations and rebirths, none of which negates any previous stage of development or personal identity. Through his daughter, David has acquired a Maori identity that will endure no matter how many further transformations he experiences.

NOTES

1. Allan J. Ryan, *Visual Voices: A Festival of Aboriginal Film and Video* (Montreal: National Film Board of Canada, 2005).

Native Hawaiian Contemporary Art: Embracing the Past/Looking to the Future

David J. de la Torre

E kō, e kō, e kō mai ana
E kō mai ana i ka lāhui o Hawai'i
E kō, E kō, E kō a mamau no na kau a kau

Sustain, sustain, sustain
Sustain the people/nation of Hawai'i
Sustain, sustain, sustain forever and for all seasons.

—chant by Kumu John Keola Lake[1]

THE INCLUSION OF NATIVE HAWAIIANS in *Changing Hands: Art Without Reservations* 2 provides a timely opportunity for re-assessing the new directions that contemporary Native Hawaiian artists have been pursuing in recent years. This exhibition sheds light on art forms that have been ignored or denied access in the past because of cultural hegemony or differing sets of aesthetic standards and disparate cultural influences. While progress has been made in opening the eyes of non-indigenous curators, academics, collectors, and critics to the art of Native peoples, the *Changing Hands* exhibition series continues this important dialogue.

Background Information

In order to grasp the current overall landscape of contemporary art among Native Hawaiians, as with other groups, it is useful to look at the combination of influences, both ancient and modern, that may have a bearing on the creative process. There are affinities between cultures where comparisons can be drawn when it comes to examining Hawai'i's current contemporary art scene. These similarities are often associated with ritual ideologies that have their foundation in nature and the environment.

Before the arrival of European explorers, most notably Captain James Cook in 1778, the indigenous people derived their appreciation of beauty through sacred relationships centered on a pantheon of deities. Hawaiians believed that gods could be found everywhere, and that they took on many shapes. Objects serving utilitarian and ritual needs were skillfully crafted from stone, plants, shells, human hair, and bones (see fig. 1). Canoe making and voyaging activities became central to the way of life of the people of Hawai'i, a theme that is often referred to in contemporary art. Dance, storytelling, and music traditions have also crossed over to affect the form and content of the visual arts. Evident in

FIG. 1. Feather-covered basketry image. *'Ie'ie* aerial rootlets, human hair, mother-of-pearl, wood, dog-tooth incisors, *olonā* netting, red *'i'iwi* and yellow *'ō'ō* feathers; 20¹/₂ x 8³/₁₆ x 12¹/₄ in. (52.2 x 20.8 x 31 cm). Courtesy of Bernice Pauahi Bishop Museum (inv. no. 24).

much recent Native Hawaiian art is a dialogue between tradition and innovation that in some works is transparent and in others represents deeper, subtle inferences in need of interpretation.

Rocky Ka'iouliokahihikolo'ehu Jensen, for example, has devoted his artistic career to preserving and documenting ancient cultural traditions through his challenging contemporary interpretations of sacred art forms; see, for example, his *Hinahanaiakamalama*, 2004 (page 51). As a sculptor working primarily in wood and stone, Jensen has a deep respect for the spiritual roots of Native Hawaiian culture as well as the empowering energy that he derives from his work as a cultural practitioner and artist. Influenced by ancient reliquary forms, his sculpture promotes a greater understanding of complex ancestral and ritual ideologies.

For Native Hawaiians, there are distinct differences that add to their uniqueness as a culture and that set them apart from other indigenous groups. Among these distinctions, the isolation of the Hawaiian Islands, as Adrienne Kaeppler points out, is important historically and remains significant today in terms of the artistic product:

> Unlike other Pacific island groups, which often had contact and trade amongst themselves, the Hawaiian Islands may well have been isolated from external influences for as long as 500 years prior to European contact, i.e., ocean-going voyages between Hawai'i and Southern Polynesia apparently ceased. Thus, the objects collected in Hawai'i on Cook's third voyage exhibit an "end point" in the material culture that is rare in world ethnology, having been derived from ancestral styles brought from the Marquesas and Society Islands without further outside influence.[2]

There are many deeply rooted historical religious and societal factors that continue to influence Native Hawaiian artists. Among the most important are beliefs in Creation and the ancient class systems. For example, *mana*, the life force or spiritual power that underlies Creation, is believed to be present in all material objects. The ancient systems of division that provided for an *ali'i* (Hawaiian royalty) thought to be descended from the gods have been revived and remain prominent today in storytelling, mythology, and the visual arts. Love of *'āina* (the land) or of *kai* (the sea) cannot be overlooked as highly significant inspirational influences for artistic expression of all kinds. Factors such as these must be considered in order to have a thorough understanding of the current art scene in Hawai'i and to avoid generalizing about Native Hawaiians and their relationship within the rich fabric of Native American art.

Interested in anthropology and writing, Kapulani Landgraf creates richly poetic, provocative installations and mixed-media works, often focusing on contemporary ecological, cultural and economic issues. She often juxtaposes photographic images with *kapa* (mulberry bark cloth) and metal objects such as nails, fishhooks, and lead weights to make powerful statements about protecting and preserving Hawaiian language and traditional knowledge of the land and sea, as in her *Make i ke kai hohonu* (*Death in the Deep Sea*), 2001 (page 66). Landgraf and others have worked proactively to change the themes of loss within Hawaiian culture to themes of resistance and cultural survival.

When most Americans think of Hawai'i, they are unaware of its unique, complex history. A few years after the British takeover of New Zealand, an incident in Hawai'i in 1843 enabled the British to make the islands a British colony, if only briefly. Subsequently, between 1848 and 1893, a strong rivalry existed between British and American interests as certain ali'i pursued British favor and religion. The French takeover of Tahiti and the Marquesas during this period made the ali'i and Americans in the Hawaiian islands very nervous. In 1848, the *Mahele* (great land division) opened up the opportunity for economic control by non-Hawaiians. Then, in 1850, foreigners gained rights to purchase and own land there. American Calvinist missionaries prominently positioned in the government and prosperous missionary-descendant merchants moved to stage a coup in 1893. These events ultimately led to the annexation of Hawai'i by the United States in 1900 and to its becoming a U.S. territory in 1901.

However, prior to foreign exploration and intervention, the Hawaiian Islands were a sovereign nation and royal kingdom. Indeed, Hawai'i is the only state in the union with a historic residence that housed a royal family, 'Iolani Palace (fig. 2). Native Hawaiians are keenly aware and proud of their monarchical past. Artists Paulette Nohealani Kahalepuna and Natalie Mahina Jensen-Oomittuk,

FIG. 3. 'Ukulele, by David Mahelona. *Koa* wood, mother-of-pearl, brass, plastic, cat gut; 20 5/8 x 5 7/8 x 2 7/16 in. (52.4 x 14.8 x 6.2 cm). Courtesy of Bernice Pauahi Bishop Museum (inv. no. 164).

for example, use mallard duck-tails, peacock hurl, and rooster or goose feathers in their delicate featherwork modeled after lei, the traditional Hawaiian garland or necklace of flowers, and *kāhili*, the royal Hawaiian standard (see Kahalepuna's three *Hand Kāhili*, 2005, page 105, and Jensen-Oomittuk's '*Anakūkulukū*, 2004, page 127).

The legacies of beloved royal luminaries such as Queen Lili'uokalani (1838–1917), Prince Jonah Kūhiō Kalaniana'ole (1871–1922), and King David Kalākaua (1874–1891), with their respective contributions toward preservation, land protection, and cultural revival, are highly revered even to this day. Moreover, a piece of pending U.S. federal legislation, the Native Hawaiian recognition bill (also known as the Akaka bill, for its principal sponsor, Senator Daniel Akaka), if passed, may help to further recognize the sovereignty of the Hawaiian people and, in the end, may or may not assist in resolving these highly charged political issues. Currently, some Native Hawaiian artists feel a sense of urgency about making history now, in the present. Restoring the island of Kaho'olawe, for example, proved to be a practical and symbolic reclamation of land for Native Hawaiians. Also, 1993 marked one hundred years since the overthrow of the Hawaiian monarchy and this, too, marked a sense of leaving behind the theme of loss and nostalgia and moving on into a new era. The struggles for recognition, subjugation, and justice continue to provide themes in Native Hawaiian contemporary art.

Kaili Chun, mentored by renowned ceramic artist Toshiko Takaezu and master woodworker Wright Bowman, is herself both a teacher and an artist, known for large-scale conceptual installations relating to cultural domination from various viewpoints. Her beautifully crafted glass-and-wood vitrines, some with hidden interior chambers, often contain plant materials in stages of decay or objects with religious associations (see page 72), offering poignant comments on control and authority.

The Landscape of Contemporary Native Hawaiian Art

During the late 1960s and early '70s, a new appreciation for Hawaiian art and culture occurred through a movement known as the Hawaiian Cultural Renaissance. Artists and performers such as the Beamer Family, Eddie Kamae, Genoa Keawe, 'Iolani Luahine, Gabby Pahinui, and the Sons of Hawai'i became leaders and cultural icons during this period. Though deeply divided at the time over issues of definition, cultural authority, and identity, the Hawaiian

FIG. 2. The façade of 'Iolani Palace, a national historic landmark completed in 1982 by architects Thomas J. Baker, C. S. Wall, and Issac Moore. Courtesy of 'Iolani Palace.

community emerged from this period with a revitalized sense of mission and renewed commitment toward increasing public awareness, respect, and appreciation for Hawaiian culture and the arts. Renewed attention was given to music, dance, voyaging, language, social awareness, and, perhaps most important, a deep respect for the kūpuna (elderly) as conveyors of history.

Keʻalaonaonapuahīnano Campton, who says that her work is "culturally and spiritually based," has deep respect for her ancestors and lineage. She creates visual metaphors in acrylic and aluminum on canvas, as in her series ʻIke Pāpālua, 2001 (page 112), reflecting the essence of prayer inspired by images of her ancestors. Through these works, she asks them for knowledge, strength, intelligence, understanding, intuitive communication, and spiritual energy.

From a multidisciplinary point of view, the overall landscape of art and cultural activity among Native Hawaiians today is impressive, and has achieved some international recognition for its artistic quality. The overwhelming success of music with slack-key guitar and ʻukulele (see fig. 3) and especially hula dance performance (see the hula dance instruments shown in fig. 4), has had an inspiring effect on other disciplines such as filmmaking, literature, and drama. Today, work of Native artists is invariably grounded in Hawaiian experience, and the culture has been reactivated by storytelling, knowledge of the islands, genealogy, a spirit of kaona (hidden meaning), and the power of the indigenous language. This ripple effect has been due in large part to a renewed commitment to the ancient island culture by artists inspired by the effects of the Hawaiian Cultural Renaissance.

Native Hawaiian visual artists are currently engaged in self-evaluation and rejuvenation. Sponsored by the Keomailani Hanapi Foundation and the Office of Hawaiian Affairs, a conference entitled "Defining Hawaiian Art" was held on the Big Island in conjunction with the Kīlauea Cultural Festival in July 2004. Involving the core leadership of the Native Hawaiian culture and arts community and led by well-respected and mature individuals, with thoughtful input from a generation of younger artists, the participants discussed strategies for making Native Hawaiian contemporary art accessible to a broader audience. A sense of "can-do" self-determination filled the daylong event with a passion and commitment for dealing with challenges and aspiring to new levels of quality. Moreover, the panelists and audience came to the conclusion that success would depend on their own leadership in helping Hawaiian culture to realize a new phase of creativity, growth, and recognition. Essentially, the Native Hawaiian art community would need to be the catalyst for change.

FIG. 4. Coconut dance rattles; ʻulīʻulī, coconut shell, chicken feathers, cotton, silk, leaf stems, wire, trade cordage, thread, wild cana seeds. Left: H. 11 1/4 in., Diam. 8 5/8 in. (28.5 x 21.8 cm); right: H. 9 1/4 in., Diam. 8 1/2 in. (23.5 x 21.5 cm). Courtesy of Bernice Pauahi Bishop Museum (inv. no. 153).

The Dialogue between Tradition and Innovation

As with most indigenous groups worldwide, Native Hawaiians are actively engaged in preserving and gaining knowledge about their traditions and cultural roots. Some highly respected cultural practitioners, known as kumu and kūpuna, act as teachers and gatekeepers of intellectual property. Through the Hawaiian language and storytelling, skills and knowledge are passed on to people of all ages, especially the younger generations, with the aim that Hawaiian culture and bloodlines will endure and not be subservient to further Western dominance.

A classically trained sculptor, Sean Kekamakupaʻa Lee Loy Browne, in his highly refined stone and metal works, demonstrates his interest in preserving and nurturing the past. With deep respect for the mother culture, he regularly returns to the past so as to be "energized and awakened by it." His sculptures Puna/Oji-san (which means "grandparent") and Kamalei ("beloved child"), both from 2003 (pages 53, 106), refer to the life cycle of the Hawaiian ʻohana (family unit), which is of primal importance not only to Native Hawaiians but to all cultures throughout the world. The execution of these works in granite, the most difficult of stones to work, evokes the endurance and longevity of the ʻohana.

With an innate determination and respect for the ancient culture, some Native Hawaiian artists are employing unusual techniques and materials as they embark on their own, learn from others, and infuse their work with a new sense of exploration. Master teachers who work with apprentices are helping to pass on their knowledge and expertise. Other professional artists are working with Native Hawaiians enrolled in undergraduate and graduate studio-art programs at the University of Hawaiʻi at Mānoa and at the Center for Hawaiian Studies.

Bernice A. Keolamauloa oʻnalani Akamine, known for her innovative, hand-blown contemporary glasswork, works out of an active glass-making studio at the University of Hawaiʻi at Mānoa, where she received her training. Her lavalike glass sculptures, inspired by the volcano goddess, such as ʻā pele, 2001 (page 111), are peculiar yet beautiful.

Ivy Hāliʻimaile Andrade makes sculptures that evoke the ancient culture, using paper pulp, kapa (mulberry bark cloth), wood, gourds, and other materials, sometimes forming containers and womblike compositions that imply a deep respect for genealogy. One of her most recent pieces, Nā Niho ʻoki, 2005 (page 114), consists of a set of beautifully crafted weapons that she made from koa wood, thirty-two shark teeth, and hemp, arranged in a circle. Here, the shark-tooth "knives" shed their usual purpose, their function having been modified from that of utility to one of landscape. Andrade is a respected, articulate leader in the arts community and is actively involved professionally with Kamehameha Schools and the Center for Hawaiian Studies.

Even so, Native Hawaiians believe that they need to create their own educational institutions in order to perpetuate their culture. The question of whether to build new schools or cultural centers in order to advance their cause, for example, represents perhaps one of the single most important issues that contemporary Native Hawaiian artists face now and for the future. Significantly, the Office of Hawaiian Affairs has recently put forward a proposal to build a $30 million cultural center in downtown Honolulu.

The physical beauty of the Hawaiian Islands serves as a constant inspiration to visual artists, as it has done for centuries. The light, the sea, the air, and the land provide incentive and enlightenment. "Lucky to live Hawai'i" is a common saying that refers to the daily reminders of extraordinary beauty in Hawai'i's natural environment.

Artist Dean Kaahanui's surfboard pieces remind us of the ocean, its power, and its place in contemporary life. His carved, functional boards refer to nature and often include stylized markings of the sacred *honu* (sea turtle), as in his *Surfboard*, 2004 (page 160), which features a carving inspired by the legend of Hono'akea (White Turtleback Island).

Indeed, Hawai'i's tropical setting is totally unlike the gray skies of the Pacific Northwest, the foggy coastlines of Oregon or Northern California, or the snow-covered mountain peaks and stark tundra of Alaska's immense northern plains. In contrast, Hawai'i's sun-drenched beaches, blue skies, aquamarine waters, and lush, tropical vegetation have inspired not only Native Hawaiians but a never-ending succession of artists, illustrators, and designers who have come to the islands in search of this beauty. Late-eighteenth-century explorers of the islands took along draftsmen such as John Webber and Louis Choris, who illustrated and recorded the people, land, and customs. During the twentieth century, accomplished artists such as Josef Albers, Jean Charlot, Morris Graves, Georgia O'Keeffe, and Pablo O'Higgins left their own cultural legacies and artistic contributions to the crossroads of the Pacific. More recently, Native Hawaiian artists have also derived new forms of expression from the abstract works of internationally known Japanese-American artists including Satoru Abe, Isami Doi, and Tadashi Sato.

Inspired by paradise and its utopian themes, Puni Kukahiko, an art student at the University of Hawai'i at Mānoa, uses popular culture to reflect on stereotypes and images associated with Hawai'i as an international vacationland. In her installation *Lovely Hula Hands*, 2005 (page 34), she engages the viewer with a set of luscious but now slowly decaying hula girls cast in chocolate. The piece showcases the bodies of indigenous women as an object of desire and entice- ment that leads to the ultimate consumption of paradise. Her work becomes a commentary on the romantic view of "the paradise con- struct" and on the negative effects that paradise seekers have had on the tourism industry. Utilizing an image of exploited sexuality, she attempts to reclaim the power and beauty of the body and the hula image itself, with the hope of luring people into learning more about Native Hawaiian culture.

Through abstract compositions such as *Saving Our Yesterdays*, 2004 (page 115), sculptor Bob Freitas tries to achieve visual and spatial balance by juxtaposing anthropomorphic forms with hard-edged geometric forms in an effort to link the past to the future. He often contrasts carefully selected materials such as *koa*, teak, stone and steel. His tabletop series features a modular construction process

that allows different components to be substituted in order to create new images.

To be certain, contemporary Native Hawaiian artists, trained or self-taught, have been influenced by the rich legacy of artistic achievement in the Polynesian islands as well as with Melanesian and Micronesian cultures. The collections and public programs of local institutions such as the Bernice Pauahi Bishop Museum, Hawai'i State Art Museum, Honolulu Academy of Arts, and the Contemporary Museum also offer rich resources for study and cultural enrichment by practicing artists.

How Specific Historical and Traditional Materials and Techniques Are Used

Inspired by traditional works in private and public collections as well as a lively regional art scene, Native Hawaiian contemporary artists continue to use many historical and traditional materials and techniques in their work. Natural substances that reflect ancient roots, including various indigenous and introduced trees and plants, are consistently used. Contemporary artists regularly turn to fine-grained woods such as *koa*, *kukui*, *milo*, and '*ōhi'a*. Other tropical and island-grown species such as guava, *kamani*, mango, spruce, and Norfolk Island pine are used for wood turning and carving by a wide range of artists.

Early Hawaiians were masters at weaving mats, baskets, fans, cordage, and nets. The indigenous culture used the leaves of the *hala* or *pandanus* tree as well as ti-leaf and coconut fibers for weaving utilitarian objects and for adorning sacred images. Today, Native Hawaiians are helping to keep these traditions alive by using ancient weaving techniques in contemporary forms. Marques Hanalei Marzan, mentored by some of the best regional weavers, frequently works in *pandanus* leaves, which he translated into bronze in his sculpture *Contemporary Artifact*, 2001 (page 165). Lehua and Kilohana Domingo offer masterful *lau hala* hats, often incorporating breadfruit and windmill motifs—intricate, modern creations finished with brightly colored feather lei hat bands, as in their *Anoni Hats*, 2004 (page 122).

Also deeply influenced by the cultural significance and meticu- lous art of ancient weaving techniques, artist Franz Kahale used the medium of clay to depict the root structure and leaves of the *hala* tree itself, in a work entitled simply *Lauhala*, 2004 (page 205). His piece is dedicated to *ho'omanawanui*, which connotes a spirit of being steadfast, patient, courageous, and persevering.

In addition to renewing interest in mats, baskets, fans, and nets, artists have also helped to revive a new appreciation for making *kapa* or *tapa*, the traditional mulberry bark cloth used for making skirts, mantles, and sleeping covers. The work of Puanani Kanemura Van Dorpe has helped to infuse *kapa* making with a new authenticity. Through research of ancient legends and chants, she rediscovered fourteen different techniques for making *kapa*. Van Dorpe is credited with making it possible for the enormous amount of *kapa* to be made for reburials on the island of Maui. Moana K. M. Eisele makes and uses *kapa* as well as ti-leaf, handmade paper, and coconut fibers in collages reflecting her deep passion for *kapa* and *kapa*-making. Employing bamboo stamps, Moana often incorporates pre-contact hand-painted designs that show a progression from the traditional to the contemporary, but maintain the intricate, subtle repetitions of Hawaiian designs, as in *Mohala Mau* (*Forever blooming forth*), 2001 (page 108). She is also known for extensive use of dyes made from native plants.

Exploring the Widest Spectrum of Materials

Native Hawaiian contemporary artists, whether trained or self-taught, are influenced by their colleagues and mainstream counterparts who make art using a wide variety of materials, including ceramics, glass, mixed-media, painting, photography, print-making, sculpture, and textiles. Innovative uses of such materials as bamboo, cement, cotton cloth, earth, enamel, glass, metal, paper pulp, and sea grass have also surfaced lately in contemporary Native Hawaiian work.

Fiber artist Pam Kawehilani Barton, who has studied in Indonesia, Japan, and the Philippines, makes use of many of these materials, especially handmade paper and *kapa*, but not limiting herself to natural fibers. Her style is to allow inner truths to emerge through her art, working spontaneously and intuitively, allowing her materials to influence her final expression. She is inspired by nature, especially the sun, moon, rain, trees, and plants, which, through her work, become personal extensions of her self. All these aspects of her art are evident in her *Paʻipaʻinahā no Hina* (*Cape for Hina*), 2002 (page 96).

Nicole Morita uses natural and found objects that are wrapped, covered, bundled up, rolled, or woven, evoking ideas about time and memory, and about the place of tradition in contemporary society. These actions—binding, wrapping, containing—serve as metaphors for protecting Hawaiian culture and its traditions. Her use of simple, minimal forms to express these ideas is exemplified by *Wāhi* (*To Bind*), 2001 (page 102).

Keone Nunes is a tattoo artist. Like voyaging, tattooing was not practiced in Hawaiʻi for many generations and needed to be relearned. Nunes went to Samoa and Aotearoa (New Zealand) to teach himself the craft. He uses traditional tools, including the albatross bone needle called the *mōlī* and the hitting stick called the *kā*. As is apparent in his *Tattoo*, 1999 (page 121, shown in a portrait photograph by Shuzo Uemoto), Nunes incorporates traditional, family-related motifs in his tattoo art, but emphasizes modern design elements. He believes that the artform needs to grow, but is respectful of its traditional context.

Ongoing Issues and Concerns

As indigenous people, Native Hawaiian artists are challenged by issues that are similar to those that confront their Native American counterparts on the mainland. Common concerns revolve around access, appropriation, copyright, reclamation, repatriation, resources, and visibility, as well as authenticity, perpetuation of their culture, preservation of objects, and profitability. The education of youth with an appreciation for culture-driven value systems that include integrity and humility are also important subject matter for Native Hawaiian artists and their families. A sensitive, respectful protocol for the re-burial of ancestral remains often engenders thought-provoking, impassioned discussions by artists and cultural practitioners.[3]

Moreover, while Native Hawaiians have a desire to share their culture with others, they want to protect their sacred imagery from exploitation by commercialism and the media. Artists are trying to learn how to mediate between respecting their traditions and being contemporary artists. In this sense, Native Hawaiian artists find themselves at a critical moment for taking control of their situation and re-writing their history. Creating and validating this new identification, re-affirming traditions and rising to a new level of artistic achievement, will require leadership and fortitude that can only be found within the Native Hawaiian art and culture community.

ʻOnipaʻa.
Stand firm.

—motto of Queen Liliʻuokalani.[4]

NOTES

I am grateful to Kaili Chun, Hikoʻula Hanapi, Kumu John Keola Lake, and Barbara Pope for their assistance with this manuscript.

1. From the transcript for the "Defining Hawaiian Art" conference held on the Big Island in conjunction with the Kīlauea Cultural Festival, July 2004. Sponsored by the Keomailani Hanapi Foundation and the Office of Hawaiian Affairs.

2. Adrienne Kaepler, "Hawaiʻi: Ritual Encounters," in James Cook, *Gifts and Treasurers from the South Seas*, ed. Brigitta Hauser-Schaublin and Gundolf Krüger (New York: Prestel, 1998), p. 15.

3. Momi Cazimero, David J. de la Torre, and Manulani Aluli Meyer, "Nā Maka Hou: New Visions, Contemporary Native Hawaiian Art," panel discussion, Honolulu Academy of Arts, 2001.

4. Mary Kawena Pukui, *ʻŌlelo Noʻeau: Hawaiian Proverbs & Poetical Sayings*, (Honolulu, Hawaiʻi: Bishop Museum Press, 1983), p. 275.

ARTISTS' BIOGRAPHIES

An asterisk (*) preceding an artist's name mentioned in another artist's biographical entry indicate that he or she is in the current exhibition, and also has a biographical entry in the section.

JACK ABRAHAM Abraham is a self-taught artist who works primarily in wood and mixed media.

ALFRED ADAMS AND PRIMROSE ADAMS Trained in the traditional manner, Primrose Adams is descended from famed Haida artist Charles Edenshaw. She has revived the ancient art of making spruce root baskets, but on a smaller scale and for a new use. The baskets are painted by her son Alfred, who was also traditionally trained—initially as an argillite carver— by his uncle, Claude Davidson. Among the public collections that include their work is the Field Museum, Chicago, Illinois.

VICTORIA ADAMS Attended San Francisco Art Institute, California; the University of Nevada, Reno, Nevada; Revere Academy of Jewelry Arts, San Francisco, California; and completed an apprenticeship with goldsmith William Burke, Mill Valley, California. Adams's work has appeared in numerous publications, exhibitions, shows and markets where she has also won many awards, and is included in several public collections, such as the Wheelwright Museum of the American Indian, Santa Fe, New Mexico.

RICHARD "RICK" ADKINS Studied with Frieda Diesing and with master artists Bill Reid and *Robert Davidson. Adkins is best known for his jewelry in precious metals, influenced by the work of his teachers and by years of studying anatomical drawings and classical art history. His work has appeared in various exhibitions in Canada and is represented in private and corporate collections in North America.

LINDA AGUILAR Received a B.A. in studio art, University of California, Santa Barbara, California. Aguilar is best known for her tightly coiled horsehair baskets decorated with shells, beads, and other materials. She has made more than 6,000 baskets, including four presented to Nobel Peace Prize winners Nelson Mandela, Desmond Tutu, the Dalai Lama, and Rigoberta Menchú Tum. Her work has been included in numerous publications and exhibitions, including *High Fiber* at the Renwick Gallery of the Smithsonian American Art Museum, Smithsonian Institution, Washington, D.C.

LAWRENCE "LARRY" AHVAKANA Attended the Institute of American Indian Arts, Santa Fe, New Mexico, and the Cooper Union School of Art, New York, New York; received a B.F.A., Rhode Island School of Design, Providence, Rhode Island. Ahvakana was head of the Sculpture Studio at the Visual Arts Center of Alaska, Anchorage; has taught sculpture and glass at the Institute of American Indian Arts, Santa Fe, New Mexico; was an artist-in-residence at the Pilchuck Glass School in Stanwood, Washington; and has lectured and conducted workshops in Alaska and New Mexico. In addition to receiving numerous public commissions, Ahvakana has had his work featured in various publications and in solo and group shows, such as *Fusing Traditions: Transformations in Glass by Native American Artists*, a traveling exhibition organized by the Museum of Craft & Folk Art, San Francisco, California. One of his early mentors was renowned Apache sculptor Allan Houser. Among the public collections that include his work: Alaska State Museum, Juneau; Portland Art Museum, Portland, Oregon; Washington State Arts Commission, Olympia.

BERENICE A. KEOLAMAULOA O'NALANI AKAMINE Studied at the California College of the Arts, Oakland, California; received her B.F.A. and M.F.A., University of Hawai'i at Mānoa, Honolulu. Akamine was co-president of the Hot Glass Hui, Hawai'i (now Hawai'i Glass Artists), and a founding member of FLUXION, a student-run alternative exhibition space. Her work has been shown in numerous exhibitions in Hawai'i, as well as elsewhere in the U.S. and abroad. She has received many awards, including fellowships from the Smithsonian Institution and a scholarship from the Pilchuck Glass School, Stanwood, Washington. Among the public collections that include her work: Peabody Essex Museum, Salem, Massachusetts; Hawai'i State Foundation on Culture and the Arts, Honolulu; Wright State University Art Galleries, Dayton, Ohio.

HAROLD ALFRED Alfred's extensive training includes fine-arts courses at Malaspina University-College, Nanaimo, British Columbia; additional coursework in design, carving, and jewelry making; and studies with master artist Tony Hunt.

DENNIS ALLEN Has lived most of his life on the Skokomish Reservation in Washington State, where he learned skills and techniques of painting and wood carving from local masters. After years of working as a logger and fisherman, Allen devoted himself to art, working primarily in wood.

LENA AMASON Received a B.F.A., University of Alaska, Fairbanks. Amason was born into a family of artists; her father is Alvin Amason, a well known Alaskan painter. She uses both traditional and modern mediums in her sculptures, exploring themes that reflect her Native heritage. Among the public collections that include her work: University of Alaska Museum of the North, Fairbanks; Alaska Native Arts Foundation, Anchorage; Alutiiq Museum & Archaeological Repository, Kodiak, Alaska.

MARCUS AMERMAN Received a B.F.A., Whitman College, Walla Walla, Washington; also studied at the College of Santa Fe, the Institute of American Indian Arts, and the Anthropology Film Center, all in Santa Fe, New Mexico. A master beadworker, Amerman also works in other mediums and performance art. His work has been featured in various publications and in many exhibitions of contemporary art, including *Indian Humor*, a traveling exhibition organized by American Indian Contemporary Arts, San Francisco, California; and *The Pathways of Tradition: Indian Insights into Indian Worlds*, George Gustav Heye Center of the National Museum of the American Indian, Smithsonian Institution, New York. Among the public collections that include his work: National Museum of the American Indian, Smithsonian Institution, Washington, D.C.; American Museum of Natural History, New York; Heard Museum, Phoenix, Arizona; Portland Art Museum, Portland, Oregon; Museum of Arts & Design, New York.

ARTHUR AMIOTTE Received a B.S., Northern State College (now Northern State University), Aberdeen, South Dakota, and an M.A. in interdisciplinary studies, University of Montana, Missoula, Montana; studied at the Institute of American Indian Arts, Santa Fe, New Mexico; and has received honorary degrees from colleges and universities in South Dakota and Manitoba. An artist, author, and educator, Amiotte has served on the Presidential Advisory Council for the Performing Arts in Washington, D.C. (1979–81), and has received numerous honors, awards, and fellowships, including a Getty Foundation Grant (1994–95) and the Honor Award for Advancement of Native American Art from the Native American Art Studies Association (1999). Amiotte's work has been featured in almost 100 exhibitions internationally, including more than 20 solo shows. Among the public collections that include his work: Denver Art Museum, Denver, Colorado; Minneapolis Institute of Arts, Minnesota; and the National Museum of Natural History, Smithsonian Institution, Washington, D.C.

 **RONALD WAYNE ANDERSON** Received a B.F.A., University of Oklahoma, Norman; and pursued graduate studies in Native American art history at the University of New Mexico. Anderson is known for his mixed-media paintings and large-scale sculptural installations. His work has been shown in numerous group shows, primarily in Oklahoma, Arizona and New Mexico, and in solo exhibitions at institutions such as the Gilcrease Museum, Tulsa, Oklahoma; Colorado River Historical Museum, Bullhead City, Arizona; and the Albuquerque Museum of Art and History, New Mexico.

 IVY HĀLI'IMAILE ANDRADE Received an A.A., Kaua'i Community College, Lihue, Hawai'i; a B.A., University of Hawai'i at Hilo; an M.F.A. in ceramics and fiber, University of Hawai'i at Mānoa, Honolulu. Andrade is currently an assistant professor at Kamakakuokalani Center for Hawaiian Studies at the University of Hawai'i at Mānoa. Her work has been exhibited locally, nationally, and internationally, and she has been the recipient of several prestigious awards.

 MURIEL ANTOINE Received a B.S./M.S. in education administration, University of South Dakota, Vermillion, South Dakota. Antoine has descended from a long line of artists and is a prolific writer who uses the pen name Anpetu Winyan (Day Woman). Her work has appeared in numerous group exhibitions including *Indian Humor*, a traveling exhibition organized by American Indian Contemporary Arts, San Francisco, California; and *Native American: Reflecting Contemporary Realities*, a traveling exhibition organized by the Craft and Folk Art Museum, Los Angeles, California. Among the public collections that include her work is the National Museum of the American Indian, Smithsonian Institution, Washington, D.C.

SONNY ASSU Received a Certificate in Multimedia Studies, University of British Columbia, Vancouver, and a B.F.A. in printmaking and digital arts, Emily Carr Institute of Art + Design, Vancouver; also studied fine arts at Kwantlen University College, Surrey, British Columbia. Assu has participated in numerous group exhibitions throughout western Canada and has been the recipient of several arts-related grants.

KERI ATAUMBI Received a B.F.A. in painting, College of Santa Fe, New Mexico; also attended Rhode Island School of Design, Providence, Rhode Island; and received an A.F.A. in 3-dimensional design, Institute of American Indian Arts, Santa Fe. Other members of Ataumbi's family are involved in the arts, including her sister, noted beadwork artist *Teri Greeves.

 SYLVESTER AYEK Studied at the University of Alaska, Fairbanks, with *Ron Senungetuk, and at Alaska Pacific University, Anchorage. Received a fellowship from Alaska State Council on the Arts, Anchorage; and was a sculptor-in-residence, Visual Arts Center of Alaska, Anchorage. Ayek has served as an instructor in numerous programs, including the Artist-in-Schools Program for the Alaska State Council on the Arts. Among the public collections that include his work: Alaska Contemporary Art Bank; Alaska State Council on the Arts, Anchorage; Anchorage Museum of History and Art; Smithsonian Institution, Washington, D.C.

 PAMELA BAKER Studied textile arts, Capilano College, North Vancouver, British Columbia; received a B.A. in fashion design in 1990, Otis College of Art + Design, Los Angeles, California. Baker is related to *Bradley Hunt and *Shawn Hunt, Northwest Coast master carver Mungo Martin, and noted Tlingit/Chilkat weaver Mary Ebbet. In 1988, after coordinating fashion shows in the U.S., Baker established Touch of Culture workshops for Aboriginal women and teens in her local community, and in 1990 founded the Touch of Culture Training Institute on the Capilano Reserve in North Vancouver, where First Nations people receive instruction in fashion design and clothing assembly. Pamela Baker's nephew is *Klatle-Bhi.

 BRIAN BARBER Received a B.F.A. in glass art, Ohio State University, Columbus; and attended Penland School of Crafts, North Carolina. Barber's work has been included in several group shows, including *Fusing Traditions: Transformations in Glass by Native American Artists*, a traveling exhibition organized by the Museum of Craft & Folk Art, San Francisco, California. He is also the recipient of several prestigious awards, such as the Hauberg Scholarship at the Pilchuck Glass School, Stanwood, Washington.

 PAM KAWEHILANI BARTON Studied at the Honolulu Academy of Arts and the Honolulu School of Art; received a B.F.A., University of Hawai'i at Mānoa, Honolulu; and has pursued additional studies at Arrowmont School of Arts and Crafts, Gatlinburg, Tennessee; the Mendocino Art Center, Mendocino, California; and in Indonesia, Japan, and the Philippines.

 RICK BARTOW Received a B.A. in art education, Western Oregon State College, Monmouth. His work has been included in many solo and group exhibitions, both nationally and internationally, including *After the Storm: The Eiteljorg Fellowship for Native American Fine Art 2001*, Eiteljorg Museum of American Indians and Western Art, Indianapolis, Indiana; *Continuum*, George Gustav Heye Center of the National Museum of the American Indian, Smithsonian Institution, New York; *Twentieth Century American Sculpture at the White House: Honoring Native America*, Washington, D.C.; and *Pacific Dragons: Contemporary Art by Established and Emerging Artists from Nations of the Pacific Rim*, Uxbridge Gallery, Howick, New Zealand. Bartow is also an accomplished blues guitar player.

 KAREN BEAVER With a Yup'ik father and a Mandan/Hidatsa mother, Beaver's mixed Native American cultural heritage is evident in her art, as are many aspects of life on the Alaskan tundra where she grew up, including skin sewing and beading pieces for powwow regalia.

ALAN BELL Not formally trained, but inspired by both traditional Native art and modern woodworking techniques, as well as the influence of a mother who quilted and a grandmother who beaded. Bell is known for his artistry in wood, and particularly for his skillful use of lamination and lathe turning to create distinctive patterns inspired by Native traditions.

SUSIE BEVINS-ERICSEN Studied art at Anchorage Community College, Anchorage, Alaska. Bevins has been an artist-in-residence at the Visual Arts Center of Alaska, Anchorage, and at Atlanta College of Art, Georgia; and attended a marble-carving workshop in Carrara, Italy. She has received several public commissions, including *Guardians and Sentinels*, exhibited at the White House, Washington, D.C.

GEORGE NIXON BLAKE Studied at the College of the Redwoods, Eureka, California, and at the University of California, Davis. Blake was director of the Hoopa Tribal Museum, Hoopa, California, and received the National Endowment for the Arts Heritage Award for his efforts to preserve traditional California Indian arts.

RANDALL BLAZE Received a B.F.A., University of Montana, Missoula. Blaze has received more than 80 prestigious awards over the past three decades, has participated in numerous national and several international exhibitions, and his works are in many public and private collections. He recently opened a gallery and art center in Pine Ridge, South Dakota, fully equipped with studios for ceramics, metalsmithing, painting, and two-dimensional design to provide workshops for students K–12 and continuing education for adults.

DEMPSEY BOB Not formally trained, but instead learned under the guidance of his parents and grandparents; also briefly attended Kitanmaax School of Northwest Coast Art, Hazelton, British Columbia. Bob's work has been presented in group shows in North America and abroad, most recently in *Totems to Turquoise* at the American Museum of Natural History, New York; and he has had several solo exhibitions, including *Dempsey Bob: Myth Maker and Transformer*, Vancouver Museum, British Columbia. He works in various mediums, but is perhaps best known for his exuberant carving style; and he has translated some of his wood sculptures into bronze. Among the public collections that include his work: Canada House Gallery, London, England; National Museum of Ethnology, Osaka, Japan; National Museum of the American Indian, Smithsonian Institution, Washington, D.C. Dempsey Bob is the uncle of *Ken McNeil.

TODD LONEDOG BORDEAUX A self-taught artist whose works include traditional and contemporary beadwork, ink drawing, sculpture, jewelry, prints, leather bags, and "storysticks," an adaptation of the "winter counts" that were made in tanned buffalo hide by his grandfather, Chief Lonedog, depicting historical episodes of the Yankton Sioux. Bordeaux's pieces have won several awards.

PARKER BOYIDDLE Attended Institute of American Indian Arts, Santa Fe, New Mexico, studying under Alan Houser, Fritz Scholder, and John Chamberlain; also studied at Pima Community College, Tucson, Arizona. Boyiddle was an artist-in-residence at the Institute of American Indian Arts, Santa Fe. He has been influenced in his art by his grandfather, who made beadwork and feather fans, and his father, who was an upholsterer and interior designer.

DAVID BRADLEY Attended University of St. Thomas, St. Paul, Minnesota; studied carving under Larry Ahvakana at the Institute of American Indian Arts, Santa Fe, New Mexico; attended University of Arizona, Tucson. Bradley also served in the Peace Corps, taking him throughout Central America and the Caribbean. He is both a painter and a sculptor, and his work has been included in many exhibitions. Among the public collections that include his work: Buffalo Bill Historical Center, Cody, Wyoming; Gilcrease Museum, Tulsa, Oklahoma; Joslyn Art Museum, Omaha, Nebraska; Museum für Völkerkunde (Museum of Ethnology), Vienna, Austria; National Museum of American Art, Smithsonian Institution, Washington, D.C.

JACKIE LARSON BREAD Attended College of Santa Fe, New Mexico; received an A.S.A. in museology, Institute of American Indian Arts, Santa Fe. One of Bread's influences as an artist was her Blackfeet Reservation grandmother's traditional beadwork. Among the public collections that include her work is the Philbrook Museum of Art, Tulsa, Oklahoma.

JESSE BRILLON Not formally trained, but grew up immersed in his culture and surrounded by elders who created important ceremonial objects; studied for a year with master artist Don Yeomans, learning basic designing and engraving techniques in silver, gold, and wood, and then moved to Hazelton, where he is currently apprenticing with artist Philip Janze.

SEAN KEKAMAKUPAʻA LEE LOY BROWNE Received a B.A. in sculpture, University of Redlands, California; and an M.F.A. in sculpture, University of Hawaiʻi at Mānoa, Honolulu. On a Fulbright Fellowship in the 1980s, Browne traveled to Shikoku, Japan and studied with Isamu Noguchi. As part of a Hawaiian awards program initiated in 1976, Browne was named one of Hawaiʻi's "living treasures" in 2001, along with *Rocky Jensen and four other notable Hawaiians. Primarily using stone, Browne makes contemporary sculptures based on ancient forms and symbols, taking inspiration from Japanese ceramics and the tools and ritual elements utilized by Native Hawaiians during the precontact period.

MARCUS CADMAN A self-taught artist, growing up in a small town on the Navajo Reservation in the Four Corners region of New Mexico; was first exposed to art by his father, who was also an artist; later studied painting at Diné College, Shiprock, New Mexico, and at San Juan College, Farmington, New Mexico. Cadman was first inspired to depict and chronicle contemporary Native American life by a Joseph Campbell reading. He combines elements from the modern world and his indigenous culture in a variety of mediums, using collage as his principal technique. He has won numerous awards.

KEʻALAONAONAPUAHĪNANO CAMPTON Received an A.A., Cabrillo College, Aptos, California; and a B.A. in studio art, University of California, Davis; studied with Wayne Thiebaud, Manuel Neri, and Robert Arneson; additional studies as a Fellow with the Pacific American Foundation, the Peter F. Drucker and Masatoshi Ito Graduate School of Management at Claremont Graduate University, Claremont, California. Campton's parents are both professional artists, and she has been influenced by a wide range of art forms, from traditional to contemporary Hawaiian; her work also includes performance art.

PHILLIP CHARETTE (AARNAQUQ) Received a B.A. in Alaska

Native studies and a B.Ed in secondary education and social sciences, both at the University of Alaska, Fairbanks; and then a master's in education, administration, planning and social policy, Harvard University, Cambridge, Massachusetts. Charette began working as a full-time artist in 2001, and specializes in Yup'ik masks, drums, and Native American flutes. Among the public collections that include his work: Coos Art Museum, Coos Bay, Oregon; Portland Art Museum, Portland, Oregon.

JUDY CHARTRAND Studied fine arts at Langara College and Emily

Carr Institute of Art + Design, both in Vancouver, British Columbia; received an M.F.A. in ceramics, University of Regina, Saskatchewan. A self-described "urban, inner-city Manitoba Cree, raised in downtown Vancouver," Chartrand grew up in a family of thirteen children. She left home at the age of fifteen and, in 1989, began working with clay. Her first exposure to hand-building clay pots was a videotape of famed Pueblo potter Maria Martinez from a local library.

KAILI CHUN Received an A.B. in architecture, Princeton University,

New Jersey, and an M.F.A., University of Hawai'i at Mānoa, Honolulu. Chun's large-scale conceptual installations focus primarily on issues related to indigenous and Native Hawaiian affairs. Among the public collections that include her work: Linden-Museum Stuttgart, Germany; Hawai'i State Foundation on Culture and the Arts, Honolulu; Hawai'i State Art Museum, Honolulu.

CORWIN "CORKY" CLAIRMONT Received a B.A., Montana

State University, Bozeman; and an M.F.A., California State University, Los Angeles. Among the numerous prestigious awards that Clairmont has received are a Ford Foundation Grant for the Arts, National Endowment for the Arts Visual Arts Grant, and the Eiteljorg Fellowship for Native American Fine Art, 2003. He was assistant vice president at the Salish Kootenai College, Pablo, Montana. His work is in such public collections as the Eiteljorg Museum of American Indians and Western Art, Indianapolis, Indiana.

GERALD CLARKE Received a B.A. in painting and sculpture, University

of Central Arkansas, Conway, Arkansas; and an M.A./M.F.A., Stephen F. Austin State University, Nacogdoches, Texas. After graduate school, Clarke taught at the university and community college for ten years. He currently lives on the Cahuilla Indian Reservation and works as an adjunct instructor of art at Idyllwild Arts Academy in Idyllwild, California.

KARITA COFFEY Attended Institute of American Indian Arts, Santa

Fe, New Mexico. Coffey's work was recently included in *Winter Camp, Honoring the Legacy: Contemporary Expressions of Oklahoma Tribal Art*, National Cowboy & Western Heritage Museum, Oklahoma City, Oklahoma; and in *Anticipating the Dawn*, Gardiner Art Gallery, Oklahoma State University, Stillwater. Among the public collections that include her work: Millicent Rogers Museum, Taos, New Mexico; Heard Museum, Phoenix, Arizona.

BARRY COFFIN Attended A.F.A., Institute of American Indian Arts,

Santa Fe, New Mexico; founding member of Artists in Support of American Indian Religious Freedom. Coffin's work has been included in numerous museum exhibitions throughout the United States. Barry Coffin is the brother of *Doug Coffin.

DOUG COFFIN Received a B.F.A., University of Kansas, Lawrence,

and an M.F.A., Cranbrook Academy of Art, Bloomfield Hills, Michigan; also studied with Anthony Caro at the University of Saskatchewan, Saskatoon. He taught at Fort Wright College, Spokane, Washington, as head of the Jewelry Department; and as an instructor at the College of Santa Fe, New Mexico/ Institute of American Indian Arts, Santa Fe. Coffin has received numerous awards, including a grant from the Ford Foundation and a National Teaching Fellowship. His work has been presented in numerous solo and group exhibitions, installations, publications, and is in various public collections. Doug Coffin is the brother of *Barry Coffin.

CHRIS COOK Initially trained as an industrial metalworker and

machinist; later received a B.A. in history, University of Victoria, British Columbia; also completed additional silversmithing courses at Camosun College, Victoria, British Columbia and came under the guidance and influence of a number of artists, including *Harold Alfred.

RANDE COOK Spent his formative years in the town of Alert Bay

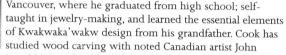

on northern Vancouver Island before moving in 1991 to Vancouver, where he graduated from high school; self-taught in jewelry-making, and learned the essential elements of Kwakwaka'wakw design from his grandfather. Cook has studied wood carving with noted Canadian artist John Livingston since 2002, exploring mask making, box making, and numerous other forms of Northwest Coast art. Cook complements his work with unusual materials such as gold, silver, and mastodon ivory.

JOE DAVID Studied art in San Marcos, Texas, and took classes at the

University of Washington, Seattle. Mask-maker, jewelry-maker, and printer, David was formally trained as a commercial artist, and in the early 1970s began carving traditional forms under the tutelage of master carver Duane Pasco, and with the guidance of noted artist and scholar Bill Holm. Mentoring other carvers, David was a founder of the Northwest Coast Indian Artists Guild in 1977, with a mission to bring international focus to Native art from the region. He also completed several public commissions with another important artist, Bill Reid, and participated in group shows throughout North America and Europe, including *In the Shadow of the Sun*, a traveling exhibition organized by the Canadian Museum of Civilization, Gatineau, Quebec, and *The Legacy*, organized by the Royal British Columbia Museum, Victoria, British Columbia. His daughter is *Lisa Marie David.

LISA MARIE DAVID Learned beadwork skills from her grandmother,

Carol Bluehorse, and carving skills from her father, master carver *Joe David. Her stepfather, William Tuifa, is also a master carver, as is her brother, Douglas David. She also learned the craft of Sioux-style leather work, and has been learning to work with cedar bark with the help of her godmother, Amelia David. She teaches Native art to children at Haahuupayak School in Port Alberni, British Columbia.

BENJAMIN DAVIDSON Comes from a long lineage of highly

accomplished carvers; has worked under the guidance of his uncle, *Reg Davidson, and also formally apprenticed with his father, *Robert Davidson, for four years of training.

REG DAVIDSON Comes from a family of artists that includes his

father, Claude Davidson, and his brother, *Robert Davidson. Reg Davidson works mostly as a sculptor, carving in wood, but also makes serigraphs and gold and silver jewelry. He is also an accomplished singer and dancer, and with his brother Robert founded the Rainbow Creek Dancers. His public commissions include a 31-foot totem pole erected at Tamagawa University in Japan.

ROBERT DAVIDSON Descendant of one of the most renowned Haida artists, Charles Edenshaw, and apprentice to another, Bill Reid. Davidson has followed in their footsteps and is recognized as a force in pushing the envelope in contemporary art of the Northwest. He is a wood and stone carver, jeweler, metalsmith, sculptor, and graphic designer, whose work has been extensively exhibited, published, and collected in North America and abroad. Among the many awards and honorary degrees he has received are Doctor of Letters, Emily Carr Institute of Art + Design, Vancouver, British Columbia; Doctor of Arts, Southern Methodist University, Dallas, Texas; and the Order of Canada. Public collections that include his work: National Gallery of Canada, Ottawa, Ontario; Donald M. Kendall Sculpture Gardens, Purchase, New York; Royal Ontario Museum, Toronto. Robert is the brother of *Reg Davidson and the father of *Ben Davidson.

PAULA RASMUS DEDE Primarily a self-taught artist; learned basic beadworking techniques from her grandmother and other beadworkers. Among the public collections that include her work is the Anchorage Museum of History and Art, Alaska.

TODD DEFOE  Received an A.F.A., Institute of American Indian Arts, Santa Fe, New Mexico. Defoe was a consultant in the casino and hotel management industry before he began in the late 1990s to focus on the art of pipe-making, working as an apprentice under a noted Ojibwe sculptor, Jeff Savage. He has had solo exhibitions at such institutions as the Heard Museum, Phoenix, Arizona, and the Wheelwright Museum of the American Indian, Santa Fe, New Mexico. Among the public collections that include his work is the Institute of American Indian Arts, Santa Fe, New Mexico.

STEVEN DEO Received an A.F.A., Institute of American Indian Arts, Santa Fe, New Mexico; and a B.F.A., San Francisco Art Institute, California; and did graduate work in painting at the University of Oklahoma, Norman, and post-graduate work in visual arts at Purdue University, West Lafayette, Indiana. Deo's work has appeared in many gallery and museum exhibitions throughout the United States. He was also a recipient of the medal for sculpture at the *Biennale Dell'Arte Contemporanea*, Florence, Italy.

KERI-LYNN DICK Daughter of artist Beau Dick, and noted for her innovative work in traditional cedar bark fiber.

KILOHANA DOMINGO Received a B.A., University of Hawai'i at Mānoa, Honolulu. Domingo has done cultural presentations at institutions across the United States, including the National Museum of Natural History, Smithsonian Institution, Washington, D.C.; and has conducted National Park Service Workshops in Seattle, New York, and other locations. Kilohana is also a recipient of a fellowship from the Native Arts Program of the National Museum of the American Indian, Smithsonian Institution, Washington, D.C. He is the son of *Lehua Domingo.

LEHUA DOMINGO Learned weaving skills from her mother; and apprenticed with Gladys Grace, who taught the *anone* style that incorporated traditional Hawaiian patterns. Lehua is the mother of *Kilohana Domingo.

CAROL EMARTHLE DOUGLAS Studied at Northwest Indian College, School of Continuing Education, Bellingham, Washington; University of Kansas, Lawrence; Haskell Indian Nations University, Lawrence, Kansas; and privately with several master weavers.

PERRY EATON Studied at Grays Harbor College, Aberdeen, Washington. Eaton is founder of the Alaska Native Heritage Center, Anchorage. Among the public collections that include his work: Le Château-Musée in Boulogne-sur-Mer, France; Alutiiq Museum and Archaeological Repository, Kodiak, Alaska.

MOANA K. M. EISELE Attended University of Hawai'i at Mānoa, Honolulu. Began working in *kapa* (traditional Hawaiian mulberry bark cloth) by organizing a series of classes supported by the State Council on Hawaiian Heritage, Honolulu. *Kapa* and other traditional Native Hawaiian materials (including dyes made from indigenous plants) are integral to her work.

JAMES FAKS Faks works primarily in silver, creating unique, hand-made "wearable art." His work has been shown at many museums and galleries, mostly in the Southwest. James Faks is the brother of *Stan Natchez.

JOE FEDDERSEN Received a B.F.A. in printmaking, University of Washington, Seattle, and an M.F.A., University of Wisconsin, Madison; and studied with Robert Graves at Wenatchee Valley College, Wenatchee, Washington. In addition to being a sculptor and printmaker, Feddersen is a writer, lecturer, and teacher; he was an art instructor at Evergreen State College, Olympia, Washington. As a sculptor, he works in a variety of mediums, including fiber and glass. Feddersen's work has been presented in solo exhibitions in numerous venues, among them the Carl Nelson Gorman Museum at the University of California, Davis; in two-person exhibitions such as *Archives*, at the Tula Foundation Gallery, Atlanta, Georgia; and in the series *Continuum: 12 Artists*, organized by the George Gustav Heye Center of the National Museum of the American Indian, Smithsonian Institution, New York. He received the Eiteljorg Fellowship for Native American Fine Art in 2001.

ANITA FIELDS Attended Oklahoma State University, Stillwater. Fields's work has been presented in many publications; in group exhibitions such as *Two by Two: Anita Fields and Rick Rivet*, Heard Museum, Phoenix, Arizona, and *The Legacy of Generations: Pottery by American Indian Women*, organized jointly by the National Museum of Women in the Arts, Washington, D.C. and the Heard Museum; and in solo exhibitions at venues including Gardiner Art Gallery, Oklahoma State University, Stillwater, and the Southern Plains Indian Museum, Anadarko, Oklahoma. Among the public collections that include her work: the Heard Museum; National Cowboy & Western Heritage Museum, Oklahoma City; Institute of American Indian Arts, Santa Fe, New Mexico; Museum of Arts & Design, New York.

BOB FREITAS Studied architectural drafting and painting in Germany, and then art, architecture, anthropology, engineering, political science and law in the United States; and has traveled extensively in Europe, Asia, and throughout the Pacific Rim region. In addition to making sculpture, Freitas is involved with securing recognition of the contemporary Hawaiian art movement.

NICHOLAS GALANIN Received an A.A., University of Alaska Southeast, Sitka Campus; a B.A. in silversmithing and jewelry design, London Metropolitan University, London, England; and will receive an M.V.A. in 2005 in indigenous visual arts, Massey University, Palmerston North, New Zealand. He has also completed apprenticeships under several master carvers in Alaska. In addition to being a sculptor in a variety of mediums, Galanin has given lectures and demonstrations, primarily in Alaska. His work has been presented in a number of group exhibitions.

 BILL GLASS, JR. Studied ceramics at the University of Central Oklahoma, Edmond, and ceramics and sculpture at the Institute of American Indian Arts, Santa Fe, New Mexico. Glass was a director and instructor at Cherokee Nation Arts and Crafts, Tahlequah, Oklahoma, and established the Bill Glass Ceramic Studio in Locust Grove, Oklahoma, which he shares with his son, *Demos Glass. He has received numerous awards for his sculptures in clay, and recently completed a public art commission from Cherokee Artists Gadugi, Inc., to research and provide Cherokee artwork along the "Passage" in Chattanooga, Tennessee. Among the public collections that include his work: Heard Museum, Phoenix, Arizona; Institute of American Indian Arts, Santa Fe, New Mexico; Atlanta History Center, Georgia.

 DEMOS GLASS Studied fine arts at Southern Illinois University, Edwardsville, and welding at Indian Capital Technology Center, Bill Willis Campus, Tahlequah, Oklahoma. Demos Glass makes sculpture in metal and wood; he has won numerous awards and has had his work shown in several exhibitions, including *Metalworks: Containers of Form, Function and Beauty,* Heard Museum North, Scottsdale, Arizona. He has also collaborated with his father *Bill Glass, Jr., and is in charge of the metals for the public commission "Passage" in Chattanooga, Tennessee.

 PAT COURTNEY GOLD Received a B.A. in mathematics and physics, Whitman College, Walla Walla, Washington. Gold's work has been presented in numerous publications and in many national and international exhibitions, including Art Train's traveling show *Contemporary Native Art* (through 2007), and *The Language of Native American Baskets, From the Weaver's View,* George Gustav Heye Center of the National Museum of the American Indian, Smithsonian Institution, New York. She has also curated exhibitions, and has received various awards and honors. Among the public collections that include her work: Portland Art Museum, Portland, Oregon; National Museum of the American Indian, Smithsonian Institution, Washington, D.C.; Peabody Museum of Archaeology and Ethnology, Harvard University, Cambridge, Massachusetts; British Museum, London, England.

 MARTHA GRADOLF Attended Indiana University-Purdue University, Indianapolis, and Glendale Community College, Glendale, California. Among the public collections that include her work is the Eiteljorg Museum of American Indians and Western Art, Indianapolis, Indiana.

 PHILIP GRAY Largely self-taught, inspired by great Northwest carvers such as David Boxly; learned carving skills from his own brother and from artist Gerry Sheena. Gray began his career as an artist in 1999 under the tutelage of Michael Dangeli. Only twenty-two years old, he has already carved one totem pole and many masks. Before learning to carve, Gray actively celebrated his heritage by dancing and singing with a Tsimshian group.

 GEOFF GREENE A self-taught artist who has studied the art of his culture for more than two decades. Currently studying bronze casting and stone sculpture at the Emily Carr Institute of Art + Design, Vancouver, British Columbia.

 STAN GREENE Attended the Kasan School of Native Art, Hazelton, British Columbia in 1977; and studied under several master carvers, including *Ken Mowatt and *Chuck Heit. Greene works mostly in wood, creating face masks, totem poles, Salish sculptures, and canoes, as well as smaller items such as rattles, spoons, and bowls; he also works in glass using sandblasting and engraving methods, and has made some silkscreen prints and paintings as well. Greene's monumental house posts were featured at the 1986 World Expo, Vancouver, British Columbia; and in 1987 he carved a 27-foot totem pole for Yokohama City, Japan.

 TERI GREEVES Received a B.A. in American Studies, University of California, Santa Cruz; also studied at Cabrillo College, Aptos, California, and St. John's College, Santa Fe, New Mexico. Greeves has received many honors, including the Eric and Barbara Dobkin Native American Woman Artist Fellowship from the School of American Research, Santa Fe, New Mexico, and numerous judges' honors at Indian markets and exhibitions. Her work has been presented in various publications, in many group exhibitions throughout the American West, and in a solo exhibition at the Fort Lewis College Art Gallery, Durango, Colorado. Among the public collections that include her work: British Museum, London, England; Montclair Art Museum, New Jersey; Heard Museum, Phoenix, Arizona; Museum of Arts & Design, New York. Other members of Greeves's family are involved in the arts, including her sister, noted jewelry designer and sculptor *Keri Ataumbi.

 ROBERT GRESS Studied at Montana State University, Bozeman, and the Institute of American Indian Arts, Santa Fe, New Mexico. Gress works in silver and is a specialist in stone inlay techniques.

 BENJAMIN HARJO, JR. Received a B.F.A., Oklahoma State University, Stillwater, Oklahoma; also attended the Institute of American Indian Arts, Santa Fe, New Mexico. Over the past two decades, Harjo's work has appeared in numerous regional and national publications, in group exhibitions at venues such as the Franco-American Institute, Rennes, France, in a solo exhibition organized in 1991 by the Wichita Art Museum, Wichita, Kansas, and in a retrospective exhibition recently organized by the Wheelwright Museum of the American Indian, Santa Fe, New Mexico. Among the public collections that include his work: Sam Noble Oklahoma Museum of Natural History, Norman, Oklahoma; Gilcrease Museum, Tulsa, Oklahoma.

 NATHAN HART Received a B.S., Bethel College, North Newton, Kansas. Hart makes sculpture in wood and clay, and has had diverse experience working within Native communities, primarily in the investment industry and in the arts.

TOM HAUKAAS Received a Ph.D., Michigan State University, College of Human Medicine, East Lansing; post-graduate work, University of South Dakota, School of Medicine and Health Sciences, Vermillion. Haukaas's sculptures and installations have been shown in many group exhibitions, such as *Gifts of the Spirit,* Peabody Essex Museum, Salem, Massachusetts, and *Lewis & Clark Revisited*, Tacoma Art Museum, Washington. Public collections that include his work: Denver Art Museum, Colorado; Milwaukee Art Museum, Wisconsin; Carnegie Museum of Art, Pittsburgh, Pennsylvania.

EMIL HER MANY HORSES Received a B.A., Augustana College, Rock Island, Illinois; graduate studies in philosophy, Loyola University, Chicago, Illinois. Her Many Horses is currently an associate curator at the National Museum of the American Indian, Smithsonian Institution, Washington, D.C. In addition to making his own art, he is a specialist in the art and culture of the Northern and Southern Plains with a focus on beadwork, and has written and lectured extensively on this topic. Among the public collections that include his work: National Museum of the American Indian, Smithsonian Institution, Washington, D.C.; Buffalo Bill Historical Center, Cody, Wyoming.

JOHN HITCHCOCK Received a B.F.A., with an emphasis on printmaking and drawing, Cameron University, Lawton, 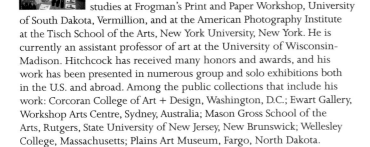 Oklahoma, and an M.F.A. in printmaking, painting, and photography, Texas Tech University, Lubbock; continued studies at Frogman's Print and Paper Workshop, University of South Dakota, Vermillion, and at the American Photography Institute at the Tisch School of the Arts, New York University, New York. He is currently an assistant professor of art at the University of Wisconsin-Madison. Hitchcock has received many honors and awards, and his work has been presented in numerous group and solo exhibitions both in the U.S. and abroad. Among the public collections that include his work: Corcoran College of Art + Design, Washington, D.C.; Ewart Gallery, Workshop Arts Centre, Sydney, Australia; Mason Gross School of the Arts, Rutgers, State University of New Jersey, New Brunswick; Wellesley College, Massachusetts; Plains Art Museum, Fargo, North Dakota.

JOHN HOOVER Studied drawing and painting, Leon Derbyshire School of Fine Arts, Seattle, Washington. Hoover, with a long career as both artist and teacher, is today one of the most influential artists from Alaska. Born to an Aleut mother and a German father, he spent his youth fishing and making art, and his participation in boat building inspired his interest in sculpture. His carvings in red cedar have been influenced by traditional Northwest Coast Indian carvings and by his travels to Japan, Taiwan and the Philippines, where he learned the woodworking techniques of those indigenous cultures. Numerous gallery and museum shows have presented his work, among them *John Hoover: Art & Life*, organized by the Anchorage Museum of History and Art. Among the public collections that include his work: Seattle Art Museum, Washington; Philbrook Museum of Art, Tulsa, Oklahoma.

CLARISSA HUDSON Apprenticed with noted regalia-maker Henry K. Bremner, Sr. in the late 1970s, and with master Chilkat weaver Jennie Thlunaut in 1986; also studied clothing design and metalsmithing at the Institute of American Indian Arts, Santa Fe, New Mexico, and studied with Preston Singletary* and David Svenson at the Pilchuck Glass School, Stanwood, Washington. Hudson has made many traditional Alaskan ceremonial robes, as well as numerous carvings, paintings, small weavings, and collages, and has taught Chilkat weaving to local Native women. Her solo exhibitions include *Blanket Statements* at the Banff Centre, Alberta. Hudson has received many honors and awards, including Heard Museum Guild Best of Show, for a work now in the permanent collection of that museum, in Phoenix, Arizona. She has also completed several public commissions in Alaska with her husband, multimedia artist Bill Hudson. In addition, she has run her own landscape gardening business, and has worked with Native dance and theater groups as costume and set designer, tour manager, stage manager, actress, and singer/musician.

BRADLEY HUNT Received a B.Ed., with a secondary art major, University of British Columbia, Vancouver. Inspired by his father, Hunt began carving at an early age, but chose a career teaching at the elementary school level, and only returned to pursuing his interest in art in the late 1970s. Bradley is the father of *Shawn Hunt.

RICHARD HUNT Apprenticed under his father, Henry Hunt, at the Royal British Columbia Museum, Victoria, after graduating from high school. Hunt is from a family of prominent artists; one of his most well-known relatives is Northwest Coast master carver Mungo Martin. After his apprenticeship, he worked as the chief carver at Thunderbird Park for twelve years. Hunt has completed many important public commissions both in Canada and abroad, including a 15-foot totem pole for the National Museum of Ethnology, Osaka, Japan; another at the City Art Centre in Edinburgh, Scotland; and a 35-foot totem pole in collaboration with *Tim Paul for the Canadian Broadcasting Corporation, Vancouver, British Columbia, which still serves as the logo for the CBC, Vancouver.

SHAWN HUNT Received a degree in studio art, Capilano College, North Vancouver, British Columbia, and a B.F.A., University of British Columbia, Vancouver; and served an apprenticeship under his father, *Bradley Hunt. Shawn Hunt makes gold and silver jewelry, and wooden totems and masks.

ROCKY KAʻIOULIOKAHIHIKOLOʻEHU JENSEN A sculptor and historical illustrator, Jensen has mounted and participated in more than 125 art exhibitions nationally and internationally. In 1978, he helped organize the first exhibition of contemporary Native Hawaiian art, at the Bernice Pauahi Bishop Museum in Honolulu. Jensen is founder and director of Hale Naua III, Society of Hawaiian Arts, and also serves as cultural adviser to many other Hawaiian organizations. He has lectured extensively in the United States; and has received regional and national awards for his contributions to perpetuating Native Hawaiian culture and the arts. Rocky is the father of *Natalie Mahina Jensen-Oomittuk.

NATALIE MAHINA JENSEN-OOMITTUK Trained since childhood in the art of Native feather work, and formally trained as a photographer. She had her first solo exhibition when she was only fourteen. Jensen-Oomittuk's work often focuses on her cultural identity. She recently completed a series of photographs depicting 25 Hawaiian women engaged in traditional occupations for an exhibition and book, *Na Kaikamahine ʻo Haumea (Daughters of Haumea)*, in collaboration with her mother, Lucia Jensen. Her work has been presented in many group exhibitions, including *Maui: Turning Back the Sky* and *Fire & Ice*. Natalie is the daughter of *Rocky Jensen and the wife of *Othniel Oomittuk, Jr.

MAYNARD JOHNNY, JR. Primarily self-taught. Maynard Johnny, Jr. creates mainly jewelry in gold and silver and graphic works, and has carved some wood panels and masks. He has been inspired by the work of many Northwest Coast artists, especially *Robert Davidson. His work has been presented in several group shows and small solo gallery exhibitions.

KENNETH JOHNSON Studied mechanical engineering, University of Oklahoma, Norman; also served apprenticeships and took specialty coursework in jewelry design. Johnson is best known for his silver, gold, and platinum jewelry featuring bold combinations of stampwork and engraving, which has been shown at numerous juried and invitational shows, and included in several group exhibitions. He was an artist-in-residence at the National Museum of the American Indian, Smithsonian Institution, Washington, D.C.

DEAN KAAHANUI Trained from an early age as a musician, and later recorded traditional Hawaiian music with various groups. Kaahanui was mentored by noted Tahitian carver Eriki Marchand and was inspired by a Marquesas carver, Joseph Kimitete.

FRANZ KAHALE Recently received a B.A. in fine arts, University of Hawai'i, Hilo. His work has been featured in many group exhibitions in Hawai'i, including the *Kilauea Hawaiian Art Exhibition* and the *East Hawaii Art Exhibition*. He also participated in the Amity Art Foundation Portfolio Project in 2003.

PAULETTE NOHEALANI KAHALEPUNA Attended Church College of Hawai'i (now Brigham Young University), Laie, Hawai'i. Kahalepuna is an accomplished fiber artist who has been perpetuating the Native art of featherwork, which she learned from her mother, Mary Lou Kekuewa. She tours throughout Hawai'i and the continental United States teaching featherwork techniques.

SONYA KELLIHER-COMBS Received a B.F.A., University of Alaska Fairbanks, and an M.F.A., Arizona State University, Tempe, Arizona. Kelliher-Combs' work has been shown in numerous individual and group exhibitions in Alaska and the contiguous United States, and in the Chongju 2005 Craft Bienniale in Chongju, Korea. Among the public collections that include her work: Anchorage Museum of History and Art, Alaska; Alaska State Museum, Juneau; University of Alaska Museum of the North, Fairbanks; Ted Stevens Anchorage International Airport, Alaska.

KATHLEEN CARLO KENDALL Received a B.F.A., Native Art Center, University of Alaska, Fairbanks, studying under noted artist and scholar *Ron Senungetuk. Kendall, known for her masks and her carved wooden panels inspired by Alaskan topography, has exhibited her work throughout the state, and has received two public art commissions from the Alaska State Government. Among the public collections that include her work: Anchorage Museum of History and Art, Alaska; University of Alaska Museum of the North, Fairbanks; U.S. Department of the Interior, Washington, D.C.

FREDERICK KINGEEKUK Trained in the traditional manner, learning carving techniques from his uncle and his father, Floyd Kingeekuk, Sr., a master seal carver. Kingeekuk is known for his unique forms and unconventional approach to traditional carving. Among the public collections that include his work is the Anchorage Museum, Alaska.

KLATLE-BHI (CHUCK SAM) Grew up surrounded by the Kwakiutl culture of mask dancing, singing and potlatching, and early on began researching and studying the works of his ancestors in museums and galleries; apprenticed for two years with master carver Simon Dick, and learned from other master carvers, too, as well as from his uncle T. Richard Baker, who had worked with Haida artists Bill Reid, *Robert Davidson, and Jim Hart. Klatle-Bhi (pronounced "Klath-Bay") is always striving for a distinctive personal style and a high level of craftsmanship. He is the nephew of *Pamela Baker.

KIM KNIFE CHIEF Received an A.F.A. in 3-dimensional art and a B.A. in museum studies at the Institute of American Indian Arts, Santa Fe, New Mexico. Knife Chief has been the recipient of several awards, including a Guest Artist Fellowship to the School of American Research, Santa Fe, New Mexico, and the Jewelry Scholarship Award from the Rhode Island Foundation, Providence.

PUNI KUKAHIKO Received a B.F.A., University of Hawai'i at Mānoa, Honolulu, and currently pursuing an M.F.A., to be completed in 2005, University of Hawai'i at Mānoa, Honolulu. Kukahiko has also taught classes on Hawaiian art and a class in studio art. Her work has been exhibited locally and in New Zealand.

JERRY JACOB LAKTONEN Attended Seattle Pacific University, Washington, and the University of Washington, Seattle. Until the mid-1990s, Laktonen worked as a commercial fisherman, and since that time has been working full-time as an artist. Among the many institutions that have commissioned work from him is the Haffenreffer Museum of Anthropology, Brown University, Bristol, Rhode Island. Among the public collections that include his work: Haffenreffer Museum of Anthropology; National Museum of the American Indian, Smithsonian Institution, Washington, D.C.; Alaska State Museum, Juneau; Anchorage Museum of History and Art, Alaska.

JEAN LAMARR Attended San Jose City College, California, as an art major, and the University of California, Berkeley. LaMarr has been a professor of printmaking at the Institute of American Indian Arts, Santa Fe, New Mexico, and at other institutions. She is well known for her works in various mediums involving contemporary interpretations of traditional Native themes. LaMarr has been the recipient of many awards and commissions, and her work has appeared in more than 300 solo and group exhibitions at institutions in the U.S. and abroad, including the Museum of Modern Art, New York. She is also the owner/director of the Native American Graphics Workshop.

KAPULANI LANDGRAF Received a B.A. in anthropology, University of Hawai'i at Mānoa, Honolulu, and an M.F.A. in visual arts, Vermont College, Montpelier. In addition to her career as an artist, Landgraf is also a free-lance photographer and the author of several books. She has received a number of awards, such as an Artist Fellowship in Photography from the Hawai'i State Foundation on Culture and the Arts (S.F.C.A.), Honolulu. Landgraf's work has been presented in group shows at numerous venues, such as the Academy Arts Center, Honolulu; Art in General, New York; and the I.A.I.A. Museum, Santa Fe, New Mexico. Among the public collections that include her work: the Contemporary Museum, Honolulu Academy of the Art, Hawai'i State Foundation on Culture and the Arts, and Kamehameha Schools, all in Honolulu; and the Bibliothèque Nationale de France, Paris.

JOEY LAVADOUR Learned to weave at age fifteen from Walla Walla tribal elder Carrie Sampson. Lavadour currently teaches at the Crow Shadow Institute of the Arts near Pendleton, Oregon, and at Evergreen State College, Olympia, Washington. Among the public collections that include his work is the Cheney Cowles Museum, Spokane, Washington; University of Oregon, Eugene.

MAYNARD WHITE OWL LAVADOUR Learned beadwork at an early age from his mother and grandmother; later, attended the Institute of American Indian Arts, Santa Fe, New Mexico. Lavadour's work has been presented in a number of important exhibitions, such as the traveling show *Lost and Found Traditions: Contemporary Native American Art, 1965–1985*, organized by American Federation of Arts, New York; and *Reflecting Lewis and Clark—Contemporary American Indian Viewpoints*, Maryhill Museum of Art, Goldendale, Washington. He received the Governor's Art Award from the Oregon Arts Commission, Salem, Oregon. Among the public collections that include his work: Burke Museum of Natural History and Culture, University of Washington, Seattle; Heard Museum, Phoenix, Arizona.

lessLIE (LESLIE ROBERT SAM) Received a B.A. in First Nations studies, Malaspina University-College, Nanaimo, British Columbia; has been studying Coast Salish art since 1995; and is currently attending the University of Victoria, British Columbia, working toward an M.A. in interdisciplinary studies, focusing on Coast Salish art. Originally inspired and encouraged by his cousin Joe Wilson, he was later influenced by other Coast Salish artists such as Manual Salazar; *Maynard Johnny, Jr.; *Shaun Peterson; *Luke Marston; and *Susan Point.

PETER LIND, SR. Began carving at age seven. Lind has spent many years teaching the skills of wood carving throughout Alaska, particularly in remote villages. He has participated in a number of juried exhibitions and received numerous awards. Among the public local and national collections that include his work is the Anchorage Museum of History and Art, Alaska.

MARY LONGMAN Received a B.F.A., Emily Carr Institute of Art + Design, Vancouver, British Columbia, and an M.F.A., Nova Scotia College of Art and Design, Halifax,; and is pursuing a Ph.D. in art education, University of Victoria, British Columbia. In addition to her career as an artist, Longman has taught and given lectures, and has also done illustrations for two books. She has received numerous awards, including a research grant from the Canada Council and the British Columbia Arts Award. Longman's work has been shown in several group exhibitions, including *Reservation X*, circulated by the National Museum of the American Indian, Smithsonian Institution, Washington, D.C., and in a number of solo exhibitions.

JAMES LUNA Received a B.F.A. in studio arts, University of California, Irvine, and an M.S. in counseling, San Diego State University, California; and has also worked as academic counselor, Palomar Community College, San Marcos, California and an instructor in studio arts, University of California, San Diego, La Jolla, California. Luna began his career as a painter, and later started creating installations and performance pieces, which he has presented at universities, art galleries, and museums throughout North America. He has received numerous awards, including Best Live Short Performance Award at the American Indian Film Festival, San Francisco, California, and a Bessie Award, Dance Theatre Workshop, New York. Luna was sponsored by the National Museum of the American Indian, Smithsonian Institution, Washington, D.C., to create a new work for the 2005 Venice *Biennale*, representing the United States.

REBECCA LYON Attended the University of Alaska, Anchorage. Lyon was awarded an Artists Fellowship from the George Gustav Heye Center of the National Museum of the American Indian, Smithsonian Institution, New York, and her work has been presented in numerous selected and juried group exhibitions at institutions including the Pratt Museum, Homer, Alaska, and the Peabody Essex Museum, Salem, Massachusetts.

JAMES MADISON Began carving at the age of eight with his grand- father, father, and uncle; later, received a B.F.A., University of Washington, Seattle, Washington, and continued his studies at Pratt Fine Arts Center, Seattle, Washington. Madison's work has been exhibited throughout Washington State.

DEBORAH MAGEE Received a B.A. in art history, Montana State University, Bozeman, and an M.Ed. at the University of Montana, Missoula. Magee obtained further training as an intern at the National Museum of Natural History, Smithsonian Institution, Washington, D.C., and the National Museum of American History, Behring Center, Smithsonian Institution, Washington, D.C. Her work was included in the exhibition *Beauty, Honor, and Tradition: The Legacy of Plains Indian Shirts* at the George Gustav Heye Center of the National Museum of the American Indian, Smithsonian Institution, New York, and in *A Warrior I Have Been* at the Birmingham Museum & Art Gallery, Birmingham, England. Magee is descended from a line of artists on her mother's side.

VALERIE MALESKU Originally trained as a carver and painter, Malesku began working in gold and silver after an apprenticeship with noted Haida artist Bill Reid.

KIM MAMARADLO Received a B.A. in visual arts, Southern Oregon 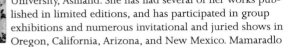 University, Ashland. She has had several of her works published in limited editions, and has participated in group exhibitions and numerous invitational and juried shows in Oregon, California, Arizona, and New Mexico. Mamaradlo is descended from an artistic family that includes George Blake* (carver and jeweler) and Lena Hurd (basketmaker).

JOHN MARSTON A self-taught artist, growing up surrounded by many artists; started carving at the age of eight with his parents, experienced carvers who taught him the legends of the Coast Salish people. Over the last fifteen years, Marston has developed his own, personal style of carving, adapting the designs of his ancestors to create contemporary totem poles, talking sticks, masks, and other traditional Coast Salish forms. Recently, he has worked with *Wayne Young, Noel Brown, and other master carvers. He is the brother of *Luke Marston.

LUKE MARSTON Grew up in a family of artists and began carving at a very early age, like his brother *John Marston. Early in his career, he sought the guidance of a well-known carver, *Wayne Young, in refining his own forms and designs and providing detailed finishing. In 1998, he began to learn stone carving as well. Luke has participated in the carving of house posts for a public school in Seattle, Washington, and a totem pole in Thunderbird Park, Victoria, British Columbia.

MARQUES HANALEI MARZAN Received a B.F.A. in fiber arts, University of Hawai'i at Mānoa, Honolulu. Marzan has taught as an instructor at the Academy Art Center of the Honolulu Academy of Arts and has traveled extensively throughout the Pacific, studying weaving techniques from the many indigenous cultures. His work has been shown locally as well as in Tahiti and New Zealand; and he has received a number of awards and scholarships, including the Hawai'i Handweavers Hui scholarship and the Pacific Handcrafters' Guild Award.

DARREN MCKENZIE Attended the Kitanmaax School of Northwest Coast Indian Art, Hazelton, British Columbia, where he studied under *Ken Mowatt; also studied at the University of Regina, Saskatchewan; Ontario College of Art & Design, Toronto, Ontario; and Medicine Hat College, Alberta. McKenzie has won visual-art grants for emerging artists three times from the Saskatchewan Arts Board. His work has been shown in western Canada as well as in the United States. Darren is the brother of *Kevin McKenzie.

KEVIN MCKENZIE Studied at Ontario College of Art & Design, Toronto; and pursued additional studies at the University of Regina, Saskatchewan, and at the Emily Carr Institute of Art + Design, Vancouver, British Columbia. McKenzie's work has been presented in solo, two-person, and group exhibitions in British Columbia; and he has received various awards and grants, including the Aboriginal Arts Development Award, First Peoples' Heritage, Language and Culture Council, Victoria, British Columbia, and a Production Grant from Canada Council for the Arts. Among the public collections that include his work is the Glenbow Museum, Calgary, Alberta. Kevin is the brother of *Darren McKenzie.

KEN MCNEIL Began his carving career when he was a teenager, guided by his uncle, noted carver and artist *Dempsey Bob. McNeil has now also taught carving, and has participated in several important collaborative commissions carving totem poles. He made one of these with master carver Stan Bevan, his cousin, at Expo '92 in Seville, Spain, which has since been returned to Canada and installed at the Kitselas Cultural/Recreational Centre, British Columbia. McNeil's work was also included in the traveling exhibition *Lost and Found Traditions—Native American Art, 1965–1985*, organized by the Renwick Gallery of the Smithsonian American Art Museum, Smithsonian Insititution, Washington, D.C.

KATRINA MITTEN A self-taught beadwork artist, currently studying fine art at Indiana University-Purdue University, Fort Wayne. Mitten's work has been exhibited at the Wright State University Art Galleries, Dayton, Ohio, and the Miami University Art Museum, Oxford, Ohio, and has won numerous awards at juried shows at the Eiteljorg Museum of American Indians and Western Art, Indianapolis, Indiana.

VALERIE MORGAN Studied applied arts at the Kitanmaax School of Northwest Coast Indian Art, Hazelton, British Columbia, learning woodcarving, jewelry engraving, and leather working; and served a long-term apprenticeship under artist *Ken Mowatt, who is known for his carved and painted wood sculptures. Morgan utilizes her knowledge of traditional Northwest Coast arts to make suede and leather clothing featuring contemporary adaptations of Native designs—wearable sculpture— and to carve narrative masks.

PETER MORIN Received a B.F.A., Emily Carr Institute of Art + Design, Vancouver, British Columbia; continued his studies at Kwantlen University College, Surrey, British Columbia, the Gulf Islands Film & Television School, Galiano Island, British Columbia, and the Synala Honours Program, University of British Columbia, Vancouver. Morin's work has been shown in a number of group and solo exhibitions. He has also curated several exhibitions and participated in panel discussions, including one that he led for the Museum of Anthropology at the University of British Columbia, Vancouver.

NICOLE MORITA Received a B.F.A., University of Hawai'i at Mānoa, Honolulu. Morita obtained further training as an intern at the Metropolitan Museum of Art, New York; the Japanese American National Museum, Los Angeles, California; and the Honolulu Academy of Arts. She has received several awards and scholarships.

KEN MOWATT Learned about his Tsimshian Nation traditions and culture from his grandparents, who raised him; attended Kitanmaax School of Northwest Coast Indian Art, Hazelton, British Columbia. In 1970, when Mowatt was studying at the 'Ksan school (the local name for the Kitanmaax School, which is housed in the 'Ksan Historical Village and Museum), he began working with other Northwest Coast artists, such as Vernon Stephens and Earl Muldoe; and he later became an instructor at 'Ksan in silkscreening and wood carving. Mowatt has created numerous

totem poles, masks, bowls, wooden shields, and silkscreen prints, many of which are in private, corporate, and public collections in North America and Europe. Among the public collections that include his works: JP Morgan Chase Bank Art Collection, New York; the City of Ottawa, Ontario.

MOLLY MURPHY Learned beadworking, hide tanning, sewing, and traditional clothing design at an early age; received a B.F.A., University of Montana, Missoula. Murphy's work reflects an interest in traditional Native arts and modern art.

STAN NATCHEZ Received a B.S., University of Southern Colorado, Pueblo, and an M.F.A., Arizona State University, Tempe. Natchez was chairman of the Humanities Department at the Orme School, Mayer, Arizona, and editorial advisor and education coordinator to *Native Peoples Magazine*. He was also a traditional dancer who performed in European capitals and across the U.S., and created the beadwork for his own elaborate costumes. Natchez's work has been exhibited extensively in group and solo exhibitions throughout the U.S. and Europe, and he still continues to participate in invitational and juried shows such as the annual Santa Fe Indian Market. Stan Natchez is the brother of *James Faks.

DAVID NEEL As a photographer, studied photojournalism at the University of Kansas, Lawrence, and at Mount Royal College, Calgary, Alberta; as a traditional carver, was taught by his mother, Ellen Neel and her uncle, master carver Mungo Martin, and trained with Kwakwaka'wakw artists Wayne Alfred and Beau Dick; also studied the great works of his Kwagiutl heritage in museum collections. Neel has had an extensive career both as a photographer and photojournalist and as an artist working in diverse mediums. He photographs contemporary Native Indian culture for publication and exhibition, and creates sculptures that bridge the divide between traditional and modern. Neel's work has been shown in numerous group and solo exhibitions at such institutions as the National Gallery of Canada, Ottowa, Ontario; the George Gustav Heye Center of the National Museum of the American Indian, Smithsonian Institution, New York; and the Seoul Arts Center, Korea. He has also received many grants and commissions. Among the public collections that include his work: Vancouver Art Gallery, British Columbia; Seattle Art Museum, Washington; National Museum of the American Indian, Smithsonian Institution, Washington, D.C.; Library and Archives Canada, Ottawa, Ontario.

MARIANNE NICOLSON Received a B.F.A. in visual arts, Emily Carr Institute of Art + Design, Vancouver, British Columbia, and an M.F.A. in visual arts and an M.A. in linguistics and anthropology, University of Victoria, British Columbia. Nicolson has had an extensive career that includes many group and solo exhibitions, among them *Reservation X*, a traveling exhibition organized by the National Museum of the American Indian, Smithsonian Institution, Washington D.C. In 1999, she was awarded an Eiteljorg Fellowship for Native American Fine Art, Eiteljorg Museum of American Indians and Western Art, Indianapolis, Indiana. Among the public collections that include her work: Museum of Anthropology at the University of British Columbia, Vancouver, British Columbia; Eiteljorg Museum of American Indians and Western Art; Vancouver Art Gallery, British Columbia.

GLEN NIPSHANK Attended the Institute of American Indian Arts, Santa Fe, New Mexico, and the Native Education Centre, Vancouver, British Columbia. Among the public collections that include his work: Institute of American Indian Arts; Heard Museum, Phoenix, Arizona; Museum of Arts & Design, New York.

ED ARCHIE NOISECAT Studied master printmaking, Emily Carr Institute of Art + Design, Vancouver, British Columbia; also completed residencies at the George Gustav Heye Center of the National Museum of the American Indian, Smithsonian Institution, New York; the Eiteljorg Museum of American Indians and Western Art, Indianapolis, Indiana; and Evergreen State College, Olympia, Washington. NoiseCat worked as a printmaker and graphic artist at Tyler Graphics, Ltd., Mount Kisco, New York and at Solo Press, New York, and as an instructor in sculpture and glass art at the Institute of American Indian Arts, Santa Fe, New Mexico. Among the numerous exhibitions that have presented his work is *Rez: Rezervation Rezurrection Reztitution*, a two-person show that NoiseCat shared with graphic artist and painter Mateo Romero at the Museum of Indian Arts & Culture, Santa Fe, New Mexico. He was recently commissioned to make a new work for the National Museum of the American Indian's new building in Washington, D.C.

KEONE NUNES Attended the University of Hawai'i at Mānoa, Honolulu. Nunes is active in various aspects of Hawaiian culture and has had a primary focus on tattoo arts for the past fifteen years.

MARVIN OLIVER Received a B.A., San Francisco State University, California, and an M.F.A., University of Washington, Seattle. He is a professor as well as an artist, serving as director of the American Indian Studies Department at the University of Washington, Seattle, where he also teaches two-dimensional design, wood carving, and art history; and he is curator of contemporary Native American art at the Burke Museum of Natural History and Culture, University of Washington, Seattle. Among the awards he has received are a National Endowment for the Arts Fellowship and a Distinguished Alumnus Award, University of Washington. Oliver's prints and his sculptures in glass have been exhibited throughout North America and in Japan.

GARY OLVER A self-taught artist, having learned to carve argillite after moving to British Columbia in 1975; now best known for his miniature carvings.

OTHNIEL KA'IOULIOKAHIHIKOLO'EHU OOMITTUK, JR. A self-taught artist who learned to carve by watching his grandfather carve in whalebone; received a B.S. in art, Western Oregon State College, Monmouth. Oomituck was later encouraged in his career by noted artist *Larry Ahvakana. Among the public collections that include his work is the Portland Art Museum, Portland, Oregon. Othniel is the husband of *Natalie Mahina Jensen-Oomittuk.

WILMA OSBORNE Has been sewing since the age of nine, descended from generations of highly accomplished skin sewers. Osborne is one of the most experienced skin sewers in the Bering Strait region in Alaska. She makes custom clothing and accessories using traditional techniques.

JUANITA PAHDOPONY Received an A.A., Cameron University, Lawton, Oklahoma, a B.A., Southwestern Oklahoma State University, Weatherford, and an M.Ed., Oklahoma City University. Pahdopony has had extensive teaching experience and has served as both a guest lecturer and a curator. Her work was featured in a recent solo show at the American Indian Community House, New York.

PAHPONEE A self-taught artist, Pahponee was named Artist of the Year by the Indian Arts and Crafts Association in 1999. Among the public collections that include her work is the Eiteljorg Museum of American Indians and Western Art, Indianapolis, Indiana.

ROSALIE PANIYAK Was taught the Native art of doll making— traditionally handed down through the maternal line—by her mother, Mary Chanarak. Rosalie, in turn, taught the art to her daughter and granddaughter. Among the public collections that include her work: National Museum of the American Indian, Smithsonian Institution, Washington, D.C.; Anchorage Museum of History and Art, Alaska.

TIM PAUL A self-taught artist; began carving in the mid-1970s at the 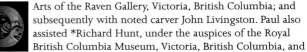 Arts of the Raven Gallery, Victoria, British Columbia; and subsequently with noted carver John Livingston. Paul also assisted *Richard Hunt, under the auspices of the Royal British Columbia Museum, Victoria, British Columbia, and he was "senior carver" for eight years at Thunderbird Park. With an extensive career both as sculptor and graphic artist, he has received numerous important public commissions. Among the public collections that include his work: Royal British Columbia Museum, Victoria, British Columbia; the Field Museum, Chicago, Illinois; Windsor Great Park, Windsor, England; University of Pennsylvania, Philadelphia, Pennsylvania; Captain Cook Memorial Museum, Whitby, England.

SUSAN PAVEL Received a B.A., Washington State University, Pullman; an M.Ed., University of Idaho, Moscow, Idaho; and a Ph.D., Washington State University, Pullman; and served an apprenticeship under master Salish weaver Bruce Miller. Pavel is the recipient of an artist-in-residence award from Evergreen State College, Olympia, Washington, and is the co-founder/director of Southern Puget Salish Weaver's Guild.

SUSAN LAURE PEEBLES Studied fine art (sculpture), University of Oregon, Eugene. Among the public collections that include her work is the Heard Museum, Phoenix, Arizona.

SHAUN PETERSON Studied examples of Salish art in museum collections to learn about the culture and art of his own people; and learned about different fields of artistic expertise and the different styles of the various Northwest Coast groups from a select group of artists including Greg Colfax, Loren White, and Steve Brown. Peterson works in a wide variety of mediums, particularly etched glass, carved wood, and graphic design. He was a participating carver for the "Founders Totem Pole" at the Pilchuck Glass School, Stanwood, Washington, and his work is featured in the traveling exhibition *Fusing Traditions: Transformations in Glass by Native American Artists* organized by the Museum of Craft & Folk Art, San Francisco, California.

DAVID RUBEN PIQTOUKUN Has had an international career, with his works shown in numerous solo and group exhibitions at institutions such as the Art Gallery of Ontario, Toronto; Vancouver Inuit Art Society; and the Staatliches Museum fur Völkerkunde (National Ethnology Museum), Munich, Germany. Among the public collections that include his work: Canada House Gallery, London, England; Art Gallery of Ontario, Toronto, Ontario; Canadian Museum of Civilization, Hull, Quebec; the McMichael Canadian Art Collection, Kleinburg, Ontario; Changchun International Sculpture Park, Laioning Province, China; Staatliches Museum für Völkerkunde.

LILLIAN PITT A self-taught, highly accomplished artist who continually reinvents her work. Pitt utilizes a wide range of materials—such as beads, feathers, shells, wire, weathered wood—to create a richly textured context for her hand-fired stoneware forms. Her work has been presented in numerous solo exhibitions, and she has received many public commissions. Among the public collections that include her work: Heard Museum, Phoenix, Arizona; Portland Art Museum, Portland, Oregon; City of Oguni, Japan.

SUSAN POINT Began her artistic career with studies at Vancouver Community College, British Columbia; and has continued to expand her repertoire to include studies in engraving, metallurgy, metal deformation, printmaking, painting, papermaking, and more. A prolific artist, Point has been the focus of many solo exhibitions in Canada and the United States. Among the sites for the many public commissions she has been awarded are Vancouver International Airport, British Columbia, and the National Museum of the American Indian, Smithsonian Institution, Washington, D.C. Among the public collections that include her work: the city of Seattle, Washington; the Province of British Columbia, Parliament Buildings, Victoria, British Columbia; Museum of Arts & Design, New York.

KIMBERLY "WENDY" PONCA

Attended the Institute of American Indian Arts, Santa Fe, New Mexico; received a B.F.A., Kansas City Art Institute, Missouri, and an M.A. in art therapy, Southwestern College, Santa Fe, New Mexico. Ponca has worked as an arts instructor at the Institute of American Indian Arts; in the Costume Department of the Santa Fe Opera, New Mexico; and as professor of drawing and design, University of Nevada, Las Vegas, Nevada. She has also been the recipient of an Artist-in-Residence award from the George Gustave Heye Center of the National Museum of the American Indian, Smithsonian Institution, New York.

KEVIN POURIER Has had the skills to carve since he was a child, but did not pursue it as an art until he was about twenty, starting with antler and then switching to buffalo horn. Collaborating with his wife, Valerie, Pourier has been creating buffalo horn jewelry with precious stones since 1992, having received numerous awards. Among the public collections that include his work: Carnegie Museum of Art, Pittsburgh, Pennsylvania; Denver Museum of Nature & Science, Colorado; Royal Museum, Edinburgh, Scotland.

THELISSA M. REDHAWK Received a B.S. in art, Eastern Oregon University, La Grande, Oregon. Redhawk's work was included in the traveling exhibition *Hitéemlkiliiksix, Within the Circle of the Rim: Nations Gathering on Common Ground*, organized by Evergreen State College, Olympia, Washington, and in *Reflecting on Lewis and Clark: Contemporary Native American Views*, organized by the Maryhill Museum of Art, Goldendale, Washington.

ERIC ROBERTSON Received a B.F.A., Emily Carr Institute of Art + Design, Vancouver, British Columbia, and an M.F.A., Concordia University, Montreal, Quebec. Robertson has done extensive teaching and curatorial work, has served as guest artist/juror for the Canada Council, and is a co-founder of the Nation to Nation artists' collective. Robertson's work has been presented in a solo exhibition at the Indian Art Centre, Hull, Quebec, numerous group exhibitions throughout Canada and the United States, and an international Sculpture Symposium, Ichon, Korea. He has received several awards/grants from the Canada Council for the Arts, as well as public commissions including *Shaking the Crown Bone* at the Museum of Anthropology at the University of British Columbia, Vancouver; *Evolving Wing and Gravity of Presence*, Seattle City Hall, Washington; and *Four Sentries on the Precipice of Post*, town of Banff, Alberta.

LARRY ROSSO Was taught to carve at an early age by his grandfather; and subsequently has worked with many Northwest Coast master carvers, including Doug Cranmer and *Robert Davidson. Rosso is known for his steamed and bent boxes, which are of outstanding design and proportion. More recently he has been carving circular panels, four of which have been installed in Vancouver International Airport.

MARCEL RUSS A self-taught artist, Russ has trained under many noted carvers, including Bill Reid, *Robert Davidson, and *Dempsey Bob.

NELDA SCHRUPP Received a B.F.A. in art/ceramics and an M.F.A. in metalsmithing, jewelry, and small sculpture, University of North Dakota, Grand Forks. Schrupp's work has been presented in group and solo exhibitions at venues such as the Northwest Art Center, Minot State University, North Dakota, and Mingei International Museum, San Diego, California. She was also artist-in-residence at the George Gustav Heye Center of the National Museum of the American Indian, Smithsonian Institution, New York. Among the public collections that include her work: Eiteljorg Museum of American Indians and Western Art, Indianapolis, Indiana; Renwick Gallery of the Smithsonian American Art Museum, Smithsonian Institution, Washington, D.C.

TANIS MARIA S'EILTIN Received a B.F.A. in printmaking, University of Alaska, Fairbanks, and an M.F.A. in mixed media, University of Arizona, Tucson. S'eiltin is currently an associate professor of art & humanities, Fairhaven College, Western Washington University. S'eiltin's works have appeared in numerous group, invitational, and solo exhibitions, including *Watchful Eyes, Native American Women Artists*, Heard Museum, Phoenix, Arizona; *Native American; Reflecting Contemporary Realities*, American Indian Contemporary Arts, San Francisco, California; and *Ee wdoowata'w ag'e: Did They Rob You?*, a traveling exhibition organized by the Institute of American Indian Arts, Santa Fe, New Mexico. S'eiltin also organized the conference "Artists of Resistance Speak Out on Protecting Cultural Heritage," under the auspices of the Seattle Art Museum, Washington; and she is one of this year's recipients of an Eiteljorg Fellowship for Native American Fine Art, with an exhibition featuring her work opening later this year at the Eiteljorg Museum of American Indians and Western Art, Indianapolis, Indiana.

JOSEPH SENUNGETUK Studied at the University of Alaska,

Fairbanks, under his brother, noted artist and teacher *Ronald Senungetuk; received a B.F.A. in printmaking and sculpture, San Francisco Art Institute, California. He is a teacher, lecturer, and coordinator of many significant programs in Alaska. Senungetuk's work has been featured in numerous solo and group exhibitions, including the Visual Arts Center of Alaska, Anchorage. He has also received several public commissions, such as *Arctic Arc*, an outdoor sculpture in Wales, Alaska, in collaboration with Michigan artist David Barr. Among the public collections that include his work: Alaska State Museum, Juneau; Anchorage Museum of History and Art, Alaska; Seattle-Tacoma International Airport, Washington.

RONALD SENUNGETUK Received a B.F.A., School for American

Craftsmen, Rochester Institute of Technology, where he studied with Tage Frid and Hans Christensen, professors of woodworking and metalsmithing; and studied in Oslo, Norway, on a Fulbright Fellowship. He also taught art at the University of Alaska, Fairbanks. Senungetuk has an extensive and international career spanning more than fifty years and is considered one of the most pre-eminent Alaskan artists. He is the brother of *Joseph Senungetuk.

SUSIE SILOOK Descended on her father's side from a long lineage

of hunters, artists, writers, and archeological workers, with her father a successful carver in his own right. A creative writer and artist, Silook was a recipient of an Eiteljorg Fellowship for Native American Fine Art in 2001. Among the public collections that include her work is the Anchorage Museum of History and Art, Alaska.

JAY SIMEON Began pursuing a career as an artist at age fourteen,

under the guidance of his first cousin, artist Sharon Hitchcock.

PRESTON SINGLETARY Studied at the Pilchuck Glass School,

Stanwood, Washington, with many of the masters of that medium. Singletary is currently a trustee of the school, and collaborated with a team of artists to install the Pilchuck Founders Pole at the Pilchuck Glass School in 2001. He has also worked with glass artists in Sweden, Finland, and Italy. Public collections that include his work: Seattle Art Museum, Washington; Museum of Arts & Design, New York; Etnografiska Museet (Museum of Ethnography), Stockholm, Sweden.

DUANE SLICK Received a B.F.A. in painting and a B.A. in art education, University of Northern Iowa, Cedar Falls, Iowa; participated in the National Student Exchange Program, studying at West Chester University of Pennsylvania, and the State University of New York at Potsdam, New York; attended the Skowhegan School of Painting and Sculpture, Maine; and received an M.F.A. in painting, University of California, Davis, California. Slick is currently chairman of the Painting Department, Rhode Island School of Design, Providence. Slick has had an extensive career of solo, two-person, and group exhibitions; has been the recipient of many prestigious awards; and served as artist-in-residence, lecturer, juror, and in numerous other professional capacities. He has also been involved in a variety of special projects and editions. Among the public collections that include his work: the DeCordova Museum and Sculpture Park, Lincoln, Massachusetts; Montclair Art Museum, New Jersey; Fort Wayne Museum of Art, Indiana.

HARRIS SMITH Harris is the father of *Steve Smith and *Rod Smith.

ROD SMITH Received his training in the traditional manner, like his

brother, *Steve Smith, learning carving and painting from their father, *Harris Smith, and their grandfather. Rod Smith began his artistic career about 1993, after leaving a job in the automotive industry. Working primarily in wood, he is inspired by the work of his father and brother, sculptor *Robert Davidson*, and the Hunt family.

STEVE SMITH Was introduced to carving and painting, like his

brother, *Rod Smith, by their father, *Harris Smith, and their grandfather. Steve Smith has been working as a full-time artist since 1990. With his artistic roots in Oweekeno Village and Campbell River, British Columbia, he has developed his own distinct, innovative style of carved and painted works, many of which are now in private collections in North America and abroad.

BENTLY SPANG Received a B.S. in art (extended sculpture) and

business administration, Montana State University, Billings, and an M.F.A. in sculpture, University of Wisconsin, Madison. Spang is an artist, curator, and educator, and has exhibited extensively throughout North America in several solo exhibitions and numerous group exhibitions, including *who stole the tee pee?*, a traveling exhibition organized by the National Museum of the American Indian, Smithsonian Institution, New York; *Indian Reality Today: Contemporary Indian Art of North America*, Westfälisches Museum für Naturkunde, Münster, Germany; *Art in 2 Worlds: The Native American Fine Art Invitational 1983–1997*, Heard Museum, Phoenix, Arizona. Spang's public commissions include *The Identity Project, Garden of Cultural Delights* at the Heard Museum.

C. MAXX STEVENS Received an A.A. and Indian Studies degrees,

Haskell Indian Nations University, Lawrence, Kansas; a B.F.A. in sculpture and ceramics, Wichita State University, Kansas with a combination Metals Certificate from the United Welding Institute, Wichita, Kansas; and an M.F.A. in sculpture, Indiana University, Bloomington. Stevens has also taught at the Rhode Island School of Design, Providence, the School of the Art Institute of Chicago, Illinois, and other important institutions. She is currently an interim dean at the Institute of American Indian Arts, Santa Fe, New Mexico. Awards include Joan Mitchell Foundation Sculpture Grant and the Site Santa Fe Regional Artist Grant.

CARL STROMQUIST A primarily self-taught artist who has focused

on the forms and designs of his cultural heritage; studied under Salish carver George Pennier and worked with glass sculpture artist Douglas Baker. Stromquist began working in glass in the early 1990s, and started carving wood in 1997, influenced by the art of *Robert Davidson, *Dempsey Bob, Charles Edenshaw, and Bill Reid. He has since created five limited-edition prints, and has been collaborating with glass sculpture artist Douglas Baker.

MORRIS "MOY" SUTHERLAND A largely self-taught artist; began

his career as a carver in the mid-1990s at the age of twenty-one, studying under several master artists in the region, starting with Joe Wilson in Alert Bay, Vancouver Island. After mastering some basic techniques, Sutherland worked with Mark Mickey and Ron Hamilton in Port Alberni, learning from them about the Nuu Chah Nulth style, his Native culture. He then worked with Victor and Carey Newman at the Blue Raven Gallery in Sooke, British Columbia, and is currently apprenticing with Nuu-chah-nulth artist Art Thompson.

NORMAN TAIT Descendant of a master carver, and educated by his elders in traditions and ceremonies; studied two-dimensional design, Kitanmaax School of Northwest Coast Indian Art, Hazelton, British Columbia, with subsequent studies in jewelry making. Tait's extensive international career includes numerous public commissions, several limited-edition prints, and many solo and group exhibitions, as well as teaching and lecturing. He established his reputation as a carver in the early 1970s with a collaborative totem pole commemorating the incorporation of Port Edward, and has since created many others, for the Field Museum, Chicago, Illinois; the Heard Museum, Phoenix, Arizona; the National Museum of Ethnology, Osaka, Japan; more recently, a thirty-seven foot pole in Scotland; and for the British Royal Family in Bushy Park, London. He is also the recipient of the Commemorative Medal from the Canadian Confederation. His nephew is *Ron Telek.

TCHIN Received a B.F.A., Rhode Island School of Design, Providence, Rhode Island; also studied at the Institute of American Indian Arts, Santa Fe, New Mexico. Tchin has participated in numerous invitational and juried shows, and his work has been published numerous times.

RON TELEK Learned to carve during his teens under the tutelage of his uncle, master artist *Norman Tait, and together they have worked on many public commissions. Telek began pursuing his career seriously as an artist in 1985. In his masks and sculptures, Telek's principal medium is wood, but he often incorporates other materials such as bone, abalone, and moose hair, In the totem poles that he creates with his uncle, the wood is left unpainted so that the natural grain will represent the faces of the figures. Among the public collections that include his work is the Museum of Northern British Columbia, Prince Rupert.

LISA TELFORD Worked as a master apprentice under traditional Haida weavers Holly Churchill (cedar garments) and Delores Churchill (basketry), Washington State Arts Commission, Olympia. Telford was an artist-in-residence at the Eiteljorg Museum of American Indians and Western Art, Indianapolis, Indiana; the Heard Museum, Phoenix, Arizona; and the George Gustav Heye Center of the National Museum of the American Indian, Smithsonian Institution, New York. She has frequently given lectures and demonstrations on Northwest Coast basketry, and her work has been shown at many institutions, including the Ohio Craft Museum, Columbus, and the Mingei International Museum, San Diego, California, and in exhibitions such as *Hitéemlkiliiksix: Within the Circle of the Rim Nations Gathering on Common Ground*, organized by Tamástslikt Cultural Institute, Pendelton, Oregon, and *The Language of Native American Baskets from the Weavers' View*, at the George Gustav Heye Center of the National Museum of the American Indian, New York. Among the public collections that include her work: National Museum of the American Indian, Smithsonian Institution, Washington, D.C.; Hallie Ford Museum of Art, Willamette University, Salem, Oregon.

DONALD TENOSO Studied at the University of New Mexico, Albuquerque, New Mexico; received an A.F.A., Institute of American Indian Arts, Santa Fe, New Mexico. Tenoso is the recipient of a number of significant awards and honors, including artist-in-residence, National Museum of Natural History, Smithsonian Institution, Washington, D.C. His work has been included in numerous exhibitions, including *Gifts of the Spirit*, a traveling exhibition organized by the Peabody Essex Museum, Salem, Massachusetts; and *Lost and Found Traditions: Native American Art 1965–1985*, traveling exhibition organized by the American Federation of Arts. Among the public collections that include his work: Institute of American Indian Arts Museum, Santa Fe, New Mexico; Sioux Indian Museum, Rapid City, South Dakota; National Museum of Natural

History, Smithsonian Institution, Washington, D.C.; Natural History Museum of Los Angeles County, California.

CHARLENE TETERS Received an A.F.A. in painting, Institute of American Indian Arts, Santa Fe, New Mexico; a B.F.A. in painting, College of Santa Fe, New Mexico; and an M.F.A. in painting, University of Illinois. Currently a professor at the Institute of American Indian Arts, Santa Fe, New Mexico, and former interim dean for arts and cultural studies, Teters is also an activist, writer, and founding board member of the National Coalition on Racism in Sports and Media in Minneapolis, Minnesota. Awards she has received include artist-in-residence, American Museum of Natural History, New York; Allan Houser Memorial Award; New Mexico Governor's Award; and being named "Person of the Week," ABC World News Tonight with Peter Jennings. Teters has lectured extensively throughout the U.S., worked as senior editor for *Native Artist* and *Indian Artist Magazines*, and has served as juror and curator on numerous occasions. Her work has appeared in many solo and group exhibitions, including *We Were Like Custer*, Center for Contemporary Arts, Santa Fe, New Mexico; *Home of the Brave*, Notre Dame College, South Euclid, Ohio; *Baseball and Playing Indian*, American Museum of Natural History, New York; and *The Art of Community*, faculty exhibition at the Institute of American Indian Arts, Santa Fe, New Mexico.

BRIAN TRIPP Studied art and served as instructor, Humboldt State University, Arcata, California. Tripp's work has been exhibited widely in venues in California, Texas, New York, Oklahoma, and New Mexico. A traditional dancer and singer, Tripp is also involved in ceremonies in northwest California and in the struggle for Native American sovereignty.

CHARLENE VICKERS Received a B.A. in critical studies of the arts, School for the Contemporary Arts at Simon Fraser University, Burnaby, British Columbia; took postgraduate classes in Native studies, Trent University, Peterborough, Ontario; studio art, Emily Carr Institute of Art + Design, Vancouver, British Columbia; and visual arts, Wexford Collegiate Institute, Toronto, Ontario. Vickers has received a number of awards and grants, including Canada Council Visual Arts Grant and the B.C. Arts Council Award.

DAWN WALLACE Received an A.A.S. in jewelry design, Fashion Institute of Technology, New York. Wallace is a jewelry designer and artist who has won numerous awards at the Wheelwright Museum Invitational for Young Native Artists and at Southwestern Association for Indian Arts annual Santa Fe Indian Market, New Mexico; and has exhibited in Alaska and Vermont. She is the daughter of *Denise Wallace.

DENISE WALLACE Attended the Institute of American Indian Arts, Santa Fe, New Mexico. Denise, along with husband Samuel, produces jewelry that is inspired by her Alaskan heritage. Their work has been the individual focus of many exhibitions, including the traveling exhibition *Arctic Transformations: The Jewelry of Denise and Samuel Wallace* organized by the Anchorage Museum of History and Art, Alaska, and has also been included in numerous group exhibitions. Among the public collections that include their work: Anchorage Museum of History and Art; Institute of American Indian Arts; Museum of Arts & Design, New York; Mingei International Museum, San Diego, California. Denise is the mother of *Dawn Wallace.

CONNIE WATTS Received a B.F.A. inter media and industrial design, Emily Carr Institute of Art + Design, Vancouver, British Columbia; and a B.I.D., University of Manitoba, Winnipeg, Manitoba. Watts has received numerous awards and grants, including Artist-in-Residence, the McMichael Canadian Art Collection, Kleinburg, Ontario; and, for her storyboard for a planned computer animation entitled *Witness*, a Visual Artist's Development Award from the Vancouver Foundation, followed by a grant from the Canada Arts Council to complete the computer animation. Her work has been featured in solo and group exhibitions across Canada and the United States, including *Circle* at the Richmond Art Gallery, British Columbia, and *Dezhan Ejan* at the Canadian Embassy, Washington, D.C. Among her many public commissions is a large Thunderbird sculpture, *Hetux*, installed at Vancouver International Airport, British Columbia.

MARGARET ROACH WHEELER Received a B.S. Ed. in sculpture, Missouri Southern State University, Joplin, Missouri; and an M.A. in fibers, Pittsburgh State University, Pittsburgh, Kansas. In addition to an numerous workshops and seminars, Wheeler has participated in the Artist-in-Residence Program sponsored by Atl-Atl, National Museum of the American Indian, Smithsonian Institution, Washington, D.C. Her work has been featured in many group exhibitions, such as *Indian Chic: A Fashion Show and Symposium*, Denver Art Museum, Colorado; and *Fashion from Native Thought*, American Indian Community House Gallery, New York.

CHRISTIAN WHITE Born into a family of artists, and encouraged as a teenager to pursue his interest in art; was taught to carve in argillite by his father, Morris White Chief Edenshaw. Although White also works in other mediums, he is best known for his highly refined miniature carvings in argillite, recently featured in *Totems to Turquoise: Native North American Jewelry Arts of the Northwest and Southwest*, a traveling exhibition organized by the American Museum of Natural History, New York. Among the public collections that include his work: Museum of Anthropology at the University of British Columbia, Vancouver; Royal British Columbia Museum, Victoria; Queen Charlotte Islands Museum, Skidegate, British Columbia.

WHITE BUFFALO No information available.

GLEN WOOD Began carving as a teenager, later attending the Kitanmaax School of Northwest Coast Indian Art, Hazelton, British Columbia; studied silver engraving with noted master artist, Philip Janze. Public commissions include a 52-foot reproduction totem pole in collaboration with *Dempsey Bob and other artists, installed at the Museum of Northern British Columbia, Prince Rupert; and in collaboration with artist Gerry Marks, a 15-foot totem pole and house front for the National Museum of Ethnology, Osaka, Japan. Limited-edition silkscreen prints have been issued after eight of Wood's paintings.

DAN WORCESTER Self-taught in the fabrication of his knife handles, Worcester attended bladesmithing school in Washington, Arkansas, the site of the original Bowie knife. His work has been acknowledged by many awards bestowed at various invitational shows.

YÁYA (CHARLES PETER HEIT) Born into a family of artists that includes uncle and noted carver Walter Harris and cousin and jeweler Earl Muldon; began carving in 1970 and was trained in a four-year apprenticeship with his uncle; also attended Kitanmaax School of Northwest Coast Indian Art, Hazelton, British Columbia; and served a two-year apprenticeship under master artist, *Robert Davidson. By the age of eighteen, YáYa was already teaching, although he was still apprenticed to his uncle, and worked on large commissions with him. YáYa's work has appeared in many exhibitions, including *Sacred Circles: 2000 Years of North American Indian Art*, a traveling exhibition organized by the Nelson-Atkins Museum of Art, Kansas City, Missouri; and *Lost and Found Traditions: Native American Art 1965–1985*, a traveling exhibition organized by the American Federation of Arts, New York.

WAYNE YOUNG Began drawing at an early age and received his first formal instruction on Northwest Coast design from his uncle, *Dempsey Bob, with additional help from another uncle, *Norman Tait. Between 1985 and 1989, Young collaborated with both uncles a series of large-scale totem poles. Many of the carvings that Young has made in his solo career are already in collections worldwide.

YUXWELUPTUN (LAWRENCE PAUL) Attended Emily Carr Institute of Art + Design, Vancouver, British Columbia. While generally known as one of the foremost Native painters in Canada, Paul has been experimenting with three-dimensional "ovoid" forms and has participated in numerous solo and group exhibitions, primarily in western Canada and the United States, including *Indigena*, Canadian Museum of Civilization, Gatineau, Quebec, and *Lost Illusions: Recent Landscape Art*, Vancouver Art Gallery, British Columbia. Among the public collections that include his work: Canadian Museum of Civilization, Gatineau, Quebec; Philbrook Museum of Art, Tulsa, Oklahoma.

BIBLIOGRAPHY

Akwe:kon Journal. *Native American Expressive Culture* 11, nos. 3 & 4 (fall and winter), Ithaca, N.Y.: Akwe:kon Press in association with the National Museum of the American Indian, Washington, D.C., 1994.

American Indian Contemporary Arts. *The Spirit of Native America*. Ed. Sarah Bates. With essay by Elizabeth Woody. San Francisco: American Indian Contemporary Arts, 1993

_____. *Indian Humor*. With essays by Jolene Rickard and Paul Chaat Smith. San Francisco, 1995.

Archuleta, Margaret, ed. *Art in 2 Worlds: Native American Fine Art Invitational, 1983–1997*. Phoenix, Ariz.: Heard Museum, 2002.

_____. *7th Native American Fine Art Invitational*. Phoenix, Ariz.: Heard Museum, 1997.

_____. *6th Native American Fine Arts Invitational*. Phoenix, Ariz.: Heard Museum, 1994.

Arnold, Grant, Monika Kin Gagnon, and Doreen Jensen. *Topographies: Aspects of Recent B.C. Art*. Vancouver, B.C.: Douglas & McIntyre, 1996.

Berry, Ian. *Staging the Indian: The Politics of Representation*. Saratoga Springs, N.Y.: Tang Museum and Art Gallery, 2001.

Canadian Museum of Civilization, ed. *In the Shadow of the Sun: Perspectives on Contemporary Native Art*. Hull, Quebec: Canadian Museum of Civilization, 1993.

Cazimero, Momi, David J. de la Torre, and Manulani Aluli Meyer. *Nō Maka Hou: New Visions— Contemporary Native Hawaiian Art*. Honolulu: Honolulu Academy of Arts, 2001.

Chalker, Kari, ed. *Totems to Turquoise: Native North American Jewelry Arts of the Northwest and Southwest*. New York: Harry N. Abrams, 2004.

Coe, Ralph T. *Lost and Found Tradition: Native American Art, 1965–1985*. Seattle: University of Washington Press, 1986.

Decker, Julie. *Icebreakers: Alaska's Most Innovative Artists*. Anchorage, Alaska: Decker Art Services, 1999.

_____. *John Hoover: Art & Life*. Seattle: University of Washington Press, 2002.

Dubin, Lois Sherr. *Arctic Transformation: The Jewelry of Denise & Samuel Wallace*. New York: Theodore Dubin Foundation, 2005.

_____. *North American Indian Jewelry and Adornment from Prehistory to the Present*. New York: Abrams, 1999.

Dubin, Margaret, ed. *The Dirt Is Red Here: Art and Poetry from Native California*. Berkeley, Calif.: Heyday Books, 2002.

Duffek, Karen, ed. *Robert Davidson: The Abstract Edge*. Vancouver, B.C.: Museum of Anthropology at the University of British Columbia, 2004.

Eiteljorg Museum of American Indians and Western Art. *Contemporary Masters: The Eiteljorg Fellowship for Native American Fine Art. Vol. 1*. Indianapolis, Ind.: Eiteljorg Museum, 1999.

_____. *Path Breakers: The Eiteljorg Fellowship for Native American Fine Art, 2003*. Indianapolis, Ind.: Eiteljorg Museum, 2003.

The Evergreen State College Longhouse Education and Cultural Center. *Hitéemlkiliiksix: Within the Circle of the Rim*. Olympia, Wash.: Hemlock Printers, 2002.

Heard Museum. *The Fourth Biennial Native American Fine Arts Invitational*. Phoenix, Ariz.: Heard Museum, 1989.

_____. *Native American Fine Art Invitational 8*. Phoenix, Ariz.: Heard Museum, 2002.

Hill, Rick. *Creativity Is Our Tradition: Three Decades of Contemporary Indian Art at the Institute of American Indian Arts*. Santa Fe, N.M.: Institute of American Indian Arts, 1992.

Hushka, Rock. *Lewis & Clark Territory: Contemporary Artists Revisit Place, Race and Memory*. Tacoma, Wash.: University of Washington Press, 2004.

Institute of American Indian Arts Museum. *The Art of Community, IAIA Faculty & Staff Exhibition, 2003*. Santa Fe, N.M.: Institute of American Indian Arts Museum, 2003.

Jonaitis, Aldona, ed. *Looking North: Art from the University of Alaska Museum*. Seattle: University of Washington Press, 1998.

Kastner, Carolyn, ed. *Fusing Traditions: Transformations in Glass by Native American Artists*. San Francisco: Museum of Craft & Folk Art, 2002.

McMaster, Gerald, ed. *Reservation X*. Seattle: University of Washington Press; and Hull, Quebec: Canadian Museum of Civilization, 1998.

McMaster, Gerald and Lee-Ann Martin, eds. *Indigena: Contemporary Native Perspectives in Canadian Art*. New York: STBS, 1992.

Monroe, Dan L., R. Conn, Richard W. Hill, Sr., S. S. Harjo, and John R. Grimes. *Gifts of the Spirit: Works by Nineteenth-Century & Contemporary Native American Artists*. Salem, Mass.: Peabody Essex Museum, 1996.

Nahwooksy, Fred and Richard Hill, Sr., eds. *Who Stole the Tee Pee?* Phoenix, Ariz.: Atlatl, 2000.

National Cowboy Hall of Fame and Western Heritage Center. *Winter Camp: Honoring the Legacy*. Oklahoma City, Okla.: National Cowboy Hall of Fame, 1999.

_____. *Winter Camp 2002: Honoring the Legacy— Contemporary Expressions of Oklahoma Tribal Art*. Oklahoma City, Okla.: National Cowboy Hall of Fame, 2001.

Nemiroff, Diana, Robert Houle, and Charlotte Townsend-Gault. *Land Spirit Power: First Nations at the National Gallery of Canada*. Ottawa: National Gallery of Canada, 1992.

Pukui, Mary Kawena. *ʻOlelo Noʻeau: Hawaiian Proverbs & Poetical Sayings* (Honolulu, Hawaiʻi: Bishop Museum Press, 1983). Originally published as *ʻOlelo noʻeau a ka Hawaii: Folk Sayings from the Hawaiian*, by Jane Lathrop Winne with Mary Kawena Pukui. Honolulu, 1961.

Rushing, W. Jackson, III, ed. *After The Storm: The Eiteljorg Fellowship for Native American Fine Art 2001*. Indianapolis, Ind.: Eiteljorg Museum, 2001.

_____. *Native American Art in the Twentieth Century: Makers, Meanings, Histories*. London: Routledge, 1999.

Ryan, Allan J. *The Trickster Shift: Humour and Irony in Contemporary Native Art*. Vancouver, B.C.: UBC Press, 1999.

Schmidt, Jeremy. *In the Spirit of Mother Earth: Nature in Native American Art*. San Francisco: Chronicle Books, 1994.

National Museum of the American Indian, George Gustav Heye Center, Smithsonian Institution. *This Path We Travel: Celebrations of Contemporary Native American Creativity*. Golden, Colo.: National Museum of the American Indian, Smithsonian Institution, 1994.

Spang, Bently and Jessica Hunter. *Material Culture: Innovation in Native Art*. Great Falls, Mont.: Paris Gibson Square Museum of Art, 2000.

Spirit Wrestler Gallery. *Kiwa Pacific Connections: A Northwest Coast Perspective*. Vancouver, B.C.: Spirit Wrestler Gallery, 2003.

Tétrault, Pierre-Léon, Dana Alan Williams, Guy Sioui Durand, and Alfred Young Man. *New Territories 350/500 Years After: An Exhibition of Contemporary Aboriginal Art of Canada*. Montreal: Ateliers Vision Planétaire, 1992.

Touchette, Charleen, with Suzanne Deats. *ndn art: Contemporary Native American Art*. The New Mexico Artist Series, no. 1. Albuquerque, N.M.: Fresco Fine Art Publications, 2003.

Wade, Edwin L. and Rennard Strickland. *Magic Images: Contemporary Native American Art*. Tulsa, Okla.: Philbrook Art Center, 1981.

Wade, Edwin L., ed. *The Arts of the North American Indian: Native Traditions in Evolution*. New York: Hudson Hills Press, 1986.

Walter, Anna Lee. *The Spirit of Native America*. San Francisco: Chronicle Books, 1989.

Wyatt, Gary. *Mythic Beings: Spirit Art of the Northwest Coast*. Vancouver, B.C.: Douglas & McIntyre, 1999.

Wyatt, Gary, ed. *Susan Point: Coast Salish Artist*. Vancouver, B.C.: Douglas & McIntyre, 2000.

Young Man, Alfred. *North American Indian Art: It's a Question of Integrity*. Kamloops, B.C.: Kamloops Art Gallery, 1998.

INDEX OF ARTISTS' NAMES

Jack Abraham – Jeff Schultz/AlaskaStock.com

Alfred Adams and Primrose Adams – Maggie Nimkin

Victoria Adams - *Deer Dancer Wears His New Striped Leggings*, Donald Neely; *Man Wearing Split Horn Bonnet with Eagle Shield*, Sara Stathus, Santa Fe, NM; *Red Bird and Morning Star Hunt for Horses*, Sara Stathus, Santa Fe, NM

Richard (Rick) Adkins – Graham Blair

Linda Aguilar – Maggie Nimkin

Lawrence "Larry" Ahvakana –Maggie Nimkin

Bernice A. Keolamauloa oʻnalani Akamine – Hal Lum

Harold Alfred – David Behl

Dennis Allen – The Legacy Ltd

Lena Amason – James Barker

Marcus Amerman – Courtesy of *American Indian Art Magazine*

Arthur Amiotte – Maggie Nimkin

Ronald Wayne Anderson – David Behl

Ivy Hāliʻimaile Andrade – Marques Marzan

Muriel Antoine – Maggie Nimkin

Sonny Assu – Dawn Vernon

Keri Ataumbi – *Tah'lee's Parents*, Craig Smith, Courtesy of the Heard Museum, Phoenix, AZ; *Martini Purse*, James Hart

Sylvester Ayek – Maggie Nimkin

Pamela Baker – www.tamararoberts.com

Brian Barber – Brian Barber

Pam Kawehilani Barton – J.D. Griggs

Rick Bartow – Rebekah Johnson, Courtesy of Froelick Gallery, Portland, OR

Karen Beaver –Maggie Nimkin

Alan Bell – Maggie Nimkin

Susie Bevins-Ericsen – *Ancient Memories: Female*, University of Alaska Museum of the North; *Primal Origins: Male*, Dan Davis, Trekker Photography

George Nixon Blake – George Nixon Blake

Randall Blaze – Anonymous

Dempsey Bob – Kenji Nagai

Todd Lonedog Bordeaux – Maggie Nimkin

Parker Boyiddle –Heather Stevenson, Santa Fe, NM

David Bradley – Dan Morse

Jackie Larson Bread – *Untitled Hanging*, Maggie Nimkin; *Connections*, David Behl

Jesse Brillon – Kenji Nagai

Sean Kekamakupaʻa Lee Loy Browne – Paul Kodama

Marcus Cadman – Aztec Media

Keʻalaonaonapuahīnano Campton – Shuzo Uemoto

Phillip Charette (Aarnaquq) – Mitchell Wiencken

Judy Chartrand – *Buffalo Soldiers*, Merle Addison; *Metis Soup Cans*, Judy Chartrand

Kaili Chun – Macario

Corwin "Corky" Clairmont – Dirk Bakker, Artbook, Huntington Woods, MI

Gerald Clarke – Gerald Clarke

Karita Coffey – Karita Coffey

Barry Coffin – Jon Blumb

Doug Coffin – Doug Coffin

Chris Cook – Kenji Nagai

Rande Cook – David Behl

Joe David – Kenji Nagai, Courtesy of Spirit Wrestler Gallery

Lisa Marie David – Kenji Nagai, Courtesy of Inuit Gallery of Vancouver

Benjamin Davidson – Graham Blair

Reg Davidson – Kenji Nagai, Courtesy of Inuit Gallery of Vancouver

Robert Davidson – *Meeting at the Centre*, Bill McLennan; *Hugging the World*, Kenji Nagai; *Identity*, Kenji Nagai

Paula Rasmus Dede – Clark James Mischler

Todd Defoe – *The New Four Directions*, Daniel Barsotti and Peter Johnson; *Improvisation #5*, Maggie Nimkin

Steven Deo – Bruce Malone

Keri-Lynn Dick – Maggie Nimkin

Lehua Domingo and Kilohana Domingo – Maggie Nimkin

Carol Emarthle Douglas – Jerry McCollum

Perry Eaton – Chris Arend Photography

Moana K. M. Eisele – Shuzo Uemoto

James Faks – Price Dewey Galleries, Santa Fe, NM

Joe Feddersen – Richard Nichol, Courtesy Froelick Gallery, Portland, OR

Anita Fields – Gina Fuentes Walker

Bob Freitas – Bob Freitas

Nicholas Galanin – Nicholas Galanin

Bill Glass, Jr. – Bill Glass, Jr.

Demos Glass – Lindsey Wade, Rush-Wade Studio, Kansas City, MO

Pat Courtney Gold – Bill Bachhuber, Portland, OR

Martha Gradolf – Tom Bertolacini

Philip Gray – Graham Blair

Geoff Greene – Courtesy of The Legacy Ltd

Stan Greene – Courtesy of The Legacy Ltd

Teri Greeves – *Khoiye-Goo Mah*, Eva Heyd; *Butterfly Belt*, Maggie Nimkin; *Gkoy-Goo: The Story of My People*, Dan Morse

Robert Gress – Maggie Nimkin

Benjamin Harjo, Jr. – Alex Matos

Nathan Hart – Keith Ball

Tom Haukaas – Christine Reynolds

Emil Her Many Horses – Christopher Smith

John Hitchcock – John Hitchcock

John Hoover – David Mollett

Clarissa Hudson – Clarissa Hudson

Bradley Hunt – Maggie Nimkin

Richard Hunt – Maggie Nimkin

Shawn Hunt – David Behl

Natalie Mahina Jensen-Oomittuk – David Behl

Rocky Kaʻiouliokahihikoloʻehu Jensen – David Behl

Maynard Johnny, Jr. – David Behl

Kenneth Johnson – Michael Neese, Studio Seven Production

Dean Kaahanui – Tom Oiye

Franz Kahale – David Souza

Paulette Nohealani Kahalepuna – Maggie Nimkin

Sonya Kelliher-Combs – Kevin G. Smith

Kathleen Carlo Kendall – Chris Arend Photography

Frederick Kingeekuk – Chris Arend Photography

Klatle-Bhi (Chuck Sam) – Graham Blair

Kim Knife Chief – Kim Knife Chief

Puni Kukahiko – Hal Lum

Jerry Jacob Laktonen – *Puffin Man*, David Shultz, Home and Away Gallery; *Dream Paddles*, Jerry Jacob Laktonen

Jean LaMarr – David Behl

Kapulani Landgraf – Kapulani Landgraf

Joey Lavadour – Maggie Nimkin

Maynard White Owl Lavadour – Maggie Nimkin

lessLIE (Leslie Robert Sam) – David Behl

Peter Lind, Sr. – Roy Mullin

Mary Longman – Mary Longman
James Luna – Ted Brummond, University of Wisconsin
  Photo Service
Rebecca Lyon – Flavin Photography
James Madison – James Madison
Deborah Magee – Adam Canepa
Valerie Malesku – Graham Blair
Kim Mamaradlo – Liz Ellington
John Marston – *Creation Story Bentwood Chest*, David Behl; *Salmon Cycle
  Storage Box*, Anonymous
Luke Marston – Maggie Nimkin
Marques Hanalei Marzan – Marques Hanalei Marzan
Darren McKenzie – Anne Marie L'Hertier
Kevin McKenzie – K.C. Adams
Ken McNeil – Kenji Nagai
Katrina Mitten – Katrina Mitten
Valerie Morgan – Maggie Nimkin
Peter Morin – Merle Adison
Nicole Morita – Shuzo Uemoto
Ken Mowatt – Maggie Nimkin
Molly Murphy – Chris Autio
Stan Natchez – David Behl
David Neel – David Behl
Marianne Nicolson – Bob Matheson, Courtesy of the Art Gallery
  of Greater Victoria
Glen Nipshank – Maggie Nimkin
Ed Archie NoiseCat – Courtesy of Cline Fine Art
Keone Nunes – Shuzo Uemoto
Marvin Oliver – Robert Vinnedge
Gary Olver – Graham Blair
Othniel Ka'iouliokahihikolo'ehu Oomittuk, Jr. – Michael Jones
Wilma Osborne – Maggie Nimkin
Juanita Pahdopony – Benson Warren
Pahponee – Azad Photography
Rosalie Paniyak – Maggie Nimkin
Tim Paul – Kenji Nagai, Courtesy of Spirit Wrestler Gallery
Susan Pavel – Mary Pavel
Susan Laure Peebles – Maggie Nimkin
Shaun Peterson – Duncan Price
David Ruben Piqtoukun – Neil Kinnear & Lesley Chung, Ontario
Lillian Pitt – Dennis Maxwell
Susan Point – *A Gift for Qulqulil*, Kenji Nagai; *Return*, Mike Zens
Kimberly "Wendy" Ponca – Kimberly "Wendy" Ponca
Kevin Pourier – Maggie Nimkin
Thelissa M. Redhawk – Bill Salmon
Eric Robertson – Kelowa Art Gallery
Larry Rosso – Graham Blair
Marcel Russ - Kenji Nagai, Courtesy of Inuit Gallery of Vancouver
Nelda Schrupp – Maggie Nimkin
Tanis Maria S'eiltin – Dirk Bakker, Artbook, Huntington Woods, MI
Joseph Senungetuk – Clark James Mishler
Ronald Senungetuk – Ronald W. Senungetuk
Susie Silook – Maggie Nimkin
Jay Simeon – Graham Blair
Preston Singletary – Russell Johnson
Duane Slick – Stan Chong
Harris Smith – Maggie Nimkin
Rod Smith – Maggie Nimkin
Steve Smith – Maggie Nimkin

Bently Spang – Maggie Nimkin
C. Maxx Stevens - Kitty Leaken
Carl Stromquist – Maggie Nimkin
Morris "Moy" Sutherland – Graham Blair
Norman Tait – Maggie Nimkin
Tchin – Maggie Nimkin
Ron Telek – Maggie Nimkin
Lisa Telford – Craig Smith, Courtesy of the Heard Museum, Phoenix, AZ
Donald Tenoso – Maggie Nimkin
Charlene Teters – Keith Howard
Brian Tripp – Maggie Nimkin
Charlene Vickers – C. Vickers
Dawn Wallace – Maggie Nimkin
Denise Wallace – Maggie Nimkin
Connie Watts – Kenji Nagai
Margaret Roach Wheeler – Gary Polmiller
Christian White – Kenji Nagai, Courtesy of Spirit Wrestler Gallery
White Buffalo – Keri Allen
Glen Wood – Suss Juelsberg
Dan Worcester – Maggie Nimkin
YáYa (Charles Peter Heit) - Kenji Nagai
Wayne Young – Maggie Nimkin
Yuxweluptun (Lawrence Paul) – ANZAI Siego, Courtesy Aomori
  Contemporary Art Centre